ISBN 978-1-330-44277-7
PIBN 10062877

1 MONTH OF
FREE
READING

at
www.ForgottenBooks.com

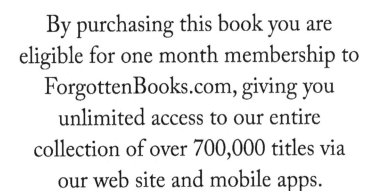

By purchasing this book you are eligible for one month membership to ForgottenBooks.com, giving you unlimited access to our entire collection of over 700,000 titles via our web site and mobile apps.

To claim your free month visit:
www.forgottenbooks.com/free62877

Similar Books Are Available from
www.forgottenbooks.com

———————————

Every Man a King
Or Might in Mind-Mastery, by Orison Swett Marden

Self-Help
With Illustrations of Conduct and Perseverance, by Samuel Smiles

Improvement of the Mind
by Isaac Watts

A Dictionary of Thoughts
by Tryon Edwards

Methods of Obtaining Success
by Julia Seton

The Power of Truth
Individual Problems and Possibilities, by William George Jordan

How to Get What You Want, Vol. 1
by Orison Swett Marden

How to Be Happy Though Married
by Edward John Hardy

Self Development and the Way to Power
by L. W. Rogers

Beginning Right
How to Succeed, by Nathaniel C. Fowler

How to Make Money
Three Lectures on "The Laws of Financial Success", by B. F. Austin

The Pursuit of Happiness
A Book of Studies and Strowings, by Daniel Garrison Brinton

Your Forces, and How to Use Them, Vol. 1
by Prentice Mulford

Conquering Prayer
Or the Power of Personality, by L. Swetenham

He Can Who Thinks He Can, and Other Papers on Success in Life
by Orison Swett Marden

The Power of Thought
What It Is and What It Does, by John Douglas Sterrett

Plenty
by Orison Swett Marden

The Practice of Autosuggestion By the Method of Emile Coué
Revised Edition, by C. Harry Brooks

Thinking for Results
by Christian D. Larson

Calm Yourself
by George Lincoln Walton

THE

PHILOSOPHY

OF

NECESSITY

OR

LAW IN MIND AS IN MATTER.

BY

CHARLES BRAY.

THIRD EDITION, REVISED AND ABRIDGED.

"Everything that exists depends upon the past, prepares the future, and is related to the whole."—OERSTED.

LONDON:

LONGMANS, GREEN, AND CO.,

AND NEW YORK: 15 EAST 16th STREET.

1889.

WORKS BY THE SAME AUTHOR:

PHASES of OPINION and EXPERIENCE during a LONG LIFE; an Autobiography. With Portrait. Crown 8vo. 3s. 6d

The SCIENCE of MAN: a MANUAL of Anthropology, based on Modern Research. Second Edition. Crown 8vo .6s.

The EDUCATION of the FEELINGS: a Moral System. Revised and Abridged for Schools. Crown 8vo. Fourth Edition, 2s. 6d.

LONGMANS AND CO.

PREFATORY NOTE TO THIRD EDITION

THIS work was first published in 1841, in two octavo volumes, and comprised, First, an Exposition of the doctrine of the Philosophy of Necessity, or the Law of Consequences, in its relation to Mental Science; Secondly, in its relation to Ethics; and Thirdly, an application of its principles to the social questions of the day. In the present abridged form this third part has been omitted as being mostly out of date, and only so much of its statistics and observations have been given in an appendix as may be of interest in their bearing upon the present condition of Society, and upon questions for its amelioration which are still in agitation. With regard to those questions concerning the laws of our being which are never out of date, it has been thought well to preserve, in an accessible form, the conclusions arrived at by a fearless thinker, who worked out for himself a theory as to the purpose of existence that satisfied his own mind, and became to him a cheerful philosophy which intensified his enjoyment of all things good and pleasant, helped him to bear the troubles of life, and to meet the end in a spirit as bright as it was resigned.

Throughout the present work Mr. Bray freely used the thoughts and words of other writers when they served his purpose, and in the Preface to the First Edition, he says, " I am induced to lay my own reflections before the public in the hope that the result of that labour which was necessary to satisfy my own mind may be in some degree a saving of labour to others."

However much his views may differ from received opinions, they were those of one who was, in the words of a philosophical friend, " an earnest inquirer after truth, whose devotion to all that is good and generous and noble was an elevated religion in itself, and who to his high conceptions of life and nature was true to the last."

CONTENTS.

PART II.—MENTAL SCIENCE.

* Chapter III., on the " Analysis of the Mental Faculties," phrenologically considered, is omitted in this edition.

APPENDIX.

THE
PHILOSOPHY OF NECESSITY.

INTRODUCTION.

The Philosophy of Necessity is the "reason why" of Necessity. Necessity implies Law or a constant and invariable order of events in the physical and also in the moral world. Reason is exercised in the knowledge and calculation of this fixed order, and if in any department of Nature this order did not reign, in that department there could be no exercise of reason. This is the "reason why" of "Necessity."

"Man, the servant and interpreter of Nature, can only understand and act in proportion as he observes or contemplates the order of Nature; more he can neither know nor do."

It is now generally admitted that Lord Bacon has defined in the above fundamental principle of the inductive Philosophy, the extent of the knowledge of which man is capable; what Nature has really enabled him and what she has forbidden

B

him to do. For want of a clear perception of the boundaries of his mind, which Nature herself has fixed, man has in all ages dogmatized upon endless subjects, which from the very constitution of his being, are beyond his reach; and has formed, and is continually forming, theories upon points which lie beyond the range of his powers. Much speculation would be saved, much pernicious error would be prevented, if we would always keep in view that it is the *order* of Nature alone, whether as relating to matter or to mind, that we are capable of observing and understanding; that we can know neither the beginning nor the end of things, but can only observe what is. We can know in itself, neither the real nature of matter nor of mind, but only the order in which one event follows another, or in which one sensation follows another. " To aspire to the knowledge of more than phenomena,—their resemblances, co-existences, and successions,—is to aspire to transend the inexorable limits of human faculties. To *know* more, we must *be* more."*

Doubtless it is difficult to believe that all Science must be resolved into the knowledge of antecedence and consequence—of cause and effect —of the powers of nature; for the power of

* Lewes's "Biographical History of Philosophy," p. xvi. See Dr. Thomas Brown's "Theory of Cause and Effect," and his 7th Lecture on the "Philosophy of the Human Mind;" also, "First Principles," by Herbert Spencer, Part I., "The Unknowable."

producing a given effect, and the cause, or the invariable antecedent of such effect, are all synonymous terms; yet such, if we strictly analyse our knowledge, will be found to be the case, and that nothing is really known to us but this relation of things to each other and to ourselves. Thus one billiard ball striking another, communicates motion to it; yet, simple as this may appear, we know not how or why it does so. We say the striking is the cause of the motion; but we do not know why one body striking another should communicate motion to it, especially as it might be proved that it does not touch it. All we know is that the motion invariably follows what we call the striking. Again, heat converts water into steam; the expansive force of steam acts upon the piston; and the piston, by the intervention of many further antecedents, produces many further effects. Here again, all we know is that such causes, *cæteris paribus*, will invariably produce the same effects; in other words, we know the relation of heat to water, of water to steam, of steam to the piston, and of the piston to what it has to perform. This kind of knowledge may be called certain or Positive, because it may be *proved*,—that is, it is knowledge of what may be made to take place again in the given or recognised order. But it will be said that independently of the knowledge of the *order* of nature, and of the relation of things to one another, we possess a knowledge of things as individuals and also of their qualities. This, however, is only a knowledge of their relation to us. What we call individual existences and their qualities is the effect such existences have upon the senses, and the senses upon the brain; it is the first link in the chain of sequences.

Again, we know that due proportions of oxygen and hydrogen form water; that sulphur, nitre, and charcoal, form gunpowder; and that a spark applied to the latter mixture causes an explosion. But we know not how or why all this should take place; why a spark should have this relation to gunpowder, *i.e.*, why it should have this *power*, or be the cause, or invariable antecedent of its explosion. We know it as we can only know everything else, by experience, from having observed that such is the ORDER OF NATURE. Now as regards our knowledge of the relation that this explosion bears to ourselves, it is exactly of the same character, merely the knowledge of the sequence of events. The powder acts upon the air and the air upon the tympanum, and the tympanum upon the nerves and the nerves upon the brain, and the action of the brain is the only antecedent we can trace before the sensation which apprises us of the explosion. To say that the brain acts upon the mind is introducing a link in the chain for which, in the present state of our knowledge, we have no warrant. Not that I would be understood to affirm that the brain *is* the cause of the sensation; but the action of the brain is the invariable antecedent of sensation, and we have no knowledge at present of anything between ; to add a link to the chain of causation is as unphilosophical as to leave one out. To make discoveries in science, therefore, is merely to show what antecedents precede such and such consequents; what causes invariably produce such and such effects; and by this knowledge we are enabled to adapt our relation to external things, or their relation to us, so as to produce the effect we wish. Thus to know, with the vulgar, that the explosion produces the sound, is only available knowledge to a certain extent; to learn that the gunpowder acts upon the air is a discovery in science, and the various other links between are essential to *certain* knowledge ; for by an alteration in the air, the tympanum, the nerves, or the brain, a different effect would be produced, *i.e.*, the relation of the gunpowder to ourselves would be changed; or if a link were yet undiscovered and left out we might infer that the same cause did not always produce the same effect. Knowledge becomes certain in proportion as we discover the invariable antecedent to the consequent; it is therefore less certain where Life is concerned than it is in Physics, and still less so where sensation is added to Life. In the action of medicine upon the body it is seldom that the same remedy will produce precisely the same effect in cases which appear to us to be similar ;

the reason of which is that so little is at present
understood of vitality that there may be many
circumstances in each case which we are unable
to calculate upon, any one of which might be
sufficient to produce the different result. Knowledge
is so much more uncertain when Sensation is added
to Life that invariable antecedence and consequence
is here supposed to cease, the same necessary
relation between cause and effect not being held
to exist in mind as in matter. But this is an
error, arising from the circumstance that the causes
that produce mental phenomena are not always so
perceptible as those that admit of more direct
experiment. There is exactly the same connection
between every action of the mind and its cause as
between things external to the mind; and not
the slightest change takes place in the mind, nor
the most transient idea passes through it, but has
its cause; which cause is always adequate in the
same circumstances, to produce the same effect;
and it is only by such admission that we can infer
the existence of anything external to ourselves, or
even the existence of what we call ourselves. It
is of very great importance that we should clearly
see that the *self* of the conscious being is nothing
but an object of observation, known only as everything else is known, by the chain of necessary
antecedents and consequents. Thus all we can
know of the mind of man is its successive changes
which are best observed in others—in their effects

or consequences; mere reflection on consciousness has produced all the errors of Metaphysics. We see at once what a wide field is cleared when we are obliged to admit that we know nothing of matter in itself, or of mind in itself, for all the speculations based on the *essential* difference in their nature at once fall to the ground, and materialist and immaterialist can no longer be said to exist.

The object of all Science, therefore, is to show the relation of things to each other and to ourselves so as to anticipate events. To this it is limited. "All that we know is, nothing can be known," is true in one sense, for we know nothing of the essential nature of anything or of *how* any one cause produces its effect. One thing invariably precedes another, and we say that it has the *power* to produce it; but what this power is, or what makes the connexion, or whether the relation will always exist or has only been established for a time, we do not know, neither is it necessary, as far as we can see, that we should know, for the knowledge of the *order of nature* is all that is requisite for the proper exercise of reason, and for the perfection of our happiness Let us not then feel ourselves degraded by the idea that the most diligent research has done no more, and can do no more than trace the relation of things here, and discover but a part of the *order of nature*; and since our inquiries can but end in the discovery of the relations of things as discernible by our present faculties, let us cease from all those fruitless attempts to attain to knowledge upon subjects beyond the comprehension of beings in our scale of intelligence, which have hitherto so retarded the Science of Mind, and prevented the happiness of man from bearing any proportion to the means of happiness afforded him.   Locke says, "We shall not have much reason to complain of the narrowness of our minds, if we will but employ them about what may be of use to us, for of that they are very capable; and it will be an unpardonable as well as childish peevishness, if we undervalue the advantages of our knowledge, and neglect to improve it to the ends for which it was given, because there are some things set out of reach of it."   Bacon says "the real cause and root of almost all the evils in science is this:—that falsely magnifying and extolling the powers of the mind, we seek not its true helps."

My object in the present treatise is to pursue this inductive method of inquiry in investigating the nature of man; his place in creation; the character of his mind; and particularly to trace to its legitimate consequences the doctrine of philosophical necessity, which the connexion between cause and effect implies.   I would show that the mind of man is not an exception to nature's other works; that like everything else it has received a determinate character; that all our knowledge of it is precisely of the same kind as that of material things, and consists in the observation of *its order* of action, or of the relation of cause and effect. This is a truth which, although acknowledged by many writers, has never yet been made of sufficient importance in the science of Mental and Moral Philosophy. It has either been considered as a mere abstraction of no practical use, or else avoided and stifled as leading to fatalism, and otherwise dangerous in its tendency. But I hope to be able to show, on the contrary, that upon this truth *alone*,—however it may be said to militate against man's free-will or accountability, in some acceptation of the terms,—our Educational and Political systems can be properly based, in accordance with the nature of the being to be educated and governed. If in setting a steam engine to work the engineer were to leave much to its *free will*, the work would be but badly performed. So as relates to man, if in our educational systems the causes are inadequate to the intellectual and moral results we desire, his *free will* will not supply the deficiency.

That the same certain and calculable laws exist in the departments of Life and Mind as in Physics is daily being made evident by Statistics. Uncertainty may exist in individual cases, or in a limited field of observation, but it is proved that in a larger field, in a given number of cases, invariable results may always be looked for. Thus, in a recent

Report of the Registrar-General on the population of England, he shows the "law" to be that one person out of every 45 living at the commencement of any year will die within that year. The departure from this law is very trifling, and the most valuable applications of it are already made by Life Insurance Companies and others who base their calculations upon the absolute certainty of its invariability. In the 12th Annual Report of the Registrar-General we are informed "it may be broadly stated that 27 in 1,000 men of the population, of the age of 20 and under 60, are suffering from one kind of disease or other; that several of the diseases are of long duration, that others are recurrent, and that some are hereditary." But Statistics now show that a similar uniformity is found to prevail where mind is concerned as in matter. M. Quetelet has furnished tables relative to crime in France, by which he shows that "law" is equally certain and calculable with respect to crime as to deaths. The same effects have followed similar inquiries in this country. M. Quetelet says "the possibility of assigning beforehand the number of the accused and condemned which should occur in a country, is calculated to lead to serious reflections, since it involves the fate of several thousands of human beings, who are impelled, as it were, by an irresistible necessity, to the bar of the tribunal, and towards the sentences of condemnation that there await them. These conclusions flow directly from the principle, already so often stated in this work, that effects are in proportion to their causes, and that the effects remain the same, if the causes which have produced them do not vary."

Year by year the same number of persons commit suicide, varying a little with varying circumstances. In London about 240 persons every year make away with themselves, while in 1846, the year of railway panic, 266 committed suicide. The number of marriages are not regulated as is ordinarily supposed by Love, but by the price of corn, that is, by the cheapness of provisions and by the rate of wages.

To show the influence of numbers in reducing apparently inextricable uncertainty to mathematical certainty, we will take as an illustration the hairs on our head. It might be supposed that the hairs on no two persons heads were exactly the same in number, but if we presume that the greatest number of hairs on any one person's head is 250 thousand, then all persons above that number must agree in the number of their hairs with one of the 250 thousand, and in a million there must necessarily be four alike. Varied as is human character and disposition,—as the hairs of our head, yet in the broad features there is considerable agreement; and, supposing the variety to be expressed by 1,000 or 10,000, then there would be ten persons in every 10,000 or 100,000 who would, in similar circumstances, act exactly alike.

" Everything throughout creation," says one of
the most philosophical writers of the present day,
" is governed by law : but over most of the tracts
that come within the active experience of mankind,
the governing hand is so secret and remote that
until very large numerical masses are brought
under the eye at once, the controlling power is not
detected. To an appreciating mind there is something attractively beautiful in the delicacy with
which laws of unswerving regularity and resistless
force are withdrawn from view, masked behind
an apparently inexhaustible variety, an independence and spontaneity of action, and a playfulness
of 'accident,' seemingly without control or bounds.
It is impossible too much to admire this indulgent
feature of creative and administrative power, which
permits thus its graciousness to be lost to general
sight in the success of the very illusion employed.
The whole vocabulary of those who talk of 'chance'
and 'luck' attest the matchless lightness and
elasticity of gait which disguise the majestic onward
tread and movement of natural law. Statistics are
the touchstone under which the illusion at once
vanishes. Like some potent chemical test it 'pre-
cipitates' at once, and exposes to view the latent
law so skilfully held in solution." It is in this wide
space that man finds room for an almost infinitely
varied field of action for what he calls his freedom
of will, and which is the source of an infinitely
varied series of sensations, productive of much

more happiness than were his actions apparently more "fixed in fate." But of course unless what is called "free-will" were ultimately governed by law as everything else is, man's actions could never be calculated, and a "Social Science," or a science of human nature, would be an impossibility. But "forgetfulness as well as free-will is under constant laws," for a late return, made by the Post-Offices of London and Paris, shows that we can calculate, that is, exactly foretell, the number of persons who will forget every year to address their letters.

"To those who have a steady conception of the regularity of events," says Buckle, "and have firmly seized the great truth that the actions of men, being guided by their antecedents, are in reality never inconsistent, but however capricious they may appear, only form one vast scheme of universal order, of which we in the present state of knowledge can barely see the outline,—to those who understand this which is at once the key and the basis of history, the facts just adduced, so far from being strange, will be precisely what would have been expected, and ought long since to have been known. Indeed the progress of inquiry is becoming so rapid and so earnest, that I entertain little doubt that before another century has elapsed, the chain of evidence will be complete, and it will be as rare to find an historian who denies the undeviating regularity of the moral world, as it now is to find a philosopher who denies the regularity of the material world."*

Bolingbroke observes that "Mankind, bred to think as well as speak by rote, furnish their minds as they furnish their houses or clothe their bodies, with the fancies of other men, and according to the mode of the age and country. They pick up their ideas and notions in common conversation or in the schools. The first are always superficial, and both are commonly false." Holding fast then to the principle of the inductive philosophy, and regardless of mere opinion, however prevalent, I shall proceed to the elucidation of the doctrine of Philosophical Necessity and its Applications, to the consideration of the Constitution of Man, and its relation to all that surrounds him.

* "History of Civilization in England, p. 31.

PART I.
MORAL SCIENCE.

CHAPTER I.

EXPOSITION OF THE DOCTRINE OF PHILOSOPHICAL
NECESSITY.

THIS subject has generally been considered as
one of unusual difficulty, for the proper treatment
of which human reason is scarcely adequate. But
this view of it arises, not so much from any real
abstruseness in the question itself, as from the
apparent opposition which the doctrine offers to
established opinions, and even to common sense
itself. Many, therefore, and perhaps the greater
number of those who have had their attention
called to it, and who have not been able to resist
the evidence upon which it stands, have found it
necessary to admit the opposite doctrine of freedom
of will also; the incompatibility of the two, although
allowed to be somewhat of a mystery, being a less
difficulty with them than the giving up of many
pre-established opinions.

There is, perhaps, no proposition that admits
of stronger proof, or that can be more logically,
if not mathematically, demonstrated; but its sup-

posed tendency has mystified an otherwise plain
question. Many have admitted and proved the
doctrine of philosophical necessity, to serve a
sectarian purpose, who, when that object has been
answered, have discarded it as of no farther use;
as a mere abstraction, having no practical bearing
upon any one of the important interests of mankind; and even of mischievous tendency, when
permitted to escape from the closets of philosophers and to circulate amongst the vulgar. The
author of "The Natural History of Enthusiasm,"
for instance, in his introductory Essay to Edwards'
"Inquiry," considers the doctrine, the truth of
which he appears not to deny, as useless when
applied to questions of "common life, affecting the
personal, social, and political conduct of mankind,
or as applied to Theology and Christian doctrine,
or to the physiology of man, or to the higher
metaphysics." But no truth is unimportant, still
less pernicious, and we think it may be shown that
this doctrine, so far from being valueless to man in
a practical sense, has a most important bearing
upon all his best interests, and is also fundamental
to all just views of the Divine Government.

Jonathan Edwards has hitherto been considered
unanswerable. The following passages from the
"Inquiry concerning Freedom of Will," contain the
argument in its support, as stated by him :—

"*The argument from cause and effect.*

"Nothing comes to pass without a cause. What

is self-existent, must be from Eternity and must be unchangeable; but as to all things that *begin to be*, they are not self-existent, and therefore must have some foundation of their existence without themselves. That whatsoever begins to be, which before was not, must have a cause why it then begins to exist, seems to be the first dictate of the natural and common sense which God has implanted in the minds of all mankind, and the main foundation of all our reasonings about things past, present, and to come. If once this grand principle of common sense be given up, that what is not necessary in itself must have a cause—and we begin to maintain that things may come into existence and begin to be, which heretofore have not been of themselves without any cause—all our means of ascending in our arguing from the creature to the Creator, and all our evidence of the being of God is cut off at one blow. In this case we cannot prove that there is a God, either from the being of the world and the creatures in it, or from the manner of their being, their order, beauty, and use. Should we admit that things may come to pass without a cause, we should be without evidence of the existence of anything whatever but our own immediate, present ideas and consciousness. For we have no way to prove anything else but by arguing from effects to causes; from the ideas immediately in view, we argue other things not immediately in view; from sensations now excited in us, we infer the existence of other things without us as the causes of these sensations; and from the existence of these things we argue other things, which they depend on as effects on causes. We infer the past existence of ourselves, or anything else, by memory : only as we argue that the ideas which are now in our mind, are the consequences of past ideas and sensations. So if there is no absurdity or difficulty in supposing *one thing* to start out of non-existence into being, of itself, without a cause, then there is no absurdity or difficulty in supposing the same of millions of millions. For nothing, or no difficulty multiplied, still is nothing or no difficulty; nothing multiplied by nothing does not increase the sum.

" Now, according to the hypothesis of some, of the acts of the will coming to pass without a cause, it is the case in fact, that millions and millions of events are continually coming into existence, contingently without any cause or reason why they do so, all over the world, every day and every hour through all ages. So it is in a constant succession in every moral agent. This contingency, this effectual *no* cause is always ready at hand to produce this sort of effects, as long as the agent exists, and as often as he has occasion.

" If it were so, that things only of one kind, viz., acts of the will, seemed to come to pass of themselves, but those of this sort, in general, came into being thus; and it were an event that was continual and that happened in a course, wherever were capable subjects of such events, this very thing would demonstrate that there were some cause of them, which made such a difference between this event and others, and that they did not really happen contingently. For contingence is blind, and does not pick and choose for a particular sort of events. Nothing has no choice. This no-cause, which causes no existence, cannot cause the existence which comes to pass to be of one particular sort only, distinguished from all others.

"Some suppose that volition can arise without a cause, through the activity of the nature of the soul; but I can conceive of nothing else that can be meant by the soul's having power to cause and determine its own volitions, as a being to whom God has given a power of action, but this, that God has given power to the soul, sometime, at least, to excite volitions at its pleasure, or according as it chooses. And this certainly supposes in all such cases, a choice preceding all volitions which are thus caused, even the first of them, which runs into an absurdity.

"A great argument for self-determining power is the supposed experience we universally have of an ability to determine our wills in cases wherein no prevailing motive is presented. The will (as is supposed) has its choice to make between two or more things that are perfectly equal in the view of the mind; and the will is apparently altogether indifferent ; and yet we have no difficulty in coming to a choice ; the will can instantly determine itself to one, by a sovereign power which it has over itself, without being moved by any preponderating inducement. The very supposition which is here made directly contradicts and overthrows itself. For the thing supposed wherein this grand argument consists is, that among several things, the will actually chooses one before another, at the same time that it is perfectly indifferent, which is the very same thing as to say the mind has a preference at the same time that it has no preference.

"To suppose the will to act at all in a state of perfect indifference, either to determine itself or to do anything else, is to assert that the mind chooses without choosing. To say that when it is indifferent it can do as it pleases, is to say that it can follow its pleasure when it has no pleasure to follow. And, therefore, if there be any difficulty in the instances of two cakes, or two eggs, &c. ; concerning which, some authors suppose the mind in fact has a choice, and so in effect suppose that it has a preference, it as much concerns them to solve the difficulty, as it does those whom they oppose.

"It will always be among a number of objects in view, that one will prevail in the eye, or in idea, beyond others. When we have our eyes open in the clear sunshine many objects strike the eye at once, and innumerable images may be at once painted in it by the rays of light; but the attention of the mind is not equal to several of them at once; or if it be so, it does not continue so for any time. And so it is with respect to the ideas of the mind in general; several ideas are not in equal strength in the mind's view and notice at once, or, at least, do not remain so for any sensible continuance. The involuntary changes in the succession of our ideas, though the cause may not be observed, have as much a cause as the changeable motion of the motes that float in the air, or the continual, infinitely various, successive changes of the unevenness on the surface of the water, so, though the falling of the die be accidental to him that casts it, yet none will suppose that there is no cause why it falls as it does.

"Concerning liberty of will consisting in indifference, the very putting of the question is sufficient to show the absurdity of the affirmative answer; for how ridiculous would it be for any one to insist that the soul chooses one thing before another, when at the same time it is perfectly indifferent with respect to each! This is the same thing as to say the soul prefers one thing to another, at the very same time that it has no preference. And should it be inquired whether volition is a thing that ever does, or can, come to pass contingently; it must be remembered that it has been already shown, that nothing can ever come to

pass without a cause or reason why it exists in this
manner rather than another; and the evidence of
this has been particularly applied to the acts of the
will. Now, if this be so, it will demonstratively
follow, that the acts of the will are never contingent, or without necessity in the sense spoken
of, inasmuch as those things which have a cause or
reason of their existence must be *connected with
their cause.*

"If liberty consist in that which Arminians
suppose, viz., in the soul's determining its own acts,
having free opportunity, and being without all
necessity : this is the same as to say, that liberty
consists in the soul's having power and opportunity
to have what determinations of the will it pleases
or chooses. And if the determination of the will
and the last dictates of the understanding be the
same thing, as Dr. Clarke affirms, then liberty
consists in the mind's having power to have what
dictates of the understanding it pleases, having
opportunity to choose its own dictates of understanding. But this is absurd; for it is to make
the determination of choice prior to the dictate of
the understanding and the ground of it, which
cannot consist with the dictate of the understanding's being the determination of choice itself."

This argument from cause and effect I consider
to be conclusive, although the connexion between
antecedent and consequent, or cause and effect, be
not considered as a necessary connexion, but one

established and upheld for a particular purpose. Edwards' argument from foreknowledge, which need not here be reproduced, would appear to be less satisfactory; for the idea of prescience not being derived from experience, our knowledge upon the subject cannot be of such a character as to admit of our drawing logical inferences from it.

We shall now proceed to a more practical elucidation of the subject.

The doctrine of Necessity, in plain language, means that a man could in no case have acted differently from the manner in which he did act, supposing the state of his mind, and the circumstances in which he was placed, to be the same; which is merely saying, that the same causes would always produce the same effects. Men are prone to suppose that they could have done otherwise, because, in reviewing their conduct, its consequences—the experience resulting from it—are mixed up with the motives that decided them before, so that if they had to decide over again, different circumstances must be taken into the calculation. Suppose a case : A man has to decide upon some speculation in business; his conduct is voluntary, that is, it is free from external compulsion, he is at liberty to do what he shall *will* to do ;—what is to determine his will? Surely we need not consult Edwards to tell us that his *will* will be determined by the " greatest apparent good," not, perhaps, in the opinion of other people, but in his own opinion at the moment. This good is the *motive* which governs his will.

To suppose that the man is not governed by motives, or even to suppose that he acts contrary to motives, does not make the action less necessary; for there must be a cause why he acts in one way rather than another, and the cause must be sufficient to produce the act; for "Nothing comes to pass without a cause."

But upon what will the motives that decide the will depend? Upon the mental constitution of the individual, and upon the circumstances in which he is placed. If he has a strong sense of justice, he will consider whether what he is about to do is perfectly honest; if he is a benevolent man, he will take care to do nothing likely to injure his fellows, and so on with respect to all the natural feelings of which the mind consists; they will impel to action, or restrain, according to their natural or acquired strength, and the direction they may have received from education. The intellectual faculties have reference to the circumstances which influence the determination of his will; they examine how far the speculation is likely to succeed, and the correctness of the judgment will depend upon the strength of the reasoning powers, the education they have received, and a more or less complete view of all the circumstances. If, however, it be admitted, as it frequently is, that a man *must* now in any given instance believe what appears to him to be true, and also act upon that belief in determining "the greatest apparent good," yet it is thought that at some previous time he might have gained more knowledge which would now have enabled him to believe differently and to choose more wisely; but it will be found that if the present belief and motions to action are without his own control, and he *must* believe and act as he does, then every influence that has previously tended to make his mental constitution what it now is, and everything that produced the circumstances in which he is now placed, has been, in like manner, dependent upon causes over which he had no control.

In what, then, does the Liberty which man feels that he possesses consist? Certainly not in the being able to act without motive, or contrary to the strongest motive; but in freedom from external compulsion; in the wide field of action open to him, and in the almost infinite number of paths to the objects of his desires lying open to his choice. The brutes approach their objects directly, impelled by one or more simple instincts, while Reason offers to man a hundred different ways of approach, a vast variety of different means by which his aim can be accomplished; and he can suspend its pursuit until he finds the proper path, for he knows that if he takes the wrong direction out of the many that she presents to him, pain and suffering will be the consequence of his error. Reason thus calls into activity a great variety of feelings, and keeps up an endless succession of sensations. If a man would eat, he is not confined to one or two simple articles of diet, but he can vary his food to suit his palate. Would he lay up store for a future day—his stock is not of one kind only, like that of the bee, nor is his warehouse, like the hive, of one particular construction, however perfect; but this desire, in combination with others, gives rise to the diversified products of commerce and the arts. Would he train up his offspring—he does not act instinctively but adapts his treatment to the requirements of the mental and bodily constitution of his child, excited by all the hopes and fears of parental solicitude, which reason suggests. But because his choice of any one mode of action is still determined by the strongest motive, this kind of liberty does not take man from under the governance of necessity.

That which has most mystified this subject, and made men think the doctrine of necessity contrary to common sense, or what they imagine to be intuitive evidence, is the supposition that it annihilates the *free agency* of man: they reason in this way—we feel that we have the power to do as we please ; we are not obliged by any physical necessity to do anything ; we have the perfect control of our own actions ; are we not then free agents ? But true necessity is not opposed to that which is voluntary, but to that which is contingent. It is undoubtedly true, therefore, that man can always do as he pleases; but what he pleases to do will ever depend upon his mental constitution (which is only another word for himself) and the circumstances in which he is placed. This is no more than saying that man possesses a definite constitution, and that he must act according to it. Locke says in his Essay, "As far as man has power to think or not to think, to move or not to move, *according to the preferences or direction of his own mind,* so far is a man free." Here the only liberty acknowledged is that of acting according to the internal mechanism of a man's mind. He says also, "The mind having in most cases, as is evident in experience, a power to suspend the execution and satisfaction of any of its desires, and so of all, one after another, is at liberty to consider the objects of them, examine them on all sides, and weigh them with others. In this lies the liberty a man has. He has the power to suspend the execution of this or that desire, as every one daily may experience in himself: this seems to me the source of all liberty. In this seems to consist that which is, as I think, improperly called free-will." But this power of suspension is quite consistent with the doctrine of necessity; for, if we delay the performance of any action, it must be because we have a motive for doing so, and that motive is the necessary cause. Each manifestation of force can be interpreted only as the effect of some antecedent force, and as Kant says — "Every action or phenomenon, so far as it produces an event, is itsel[.] an event or occurrence which presupposes another state wherein the cause is to be met with ; and thus everything that happens is only a continuation of the series, and no beginning *which occurs of itself* is possible : consequently, all the actions of the natural causes in the succession are themselves again effects." · In fact, the Universe is one General Effect, both in Mind and Matter, and there is but one Supreme Cause.

Spinoza says—" In no mind is there an absolute or free volition ; but it is determined to choose this or that by a cause, which likewise has been fixed by another, and this again by a third, and so on for ever.[*] But he also says, and this by some is held to contradict the above : " moreover, it is to be observed, although the mind is influenced by external circumstances to affirm or deny anything, nevertheless, it is not in itself so swayed as to be forced by external things, but always in its own nature remains free." *True Freedom, as we have before said, is where a being is able to act by the law of its own nature without external compulsion.* This is the freedom which we all feel that we possess : this is the freedom for which Kant contends, based upon what he calls *practical* reason; this is evidently what Locke means, and also Spinoza when he says the mind is not " so swayed as to be *forced by*

---

[*] *Tractata Theologica-Polit,* ch. xii, sec 22.

external things." This in fact is the only freedom of which we can conceive, but it is not at variance either in God or man with necessity, and belongs alike to mind and matter. Man acts spontaneously by the law of his own nature, and so does every atom equally in accordance with its tendencies ; but in God we believe such nature to be self-existent, original, eternal ; in man and matter it is derived. Of course we cannot speak dogmatically of the nature of God, for we really know nothing ; but in this sense he must be the most free as well as the most " necessary " of all beings. We can conceive a hundred courses open to man, ninety-nine of which from his limited intelligence may be wrong (limitations of *real* freedom), but we cannot conceive of supreme intelligence taking more than one course——the right. Thus as we rise in the scale of intelligence, is the path of duty narrowed to us, and we lose that spurious freedom for which the advocates of free-will so strenuously contend.

Motive is to voluntary action in the moral world, what cause is to effect in the physical, and the order of nature is as fixed in the world of mind as of matter ; for if the course of nature were not as fixed in the moral world as in the physical ; if calculable laws did not regulate one as well as the other, man's reasoning power, which depends for its exercise upon the uniformity of events in both, would be of no use. If man could refuse to be governed by motives ; if his conduct did not depend upon springs of action which could be calculated and relied upon, the superiority of his organization, which now raises him so eminently above the brute creation, would have availed him nothing. Reason is dependent for its exercise upon experience, and experience is nothing more than the knowledge of the invariable order of nature, of the relations of cause and effect. Man observing these sequences and expecting them to occur again in like circumstances, shapes his conduct accordingly. In the first ages of the world, when succession was only observed in a few simple things, such as the rising of the sun from day to day, it was thought that the same free will now attributed to man, belonged to the physical world also; that events might come to pass, or they might not, and the term *chance* denoted this uncertainty. But increased knowledge has tended to abolish this term, by showing the uniform manner in which events follow one another, and that under similar circumstances the same results may be expected to follow. The explosion of gunpower could not be predicted by the analysis of its parts, and the simplest phenomena were all at first at an equal distance from human sagacity. Having observed then the order of nature, we can anticipate events and regulate our conduct accordingly, suiting our circumstances to this known order of events; we regulate our conduct by what we expect to result from it, by making use of the same causes to produce the same effects.

Admitting that this is a proper definition of the exercise of reason, it follows that if this uniformity did not exist, the exercise of it would be as likely to be ruinous as serviceable to us; our knowledge would in no way avail us, for we could not predict that things would occur again as we had before observed them. All the discoveries that man has made in the arts and sciences, everything in fact that has tended to ameliorate and raise his condition, depend on this known order of nature, and rest upon its immutability.*

Because the causes of human actions have been

---

*"Although there are phenomena, the production and changes of which elude all our attempts to reduce them universally to any ascertained law; yet in every such case, *the phenomenon, or the objects concerned in it, are found in some instances to obey the known laws of nature.* The wind, for example, is the type of uncertainty and caprice, yet we find it in some cases obeying with as much constancy as any other phenomena of nature the law of the tendency of fluids to distribute themselves so as to equalise the pressure on every side of each of their particles; as in the case of the trade winds, and the monsoons. Lightning might once have been supposed to obey no laws; but since it has been ascertained to be identical with electricity, we know that the very same phenomenon, in some of its manifestations, is implicitly obedient to the action of fixed causes. I do not believe that there is now one object or event in all our experience of nature, within the bounds of the solar system at least, which has not either been ascertained by direct observation to follow laws, of its own, or been proved to be exactly similar to objects and events, which, in more familiar manifestations, or on a more limited scale, follow strict laws: our inability to trace the same laws on the larger scale, and in the more recondite instances being accounted for by the number of complications of the modifying causes, or by their inaccessibility to observation."— Mill's *System of Logic,* c. II, p. 116.

hidden from us like those of physical action in the first ages of the world, such actions have been supposed to be contingent, to depend upon chance and not to follow the same law of invariable sequence; but if this were really the case—if the doctrine of philosophical necessity were not true, the regularity of events in the physical world would little avail us, neither would they afford sufficient foundation for morality and prudence, as the voluntary conduct of our neighbours enters into almost all those calculations upon which our plans and determinations are founded.

"A person well acquainted with the necessary order in which events follow each other, (*i.e.*) well skilled in the ordinary movements of the machinery of life, may with confidence, if not with absolute assurance of success, risk his most important interests upon the issue of well concerted plans. Skill and sagacity in managing the affairs of common life, or wisdom in council or command, is nothing else than the knowledge of the fixed laws of matter and mind, which together dictate the intricate movements of the great machine of the social system. It must be upon the immovable substratum of cause and effect, of motive and voluntary action, that our calculations of futurity are formed, and it is upon this basis alone, that a wise man rests his hopes and constructs his plans."

"Correctly conceived, the doctrine [called Philo-sophical Necessity is simply this: that given the motives that are present to an individual mind, and given likewise the character and disposition of the individual, the manner in which he will act may be unerringly inferred : that if we know the person thoroughly, and knew all the inducements that are acting upon him, we could foretel his conduct with as much certainty as we can predict any physical event. This proposition I take to be a mere interpretation of universal experience, a statement in words of what every one is internally convinced of."*

It has been said, however, that "on the supposition that man is not a free agent—the master of his own sentiments and conduct, but on the contrary subject to the laws of physical causation which rule in the material world—conscience—the moral sense, though an essential part of his nature, has no foundation in it. It bids him do this, and restrain from that; though he has no power to determine what he shall do, being himself absolutely disposed of by laws as inviolable as those which keep the earth in her orbit, and provide that summer and winter, seed time and harvest, shall not fail. Any theory which fails to recognize man's moral freedom converts his nature into an incoherent delusion, to which we find nothing analogous in the other arrangements of the universe. Admit, however, human free agency, and this incongruity

* "System of Logic."

D

vanishes—conscience ceases to be ' a redundant
endowment.' "*

But this objection arises from the limited
use of language at our command, and from our
thus applying "necessary" to voluntary action
in the same sense as we do to the laws of *physical
causation.* Voluntary action is as much dependent
upon the laws of mind as matter upon the laws of
physics. As Priestley says—"It must be understood that all that is ever meant by *necessity in a
cause,* is that which produces *certainty in the effect.*"
The proper answer then to the above objection of
the " National" is, that man is not only governed
by the external laws of nature, but by the internal
nature or laws of his own mind, of which conscience
is one. The pain of burning keeps him out of the
fire and protects his body; the pain of conscience
keeps him from doing what he considers wrong and
protects his mind or moral being. As Buckle says,
" On the one hand we have the human mind obeying
the laws of its own existence, and, when un-
controlled by external agents, developing itself
according to the conditions of its organization. On
the other hand we have what is called nature,
obeying likewise its laws; but incessantly coming
into contact with the minds of men, exciting their
passions, stimulating their intellect, and therefore
giving to their actions a direction which they would

* "National Review," Jan. 1858.

not have taken without such disturbance. Thus we have men modifying nature, and nature modifying man; while out of this reciprocal modification all events must necessarily spring."

However it may suit the wants of certain creeds to deny the necessity of all our actions, yet those who adopt them, acknowledge it in action, if they deny it in words. Do not such persons expect from certain moral inducements to produce a certain voluntary line of conduct? All the arguments they use to excite our hopes or fears, proceed upon the supposition that mind is subject to certain laws, and that if their arguments are efficient as a cause, the effects desiderated will invariably follow. "Do you think such motives are sufficient to induce him?" is a question with them as pertinent as "Do you think this lever has the power to raise that weight?" But, say the advocates of freedom of will, necessity is not here implied, for though we are obliged to admit a connexion between motives and actions, yet this connexion does not appear to us to amount to a certainty. The mind possesses an inherent activity, by which it can at pleasure dissolve this connexion; consequently when motives are presented to induce a particular line of conduct, it is not done with certain expectations of success, and we are not always disappointed if we fail. We make a reservation for a certain liberty of will a person is supposed to possess, which may cause him to resist all our inducements. This objection is as forcible when applied to matter as to mind. It arises from our not being sufficiently acquainted with the causes necessary to produce the effect we wish. A philosophical experiment may succeed ninety-nine times and fail the hundredth, not from any liberty of will that the materials possess, but from some counteracting cause that has crept in of which we are ignorant, but which farther investigation may discover. So with respect to mind, if our arguments are not successful, it is because they are not forcible enough, or they do not apply to the state of mind of the individual, or there is some prejudice still unmoved; and not from any power he may possess of refusing to be moved, by a motive strong enough for the purpose. In the latter case, as in the first, we must not ascribe our failure to the free will of the individual, but to our own ignorance of how to move him, and if we would succeed, we must look in both cases for the hidden cause of the failure.

The character of a man is the result of the organization he received at birth, and all the various circumstances that have acted upon it since, and these, if that were possible, being given, a mental philosopher would predict the line of conduct that will be invariably pursued by each individual, as readily as the chemist can predict the exact result of the mixture of any chemical substances. Man, like everything else around, has received a definite constitution and he is no more capable of acting contrary to that constitution, and of refusing to be acted upon by the influences that everywhere surround him, than the atoms of matter are capable of resisting the impulses of attraction and repulsion, and the various affinities from which result all the beneficial order and arrangement of the present material system. The same disastrous effects might be expected to result in the one case as the other; for if matter refused to obey the laws that pertain to it, we could not depend upon the causes that are capable of producing certain results to-day being efficient to the same ends to-morrow; and if there were no certain connexion between motive and action, we should never be able to predict what men would be from what they had been; thus reason would be of no use, all progression would cease, and man would be as the beasts, moved by immediate impulses, and confined to an equally limited range of ideas and enjoyments.

CHAPTER II.

THE APPLICATION OF PHILOSOPHICAL NECESSITY TO RESPONSIBILITY, PRAISE AND BLAME, REWARD AND PUNISHMENT, VIRTUE AND VICE.

So clear is the evidence in favour of Philosophical Necessity that it would never for one moment have been doubted if it had not been for its supposed consequences. It was supposed to lead to fatalism—to the doctrine of non-responsibility, and consequently to be subversive of the very foundations of morality. We should never attempt, however, to stifle truth from its supposed consequences, but either make it harmonise with other truth or quietly wait till we can. If we had followed this course in this direction we should earlier have discovered that Induction applies to Mind as well as to Matter—and that as the great desideratum in Nature is Unity, Law, and Order, we should not have left it out of one-half creation, and that the most important, and having banished Miracle and the Supernatural from the physical world, we should not have left it in the world of mind and morals. We should have been able to banish half the misery of life that arises from the supposition that things might have been otherwise, that they ought to have been otherwise, and at the

same time we should have banished the source of
at least one half of the crime in the world, that
arising from the feeling of revenge and the desire
of what is called retributive justice, and the origin
and use of what is called "evil," would have been
made much clearer. We shall now proceed to trace
the doctrine to its legitimate consequences.

RESPONSIBILITY.—If a man's actions are determined necessarily by the previous state of his mind,
and the circumstances or influences to which he is
exposed, and if, consequently, no action of his life
could possibly have been different from what it
actually was, in the circumstances,—responsibility,
in the sense in which it is generally used, is without
meaning. A man is usually considered to be
responsible, or accountable, for having acted in a
certain manner, because it is supposed that he might
have acted differently; but this not being the case,
all responsibility for such actions would be unjust;
besides, as such actions are *already past* and
perfectly *inevitable*,—for actions that are already
past God himself could not prevent,—it is evident
that any such responsibility would be as useless
and absurd as it would be unjust. Is then man
not accountable for his actions? Most certainly he
is, for he can never get away from their consequences, and these are made pleasurable or painful
as the actions are right or wrong. All true
responsibility must have reference to the future,

never, as is commonly supposed, to the past. The Creator has attached responsibility in the shape of inevitable pain, moral or physical, to every breach of his laws ; or if not in all cases of positive pain, of diminution or loss of happiness. He has given to man a frame, " fearfully and wonderfully made," and his happiness is dependent upon the proper regulation and protection of its complicated mechanism. If he does anything that has a tendency to injure this constitution, either bodily or mental, pain follows and obliges him to desist. Thus, if he puts his hand into the fire, he is subjecting it to an influence that would soon destroy it, and with it all the powers and pleasures that are dependent upon its use ; the pain that he feels, therefore, or the punishment that is inflicted upon him for doing so, quickly obliges him to take it out. Here, then, he is responsible for the ignorance or carelessness that induced him to put his hand where, from the relation that heat bears to the body, it must be injured; and this *whether the action be voluntary or not ;* for the object of the pain being to deter the individual and others from the breach of this law, the pain must be attached to the act. So also with reference to the mind; if a man commits an act of injustice or treachery, he suffers its consequences in the distrust and resentment of his fellow-men, though his evil action be the result of bad education and temptation ; because the certain connexion of such conduct with such consequences, is necessary to make men attach importance to good education and to the avoidance of temptation. If a man says what is false, he suffers from not being believed for the future, and so every fault has its unpleasant consequences. Not an evil thought can pass across the brain without leaving its trace, in less aptitude for good, and therefore for pleasurable sensation. This view involves a much stricter responsibility than the common one, for we are thus accountable to our Maker for the breaking of his laws, whether such breach proceeds from our ignorance, our convictions, or our feelings; whether our actions be voluntary or involuntary, or proceed from free will or necessity; and we are made to suffer for that which is already done, in order that the further evil may be prevented which would ensue from the repetition of the offence. Man is, thus, not only responsible for that portion of his happiness which depends upon his own body and mind, but for that which he derives from the great body of Society, of which he is a member; and if he commits any offence against this latter, that is, if he inflicts any injury upon it, he is accountable in the same sense, and in no other. For such breach of the moral law he suffers, or ought to be made to suffer, just so much as will prevent the same fault in future. If its recurrence could be prevented without any suffering at all, we only do an injustice to the individual in subjecting him to it, since he

could not have acted otherwise. If we are made to
suffer, then, it is for protection, and "punishment"
is *for our own good;* and to ask to be relieved from
it, or to have our sins forgiven, would be asking for
that which would do us an injury. "Forgiveness
of sins" then is out of the question. To suppose
that God is angry and wishes to take vengeance, is
transferring human passion to the Creator, and to
ask Him to interpose miraculously to save us from
the consequences of our actions, would be asking
for the greatest curse he could bestow upon us, for
such consequences are all that reason has for its
guidance. "Forgiveness of sins," "Atonement,"
"Vicarious Sacrifice," are all based upon the
common but erroneous notions of the nature of
"Sin" and the use and necessity of "punishment."
Then "let the dead past bury its dead." The past
is past and cannot be altered or recalled, and what
is more, *nothing could have happened differently.* The
full conviction of this truth would save half the
misery there is in the world, which is made up of
vain regrets for events which it is supposed might
and ought to have been otherwise. Experience, or
knowledge of the consequences of the past, ought to
guide our conduct for the future, but REMORSE
should be banished from the world. Repentance,
so far as it consists of a full perception of evil
consequences, and sorrow and humiliation for the
state of mind which caused them, and which may
therefore influence our coming actions, is a rational

and wholesome feeling,—but when, as is too generally the case, remorse is mixed with it, it is a useless sacrifice of happiness based upon popular error.

PRAISE AND BLAME.—Upon a cursory view of the subject, the difficulty naturally arises, that if actions could not have been otherwise under the circumstances, then merit and demerit are mere names, denoting only the character of certain actions; and that, in consequence, man is not, properly, the subject of praise and blame. Upon reflexion, however, it will be found to be just the reverse; for if there were no necessary connexion between motives and actions, if we might refuse or not to be guided by the former, then, indeed, all praise and blame would be useless; for we praise a certain line of conduct because it is right and in order that it may be pursued, or we blame it that it may be forsaken, and our approbation or disapproval act as motives that are calculated to produce one kind of action more than another.

We naturally approve of, or praise, that which is agreeable to us, and disapprove of, or blame, that which is disagreeable; and that this sense of what is pleasant or unpleasant to us, may have proper weight with those upon whom our happiness in a great measure depends, nature has given us a disposition by which such praise or blame becomes a great source of enjoyment or discomfort, and a strong motive to incite to some actions and to restrain from others. The expression of praise and blame, of approbation or disapprobation is therefore, necessary and proper, although we could in no case act otherwise than we did act under the circumstances. What a complete revolution will take place in society when the expression of this praise and blame shall be no longer made instinctively, but be brought into accordance with the doctrine of necessity! A child knocks its head against the table, and thinking the table had a choice in the matter, turns round and beats it. So man, "a child of larger growth," knocks his head against some rough corner of another's disposition,—he meets with some injury or offence, and not knowing, or not thinking, that the offender could not possibly have done otherwise, he acts as instinctively as the child, and expresses his disapprobation in all probability in the same way. What, however, would be the conduct of a person brought up from infancy as a disciple of necessity? He would know, that of whatever action a person might have been guilty against him, in the state of such an individual's views and feelings, he could not have acted differently, and that it would be as absurd to give way to the feeling of anger in this case as in that of the child : that to produce a different effect towards himself he must alter the cause, that is, he must change the views and feelings of the offender towards himself. If the offence were a personal insult, and the object were to prevent it in future—if knocking the person down were the best mode of doing this, why then knock him down; but this display of the combative propensity would probably produce a similar exhibition on the part of the other, and if they were well matched they would leave off just where they began. But if inquiry were calmly made into the motive of the insult, and the cause removed if possible—according to the dictates of the moral feelings, with kindness and justice—in the generality of cases there would be no fear of its repetition. It can only be this mode of looking at injuries, and the temper of mind consequent upon it, that can give that "soft answer which turneth away wrath." By the predominance of feelings, the produce of opposite views to these. many minds dwell in a state of perpetual irritability, occupied in resenting not only real injuries, but imaginary offences; and is is a question, whether a larger amount of unhappy feeling in the world is not occasioned by the latter class than the former.

The evils resulting from the ordinary mode of considering this subject are very numerous. The common notions concerning merit and demerit, praise and blame, and responsibility, give rise to the worst abuses of our selfish propensities, to envy, hatred, malice, and all uncharitableness. If we were early taught to feel and know that a man's character is the result of his mental constitution, and the circumstances in which he is placed, all such feelings would be kept in check from the mere absurdity of giving vent to them. True, the exhibition of anger and of those feelings that induce us to take immediate vengeance for an offence, may to a certain extent, have the effect of preventing offences; and among the inferior animals this is apparently the legitimate and only mode of doing so; but man possessing additional faculties, his reason enables him to foresee the direct consequences of open violence, and to avoid them, whilst producing *secret* and much more complicated mischief. How is it possible to "Love our enemies, to bless them that curse us, and to do good to them that hate us," so long as we look upon them as the cause of our suffering in the sense that they had liberty to do otherwise? But when they are considered as mere instruments, as acted upon by causes over which they had no control, then indeed we may "love our enemies," love them as fellow-creatures, pity them as being in all probability greater sufferers than ourselves, and with calmness and reason, guided by benevolence and justice, endeavour to remove the cause of their enmity; or if that be impossible, to guard ourselves against it with as little suffering as may be to them.

It may be said, perhaps, it is impossible but that by a law of our nature we should hate that which is unpleasant to us. This is true, but let the feeling receive its right direction, let us hate *vice,* not the *vicious*. The precautions we take to secure ourselves against that which injures us, are not necessarily connected with our hatred of the injurer. We guard ourselves sedulously against the poison of the viper, and the destructive propensities of the tiger, although, knowing as we do that their power and disposition to injure is the inevitable condition of their nature, we cannot be said to hate them.

A man cannot be a true Christian or a true philosopher, until he is a practical Necessitarian. It is then only that he can exercise a perfect control over his own feelings, and cease to be acted upon, to his own discomfort, by the bad feelings of others. It is then that he feels himself master of his own fortune in the strictest sense of the word, for he knows that nothing is uncertain, but that he has only to seek and apply the proper cause, and the effect desired will inevitably follow.

REWARD AND PUNISHMENT. After considering Responsibility, and Praise and Blame, little remains to be said under this head. We have shown that the responsibility of man consists in his experiencing always the natural and necessary results of his actions, and that praise and blame, and consequently reward and punishment, can be employed by the Necessitarian only as motives to the adoption or abandonment of any given line of conduct. Desert and merit being entirely out of

the question, where a man could not possibly have
acted otherwise than he did act, so also are all
rewards to which a man may consider himself
entitled. The rewards of nature are the pleasureable sensations, the happiness consequent upon the
study and observance of, and obedience to, her
laws; her punishments are the pain that follows
the breach of them. It is in this way that Nature
is more powerful than mere doctrine all over the
world, and it is well for mankind that she is so, for
had man been a free agent, such as he is represented, capable of observing and following the
pernicious creeds and dogmas that selfishness has
never failed to instil into his mind, he must long
since have ceased to exist on this earth. But in
spite of what a man professes to believe, he cannot
help invariably seeking, in practice, that which is
pleasureable, and avoiding that which is painful;
and this it is that secures to him, on all occasions,
the object of his being, a balance of enjoyment;
and preserves that consistency in his conduct, which
would be lost, if his actions were guided solely by
his opinions. This balance of enjoyment is the
natural reward which a man receives for having
sought for happiness where it was to be found; but
given to him without any desert on his part. So
suffering is the punishment that nature inflicts
upon those who have sought for happiness where
it was not to be found. But we nowhere find
nature inflicting this punishment, excepting for the

good of the person offending, or of society at large, which, as man is necessarily a part of society, is the same thing; for where a man has offended against the physical or organic laws of his being, so that the pain or punishment resulting can be of no use in a remedial point of view, the pain does not last long, for death mercifully takes him from this state of existence.

But, says the advocate of freedom of will, it is not enough that punishment should be merely remedial, that it should merely have for its object the prevention of the repetition of the offence—a criminal should be made to suffer in exact proportion to the fault he has committed; and this idea of retributive justice, as it is called, but more properly vengeance, lies at the foundation of all criminal codes throughout society, is the main cause of their inefficiency, and of a vast amount of unnecessary suffering. It is assumed that by allotting a certain amount of suffering to a certain amount of "sin" all wrong is made right, and God is necessarily satisfied; but to the consistent Necessitarian, any punishment beyond such as is requisite for the purpose of amendment, must appear an *injustice* of the highest degree towards the individual upon whom it is inflicted, because it is evident that under the circumstances in which he was placed, and with his views and feelings, his conduct was inevitable   Our Criminal Codes

E

cannot be radically reformed and made effectual until this view of the question with respect to accountability and punishment becomes general; until the very idea of retribution be dismissed from our thoughts, and, consequently, the principle of it from our Institutions. The wicked must be regarded as the truly unfortunate of the earth, and punishment the means which true kindness would dictate of correcting vicious habits, and of clearing away the obstacles to that large amount of enjoyment of which their bad dispositions deprive them.

VIRTUE AND VICE.--But if Philosophical Necessity be true, what becomes of all the distinctions between virtue and vice? If all actions are necessary, are not all equally virtuous or vicious? They would undoubtedly be so if there were no difference between pleasure and pain, happiness and misery; but so long as there is this difference, the inherent distinction between actions must continue, as they tend either to one state or the other. Thus, if they tend, all things considered, to produce happiness, they are virtuous; if they tend to misery, they are vicious; and it would be difficult to prove any other distinction between virtue and vice, if considered with reference either to this world or another.

Much has been said and written upon this subject, and although plain in itself, so much has it been mystified, that it has become the general opinion that there is *something in actions themselves,* that places them in the one class or the other. "In

order," says Edwards, "to a thing's being morally
evil, there must be one of these things belonging
to it; either it *must be a thing unfit or unsuitable in
its own nature;* or it must have a bad tendency; or
it must proceed from an evil disposition, and be done
for an evil end." Now if it were possible to conceive of anything unfit or unsuitable in *its own
nature,* supposing that the doctrine of necessity
were unproved, it is impossible to believe it
together with the conviction that nothing could
possibly have been otherwise than it was, and that
everything was appointed by an All-wise Creator.
The same act according to circumstances, is sometimes either virtuous or vicious; thus the act of
killing a man, when done in our country's defence,
is meritorious, but when committed to suit private
revenge or interest, it is murder, and a crime of
the deepest dye. We might easily multiply
instances to show that in the moral world, there is
no difference in the character of actions, when
considered separately from their effects upon
happiness or misery, but that will be unnecessary,
as they must present themselves to every one.
"Morality is the science of the means invented by
man to live together in the most happy manner
possible." It is impossible to conceive that God
can have any other view, in laying down laws,
than the happiness of his creatures; to make man
a better is to make him a happier being.

Are all therefore to be put upon the same level

in society ? Are the vicious upon an equality with
the virtuous ? Yes, when the tiger and the lamb
are so.   When the lap dog gives place to the wolf,
when vipers are hidden in men's bosoms ; in fact,
when we prefer the company of that which gives
us   pain,   to   that   which   bestows   happiness.
Virtuous, holy, pure, and other terms of like
import, have no meaning when applied to actions
in any other sense than as they tend to happiness
or misery ; and when we speak of any kind of
discipline as having a tendency to *perfect* our
character, to make us more pure and holy, we
cannot mean anything else but that it tends to
increase our capacity of enjoyment, and our power
of adding to the happiness of all around. That
man is most perfect who is capable of giving and
receiving the greatest sum of enjoyment. Neither
can we admit that actions are virtuous or vicious,
according to the motives that dictate them, for all
motives are equal being all dependent, like the
actions to which they give rise, upon the mental
or bodily constitution and circumstances. "All
motives," says Bentham, "are abstractedly good ;
no man ever has, ever had, can, or could have, a
motive contrary to the pursuit of happiness or the
avoidance of pain." All feelings, both propensities
and sentiments, in which motives generally arise,
good or bad, whichever they may be called, are
mere blind impulses requiring the guidance of the
reason, which shows that the intellect must be

cultivated, in order that we may *do* well as *mean* well. It is not enough to *wish* to do right, we must set ourselves diligently to learn what *is* right. If we do mischief we are responsibile for it, whatever our wish or motive might have been. Benevolence and Destructiveness are equally hurtful if misdirected or unrestrained. We must be judged then by our actions, not by our motives, for we are as much responsible for the direction of our feelings as for the feelings themselves.

CHAPTER III.

ON THE ORIGIN, OBJECTS, AND ADVANTAGES OF EVIL.

"Is God willing to prevent evil, but not able?
Then he is not omnipotent. Is he able but not
willing? Then he is malevolent. Is he both able
and willing? Whence then is evil?" *   It is
probable that what we call evil is the best, if not
the only means of producing and preserving the
good. Is our calling it evil then merely a mis-
nomer, or must we not rather admit that we are
obliged to limit the power of God, and that He
cannot produce the good in its full amount without
the evil, and that one is absolutely necessary to
the production of the other?

"If the Author and Governor of all things be
infinitely perfect, then whatever is, *is right*; of all
possible systems, He has chosen the best; and,
consequently, there is no *absolute* evil in the
universe. This being the case, all the seeming
imperfections or evil in it are such only in a partial
view, and with respect to the whole system they
are good." †

"Whence then comes evil? is the question which
hath in all ages been reckoned the Gordian knot in

* Epicurus.   † Turnbull's "Christian Philosophy."

philosophy. And, indeed, if we own the existence of evil in the world in an absolute sense, we diametrically contradict what hath been just now proved of God. For if there be any evil in the system that is not good with respect to the whole, then is the whole not good, but evil, or at the best very imperfect; and an author must be as his workmanship is; as is the effect, such is the cause. But the solution of this difficulty is at hand; that there is no evil in the universe. What! are there no pains, no imperfections? Is there no misery no vice in the world? or, are not these evils? Evils indeed they are; that is, those of one sort are hurtful, and those of the other sort are equally hurtful and abominable; but they are not evil or mischievous with respect to the whole. * * * God intends and pursues the universal good of His creation; and the evil which happens is not permitted for its own sake, or through any pleasure in evil, *but because it is requisite for the greater good pursued.*"

" Natural evils proceed from the original condition of things, and are not permitted by God, but in order to prevent greater. Neither the goodness of God, nor the perfection that belongs to the nature of things, required that all natural evils should be removed: for some created beings have evils inherent in their very natures, which God must of necessity either tolerate, or not create those things in which they do inhere." *

* Archbishop King on the Origin of Evil, vol. i., p. 220.

Leibnitz says, "God has permitted evil, because it is enveloped in the best plan which is found in the region of possibles, and that divine wisdom could not fail to have chosen." Dr. Chalmers, commenting on this idea, remarks: "He could not by this hypothesis, expunge the evil that is in our actual universe, but at the expense of a shortcoming from the maximum of good that is rendered by it. We cannot positively affirm this to be true; but we can at least say, that for aught we know, it may be true."

The previous inquiry into the nature of virtue and vice is essential to the proper understanding of this question of acknowledged difficulty, and the Necessitarian is alone able to put it in its simple, true, and proper light. The supposition that man could have done differently in the state of mind and circumstances in which he was placed, has enabled Theologians to introduce most of the mystery that ordinarily is made to surround this subject. We hear consequently of supreme justice; of judicial retribution; of the sanctity of moral laws, irrespective of the tendency of such laws to produce good: of the sovereignty of the Almighty; and that the Most High must vindicate his authority, &c., as if God had some other object in his laws, either physical or moral, than the good of his creatures, or as if like some earthly potentate his dignity and self-importance could be outraged! Now all this is perfectly childish, and when we know that nothing could have happened but what did happen, equally untrue.

The doctrine of Philosophical Necessity assumes that sin and evil exist only in relation to Pain and Pleasure: whether it be the pleasure arising from physical or intellectual enjoyment on the happiness resulting from the satisfaction of the moral and religious sense: or pain, either mental or bodily, in all its different degrees, from mere uneasiness, to that agony which can be supported only for a few moments. In fact, virtue *is* *virtue* only because it promotes the one and avoids the other: and if the directly opposite course conduced to the highest good, that would be virtue and not what we now assume to be such. The virtues have all been named accordingly—in accordance with this tendency to produce the general good; it is impossible therefore, in a *general* *sense* to do evil that good may come, because if the *general* good did come from what we call evil, it would not be evil but good. The supposition that there is something in actions themselves, something unfit or unsuitable in their own nature, that renders them virtuous or vicious, has tended to involve the subject in mystery. Sin, vice, and moral turpitude, are evils from their tendency to produce pain and misery, and the question, on being extricated from all those difficulties with which the notion of man's free agency has encumbered it, assumes its simplest form, viz., what is the use of pain?

The Deity, of course, cannot but be regarded by the Necessitarian as the Author of all things, of the evil as well as the good ; and that evil has its use, and that a benevolent one, cannot be doubted by him whose knowledge of our Creator has been gathered from the numberless instances of benevolent design throughout the universe, which, whilst they manifest the power of God, show us plainly the direction of that power towards the production of the greatest possible enjoyment. If, therefore, it can be demonstrated that pain, which is the only evil, is a necessary agent for the production of this balance of enjoyment ; that it is the only effectual guardian of that system of organization upon which our happiness depends ; that it is essential even to our very existence ; will not the question in part be stripped of its mystery, and the ways of God to man be justified even to our finite comprehensions ?

To creatures possessing our modes of intelligence, there are some propositions which appear by their nature to be absurd and contradictory ; thus, that the half of a thing can be equal to the whole, and that an event which has already taken place can be caused not to have taken place, we instinctively feel to be contradictions, and the reverse of each of these propositions we constitute into an axiom which serves as a basis of reasoning. In the same way we deduce the axiom that God could not create an intelligence equal to himself ; for, to suppose

that he could do so would involve the absurdity of
two infinite existences. All created intelligences
must, there, be finite; limited in their powers of
knowing; and such limitation implies a certain
degree of imperfection which must extend throughout the whole universe of mind. But we cannot
conceive of perfect happiness consisting with any
degree of imperfection; for in the space between
finite and infinite knowledge there must be numberless things, the nature and tendency of which the
highest order of created beings cannot know, and
with reference to which they must be continually
liable to do wrong; that is, to act in opposition to
the laws which constitute the definite character
which everything has received, and in disregard of
the relation which has been established between
such objects and the subject or intelligence, thus
causing a perpetually increasing amount of dis-
arrangement. To check, therefore, that utter
subversion of order, and consequently of happiness,
which the necessary ignorance of created intelligences would occasion, a something must be
appointed which shall constantly act as a warning
whenever these laws are transgressed. It is
doubtful whether a monitor more effectual or
better adapted for the purpose than Pain could
possibly have been selected.

It is probable even that no part of the creation
is free from evil, in the sense in which we thus use
the term, as it is *the invariable accompaniment of*

that error which is consequent upon the necessary limitation of the powers of knowing. George Combe in his " Constitution of Man " has very clearly shown that " All objects that exist, animate and inanimate, have received definite qualities and constitutions, and that good arises from their proper, and evil from their improper use." The field of choice is immense, and our powers are limited; how then are we on all occasions to distinguish the proper from the improper use? Pain and pleasure attend the selection and thus guide and even dictate our choice. This is the most effectual teaching we can have, and very probably the best possible arrangement that can be made. Why then call the pain that seems absolutely necessary to warn us when we are doing wrong, that is, making an improper choice, an evil?

Not only is Pain the best schoolmaster, but much of what we call evil is nothing but the natural adaptation of beings to the necessary conditions of their existence, on the principle of " Natural Selection " by which the weak and bad are destroyed, to make room for the strong and good, which only ought to be preserved. In fact, what we foolishly call evil, is only the natural and necessary law of progress, from good, ever on to better and better. With respect to the employment of pain for the correction of error in other worlds, it must be mere matter of conjecture, for " what

can we reason but from what we know?" It
would appear however to be probable that wherever
there are beings susceptible of enjoyment there also
is pain.

CHAPTER IV.

As the capability of enjoyment is ever found to increase with complexity of structure, the power of feeling pain always increases in the same proportion. For the more complex and delicate the nervous system, and consequently the more varied and intense the powers of thinking and feeling, the more necessity has it for a protection from the numerous surrounding influences which would tend to throw it into disorder, or to destroy it. Pain, in many cases intense pain, could alone compel us to desist from subjecting our body to such influences, and thus destroying the power of enjoyment dependent upon the perfection of our organization. Extraneous substances introduced into the body, are, by a long and intricate process, fitted for becoming part of a living structure, and by a still further process are adapted not only for living, but for feeling and thinking ;—out of the same blood are formed all the different materials of which our frame consists, each new atom being deposited in its proper place, and the old materials, by a variety of processes, carried out of the system, or mixed up

with new matter to be revivified. It is necessary
that each atom should assume its proper place in
the system, and if any derangement or artificial
obstruction prevents this, we are immediately
warned and made conscious by pain that something is wrong, the pain being generally in proportion to the importance of the derangement.

We thus find man possessed of a complicated
apparatus, consisting of numerous functions; first,
those necessary for the preservation of life, and
secondly, those essential for the support of the
nervous system upon which sensation depends; and
he is surrounded on all sides with objects bearing
a fixed relation to himself, the greater part causing
pleasurable sensations, but all, when calculated to
injure him, causing painful ones. Experience, thus
tutored by pleasure and pain, is his only guide as
to what is injurious and what salutary; and real
Education consists in imparting a knowledge of
the nature and tendencies of everything around us.

It is easy to make apparent the objects and
advantages of evil, as it is denominated, in the
physical world, by showing that the benevolent
guardianship of pain alone could maintain our
bodily frames in the state requisite for the enjoyment of which they are the source. Thus, if a
person falls into the fire, pain compels him to extri-
cate himself in the most speedy manner possible;
if a limb is fractured, or any important bodily
function deranged, pain obliges him to seek a

remedy and to repair the mischief. In all these cases, the benevolent intention to the individual sufferer is evident, and he who would consider bodily pain as an evil and not as a good, is like the unruly child that quarrels with its nurse for not allowing him to play with a razor, or to drink poison. But in the moral and intellectual world, suffering, though no less remedial, is less evidently so to mankind at large; although it is incalculable the extent to which the comfort and welfare of all may be enhanced, when it is universally understood that mental as well as bodily suffering is intended to apprise us of the infringement of some important law of nature upon which the preservation of happiness depends. A large class of those sufferings which are thought to be purely mental, may, upon further investigation into the intimate connection between matter and mind, be found to be solely referrible to peculiar states of the bodily system, and may be capable of much alleviation when the corporeal functions upon which they depend shall be better known, so as to come within the province of medicine.

With respect to the sufferings to which we are liable in consequence of the relation in which we stand to society, the benevolent tendency is less obvious, by reason of our present ignorance as to the nature of that relation, and of our own mental constitutions. Our ideas of justice have been formed upon notions of free-will; we have regarded ourselves strictly as individuals, instead of mere parts of the great body of society united to it by ties quite as strong as those that unite one part of our body to another, not indeed by contiguity of atoms, but by contiguity of feeling; and it would be quite as reasonable for one part of the body to object to suffer for the derangement of another part—for the lungs to expostulate with the stomach, 'Why must I suffer for your imprudence?' as for one man to complain to the body of society, of which he forms only a member, ' Why must I individually suffer for your misdeeds ?' The same answer might be given in both cases, that, as one part of the body could not exist without the other, an injury to one is felt by all, that all may feel interested in the restoration of the injured member: that, as one man could not exist (in a state in which existence would be a blessing) without society, he suffers from the sins of another, that he may have an interest in removing the ignorance or ill-feeling from which he suffered, and in keeping every member of the general body sound. Society is, in fact, so organized, that so long as there is one of its members ill-disposed or ignorant, all are liable to pay the penalty ; and although this distribution of evil may not seem in accordance with the common notion of justice, viz., that each man should suffer only for his own misconduct, yet if it can be shown that each individual gains infinitely

F

more than he loses by such an arrangement, justice cannot be said to be outraged by a system which produces the greatest possible happiness to all; or if it can, injustice becomes the virtue and not justice.

Dr. Arnott gives a pleasing picture of the advantages we derive from living in society —" Every one feels that he is a member of one vast civilized society which covers the face of the earth; and no part of the earth is indifferent to him. In England, for instance, a man of moderate fortune may cast his looks around him and say with truth and exultation, ' I am lodged in a house that affords me conveniences and comforts which some centuries ago even a King could not command. Ships are crossing the sea in every direction to bring what is useful to me from all parts of the earth. In China, the men are gathering the tea-leaf for me; in America they are planting cotton for me; in the West India Islands, they are preparing my sugar and my coffee for me; in Saxony they are shearing the sheep to make me clothing; at home, powerful steam-engines are spinning and weaving for me, and making cutlery for me, and pumping the mines, that minerals useful to me may be procured. Although my property is small, I have post-coaches running day and night on all the roads, to carry my correspondence, and I have protecting fleets and armies around my happy country, to secure my enjoyments and repose. Then

I have editors and printers, who daily send me an account of what is going on throughout the world, among all those people who serve me. And to crown the whole, I have books; the miracle of all my possessions, more wonderful than the wishing-cap of the Arabian Tales; for they transport me instantly, not only to all places, but to all times. By my books I can conjure up before me, to vivid existence, all the great and good men of antiquity; and for my individual satisfaction I can make them act over again the most renowned of their exploits: the orators declaim to me: the historians recite, the poets sing : and from the equator to the pole, or from the beginning of time until now, by my books I can be where I please.' Such has been the effect of the combined powers of man, giving " to each individual of the civilized millions that cover the earth, nearly the same enjoyments as if he were the single lord of all."* Compare these advantages with those which an individual might possess by his own unaided powers, and it is evident how much more he gains by the social arrangement than he loses by being a part of the great whole. The object of creation is to produce the largest possible sum of enjoyment to all, considering individuals not as individuals, but only as parts of the sensitive world, and it is to the practical ignorance of this wise arrangement, and to the tendency that all have to individualize their enjoyments, that we

* Elements of Physics, Introduction, p. 26.

must attribute much of the moral evil, or mental pains, now prevalent throughout society. The advantages that ought to be derived by the race generally from the progress of civilization, are too much monopolized by the few, whose happiness, meanwhile, would be far better secured if they were made to participate only in the general well-being. The overgrown wealth which tempts the possessor to the destruction of the power of enjoyment which nature gave him, would suffice to call into healthy and vigorous action hundreds now cramped and stunted under the chilling influence of want. The excess of ease and leisure which eats into the soul of the indolent in the lap of luxury, would refresh the minds, and cheer the spirits of a multitude whose incessant toil furnishes the perverted blessing to its victim. The object and advantage of what is called moral evil then is to extend these advantages to the whole of mankind.

What then, will it be said, are crimes against the person and property, robberies and murders, good upon the whole to society? These evils bear the same relation to the body of Society, as physical evils do to our own bodies, and are intended for the same purpose—to secure the health and happiness of the system. Some vital organ is diseased, and the consequent pain drives the individual to seek a remedy before the organic functions are destroyed. Robbers and murderers are diseased parts of the body of society, and the evils resulting from the inroads of such malignants, serve to induce men to look to the causes of crime, and to apply those measures that are calculated to restrain it ; thus diminishing by the most direct means crime, and the suffering thence resulting.

It has been objected that virtue does not, in the present state, on all occasions, produce a balance of good to the virtuous. As a general rule, it is admitted that it does so, and that when the laws of nature have free operation, there are no exceptions ; but it is urged that since the laws and social institutions of mankind are at variance with the laws of nature, particular cases do occur in which a man suffers for acting virtuously.

Virtue, to the Necessitarian, mean that line of conduct which, *all* things considered, shall be productive of the greatest happiness to all. Now suppose that in consequence of some human law made for individual advantage, or the advantage of a class, a person in calculating the results of a certain action, perceives that though it may tend to the advantage of the whole, yet that he individually must suffer by it. Still the strength of his moral faculties, his innate love of virtue, and the persuasion in which he has been brought up, that virtue is the best policy, induce him to choose the virtuous path. What good arises from his suffering in the cause of virtue ? This much. The evil he suffers induces him to look to the cause—he discovers it in the unjust law, and he joins others who have felt the ill effects of the same law, in obliging legislators to repeal it. It is in this manner that the state of society is continually improved. But this particular individual may not live to enjoy the fruits of his virtue—how then is he benefited by it? He has been benefited all his life by the state of society in which he has lived having been improved by similar means: others have suffered in the past, more for him than he has for the people now in being, and he is a proportionate gainer. He reaps in this way the reward of virtue, though not of his own individual virtue.

As earthquakes, storms, and hurricanes tend to restore the equilibrium of nature's powers, a few suffering by them, but thousands benefiting, so moral tornadoes help to maintain communities in a healthy state.

By the French revolution, the moral atmosphere of France was rendered far more favourable to the growth of virtue, and, consequently, of enjoyment, to the whole of its inhabitants.

" Mr. Arthur Young has truly described the deplorable indigence of the French peasantry prior to the Revolution, and the present age has sufficiently experienced the evils arising from the miserable condition of the Irish poor. Posterity, however, will not fail to remark, that the sufferings of the peasantry in France brought about the Revolution by which the condition of the labouring poor was, in the first instance at least, considerably, and but for the enormous sins they committed during its progress would have been durably improved: and we are ourselves witnesses to the formidable weight which the Irish people have acquired, since the redundance of their population has swelled the ranks of the disaffected, and deluged their neighbours with distress. * * * The misery, therefore, which is the immediate consequence of the redundant population, which flows from political oppression, is in fact the means which nature takes to hasten the downfall of the institutions which have occasioned it; like the swelling of a limb which has been wounded or imbibed poisonous matter, it is the effort of nature to discharge the noxious substance which occasions the suffering. The benevolent laws of nature are incessantly operating for the good of man, even when their tendency is most mistaken by numerous observers. At the moment when the misery of Ireland was confidently appealed to, as demonstrating the unavoidable pressure of population upon subsistence, that very misery was the means which she was taking to terminate the distresses of the country; and heal the wounds of the social system." *

The evils of WAR present great difficulties to those who regard only its immediate effects upon a people or district; but to such as

*Alison on Population, vol. 1, p. 247.

study the history of civilization, the wars
which have accompanied its progress appear,
not as unmixed gratuitous evil, but as the
means of working out the good of evil; by forming
the character of nations; introducing light where
darkness and night before existed ; uniting by one
bond of brotherhood the people of each nation,
formerly consisting of detached individual families
or clans; breaking down old and useless institutions that had answered their ends, and now
served merely as clogs to the advancement and
happiness of society; by clearing away old and
decayed states in which, from defective institutions
and the misgovernment of ages, the balance of
happiness was reversed and turned against the
people. The wars of the Crusades, mad as they
would appear, yet were the means of spreading
throughout Europe the light that broke the bonds
of superstition, and gradually led to the Reformation, which again contributed to that freedom of
inquiry from which the present advance in science
results. The wars between France and England,
notwithstanding their many disastrous consequences,
helped to strengthen the character of both people,
and to give that spirit and hardihood by which the
greatness of each has been maintained. The wars
of the White and Red Roses, whilst they ravaged
our country and weakened the aristocracy,
emancipated the people—the masses, from civil
bondage, and led to the formation of those institu-

'tions upon which British freedom has been dependent.

"War," says Mr. Alison, "Is the great instrument by which the agency of some important laws of nature is maintained. It is the decay of military virtue which exposes civilized states to destruction from the efforts of their barbarous neighbours. Their fall does not take place till they have conferred all the benefits on mankind of which they were capable, and till their further continuance would be a misfortune to humanity. The destruction of Nineveh by the Medes, of Babylon by the Persians, of Rome by the Goths, and of Constantinople by the Turks, served only to extinguish so many branches of the human race, in which age had withered the sinews of virtue, and prosperity exhausted the sources of happiness."*

Upon the same subject Mr. Combe observes, †" There is more of benevolent arrangement in the tendency of savage and barbarous tribes, to wage furious wars with each other than at first sight appears. The Irish peasantry are still barbarous in their minds and habits, and but for the presence of a large army of civilized men, who preserve the peace, they would fight and exterminate each other. It is questionable whether the miseries that would attend such a course of action would exceed those which are actually endured from starvation. The bane of Ireland is, that her population has increased

*On Population, vol I., p. 268.   † Lectures on Moral Philosophy.

far more rapidly than her capital, morality, and knowledge. Where a nation is left to follow its own course, this does not occur. Dissension keeps down the numbers, until intelligence, capital, and industry take the lead. England prevented the Irish from fighting, but she did little to improve them."

Destruction and renovation is the great law of nature. This is infinitely better than that nations should drag out "a slow and snake-like life of dull decay" and decrepid old age. A generation of a thousand millions is swept away about every 35 years; and should it be cleared off a few years before its time, what is that to the necessity for a clear and healthy atmosphere for all the generations to come?

These are some of the effects of Evil considered with reference to society as a whole : with respect to the individuals of which the social body is composed, the subject has been partially considered in treating of Rewards and Punishments.

CHAPTER V

The greater part of mankind being imbued with a notion that the will is free, are in the habit of regarding more the objects and ends of actions, than the causes which originate them; intent chiefly upon results, the delicate and wonderful machinery that produces these results is comparatively unnoticed. A large part of that which is called "evil" in the world consists of nothing more than the wants, the desires, that furnish the motives to action, and without which we could not maintain our existence for a day. All the faculties of man, when active, constitute wants or desires. Thus he wants food, he wants some one to love, and who shall love him in return; he wants the approbation of his fellows, he wants to see every one receive that which is his due; his happiness consists in the gratification of these and other wants, and pain results when from any cause they remain ungratified. But these wants are the impelling forces which irresistibly set him in motion, securing an infinite diversity in the direction of his powers, and a never-ceasing succession of sensations.

Some of our most pressing wants have relation to the very preservation of our existence, the appetite for food, for instance : and could we have been made to live without sustenance, freedom from all liability to the pains of hunger would not compensate for the loss of the pleasures of appetite. Nor would the privilege of requiring no bread, be 'equal to the advantage we derive from the law of nature which compels us to earn it by the sweat of the brow. Laing, in his "Journal of a residence in Norway," observes : "The food best for a country is clearly that which it requires the greatest exertion of industry and skill to produce. That which requires but little of such exertion, as potatoes, would undoubtedly, reduce a nation to a low state of industry and skill. Those are in the wrong path who would reduce the rate of pauperism in England by reducing the standard of subsistence for the poor. If the English labourers, instead of considering wheaten bread and meat necessary for their proper subsistence, were to be contented with potatoes and salt herrings, the increase of pauperism among them would be in proportion to the diminished value of their food and the ease of obtaining it." "Potatoes are the worst food for a nation to subsist on, because in proportion to their nutriment as food, they require less labour, less exertion of body and mind to bring them to a state of food than any other article of human culture. The planting and digging up, the boiling or baking, are almost the only operations required with the potato; and therefore, the nation which is satisfied with a potato diet must be in a state of sloth and inactivity, bodily and mental. The most complicated manufacture, perhaps, which we have among mankind, and which in all its parts requires the most continual exertion of human industry and skill, is the production of a quartern loaf from a few seeds of wheat put into the ground."

Thus Necessity is the mother of invention. The ordinary and common wants, of our nature, of food, clothing, and lodging, always recurring and never satisfied, set us in motion, bring into action all the powers of our mind, and call for that exercise which is as necessary to the mental powers as ailment to the body. Locke says, "all our actions owe their rise to a state of uneasiness," which uneasiness is more or less intolerable as the action to which it would urge us is more or less important. The disposition to activity increases with exercise, the more we do the more we seem disposed to do; and it may with truth be said that never are we so happy as when every moment has its full employment. Take away the common wants of our nature, and you take away that which produces all this activity. So that these constantly recurring wants, so far from being infirmites in the body of society, are its very principle of life, the source of all its health and enjoyment.

It is not uncommon to hear the *solid* and *perfect*

happiness of the future state described as consisting
in total rest, inactivity, and freedom from all wants
and desires; but whatever may be the case in the
unknown world, constituted as we are with respect
to this, we can conceive of no possible degree of
happiness resulting from such a state; for all our
ideas of enjoyment are ideas of wants gratified;
and man is unquestionably infinitely the gainer by
being surrounded perpetually by wants, than he is
the loser from their occasional non-gratification.

Evil, then, is the result of the necessary limitation of our faculties, and without pain we should
have no means of knowing or avoiding what would
injure us; and none of our motives would be
sufficiently strong to induce us to seek our own
welfare. Now if a man is idle, and refuses to
perform his allotted part in the labour of the world,
nature pinches him in the stomach and obliges him
to move on. Hunger is the great conservator of all
law and order, it sets every one to work, it keeps
every one in his place, and if it is an evil at all,
every one must admit it is a very necessary one.

The ordinary idea of philosophical Christians
differs apparently but little from this view of the
nature of the evil, viz., that it is permitted by an
All-wise Providence, and that in His hands, it on
all occasions tends to good; that it is the means of
the improvement and purification of our characters,
and a preparation for a future state. But there is
considerable practical difference between the two

views. Pain, says the advocate of one, is intended
to prepare you for a future state; bear it therefore
with resignation, looking to a hereafter for the
reward of your patience. Pain, says the advocate
of the other, is the invariable intimation that you
have disobeyed some of the Creator's laws upon
which happiness is dependent here; look to its
cause, therefore, and remove it.

But if evil results from ignorance, might not
Almighty Power and Wisdom have interfered to
save us from the effects of our conduct when
injurious? Certainly, but it would be by cutting
the spirit of action and of right conduct at the
root, and we should have no interest in rectifying
error; and as the exercise of reason is based upon
the uniformity of nature's laws, any interference
with this uniformity by such special providence,
would make reason a useless, if not a fatal gift. It
may be asked is not reason itself then an undesirable gift, and would not man have been better left
to the mere guidance of Instinct as the brutes are?

Isaac Taylor, the Author of the Natural History
of Enthusiasm, says, "The reader need not be
reminded that the application of the word Instinct
comprehensively, and without distinction, to all the
actions of the brute orders. is a popular im-
propriety. One might as well call all the actions of
man rational, as all of the inferior order instinctive.
When an animal acts in a manner, which differs in
no essential circumstance to a corresponding action

in man, a delusion must be engendered by applying
to the two actions different terms. We should
confine the word Instinct to those instances in
which a course rational as to its end, is pursued by
a voluntary agent, under circumstances that forbid
the supposition that it springs from a perception or
calculation of the connexion of means and end.
The instance usually adduced, that of the construction of the honey-comb, is one of the most popular
that can be named, especially because it involves
some of the highest and most abstruse principles of
geometry. Philosophical writers must be understood to use the words reason and instinct in a
popular sense, when attributing one to man as his
prerogative, and the other to the brute as his blind
faculty. The terms reason and instinct thus
vaguely used mean, more reason and less reason.
For if the brutes were altogether destitute of
reason and liberty, in the same sense in which the
bee is destitute of both in building her cells,
rewards and punishments would have no operation
or efficiency."

Instinct appears to be a power impelling
voluntary agents to act in a single direction,
without any perception of the connection of means
and ends, and little capable of adapting itself to
circumstances; consequently it has a very limited
field of action. If, therefore, we were to be
governed entirely by instinct, in order to our
possessing the large field of action that we now

enjoy we should require ten thousand instincts at least. But all the instincts with which we are acquainted we find acting by means of organisation; and a brain containing the organs of ten thousand instincts would, it is to be feared, be inconveniently large. Man is a creature possessing a variety of instincts, which give him his purpose and disposition to act: but instead of being directed to their objects in one unvarying manner, they are put under the charge of a generalizing instinct, which we call reason, and which gives to each a liberty of acting in a hundred different ways, calling at the same time our other feelings into sympathetic action. It must be evident that this is a means of increasing our sensations a hundredfold, and it is the aggregate of pleasurable sensations that constitutes happiness, and the evil, or the painful sensations resulting from the wrong direction which our instincts sometimes take, are not in the proportion of one to a hundred of the extra sensations we receive.

Suppose that appetite in man, as in the lower animals, infallibly directed him to eat only at proper times and in proper quantities of some few things that are the most wholesome, the many evils bodily and mental, which arise from gluttony and drunkenness, would be spared, but we should lose the varied pleasures of the taste, with all the sympathetic pleasures which accompany its gratification.

G

Take another instance, the love of offspring.
Suppose that children could run about as soon as
they were born, and were protected by the perfection of their instincts; much trouble in nursing
would be saved, and all the evils of physical mismanagement; but all the pleasures, the hopes and
fears, joys and sorrows, of parental solicitude
would be lost. Perhaps nothing shows more the
folly of those who would take the place of the
Almighty and make a better system, than the fact
that the pleasures derivable from offspring, more
intense perhaps than any other, depend in a great
measure upon what may be called the evil of the
helplessness of the object.

Happiness is made up of units, of single
pleasurable sensations, and the object of nature is
to bring us into such circumstances as shall produce a constant succession of such sensations; and
even if they are partially painful, they are preferable
to the pains of ennui, "which is the absence of
sensations sufficiently acute to engage attention."
Habitual sensations also are too weak to avert
ennui, and none but habitual sensations could be
experienced by us if we were guided by infallible
instincts without the diversifying power of reason;
for all progression would cease, and comparative
stagnation would be the consequence.

CHAPTER VI.

DEATH.

" How strange is human pride !
I tell thee that those living things,
To whom the fragile blade of grass,
   That springeth in the morn
   And perisheth ere noon,
   Is an unbounded world ;
I tell thee that those viewless beings,
Whose mansion is the smallest particle
   Of the impassive atmosphere,
      Think, feel, and live, like man ;
That their affections and antipathies,
   Like his, produce the laws
   Ruling their moral state ;
And the minutest throb,
That through their frame diffuses
   The slightest, faintest,.motion,
   Is fixed and indispensable
      As the majestic laws
   That rule yon rolling orbs."
                              Shelley.

Such, though a poetical, is yet a logical deduction
from the doctrine of "Necessity" Man individually, and the whole world, of which
he forms an insignificant item, is one general
" effect," not a cause. He prides himself upon
his separate independent existence and freedom
of will, but he has no such existence ; he
is part only of a great whole, and he cannot be

separated. Millions of causes helped to bring him into existence and made him what he is, and millions of causes playing upon his mental mechanism produce all the effects of his varied being. He is dependent upon the human race, and the human race on the great whole of animate existence; and animate and inanimate are again inseparable. "The simplest germination of a lichen is, if we apprehend rightly, directly linked with the grandest astronomical phenomena; nor could even an infusory animalcule be annihilated without altering the equilibrium of the universe.

> ' Nothing in this world is single,
> All things by a law divine
> In one another's being mingle.'

Plato had some dim forecast of this when he taught that the world was a great animal; and others, since Plato, when they considered the universe the [manifestation of some transcendent life, with which every separate individual life was related, as parts are to the whole." *

"Everything in nature contains all the powers of nature; everything is made of one hidden stuff. The true doctrine of Omnipresence is, that God reappears in all his parts in every moss and cobweb; thus the universe is alive." †

"When we view the world as one universal effect we are at once led to the contemplation of a

---

* Lewes.　　　　　　　† Emerson.

universal Divine Agency. Does not the Infinite act on every atom? * * * God never delegates his powers; *He cannot transfer divinity to a substance:* there is no power therefore separated from himself. In Him all things have their being." *

> " All are but parts of one stupendous whole,
> Whose body nature is and God the soul."

In fact, let us look at it from whatever point of view we will, we cannot disjoin man from the rest of creation and consider him individually and separately.

Then what is death? It is simply the removal of the old worn out, and useless matter, from the great body of sentient existence, leaving that body always young and vigorous; the old matter taking new forms and immediately passing into new life. To individual man, "Death is the sleep of the weary. It is the repose, the body's repose, after the busy and toilsome day of life," and when natural and not violent it is as painless as birth— of the beginning and end of life we are equally unconscious, "the exhausted faculties sinking to their mortal repose, as they do to nightly sleep. Death is as natural as Birth, and equally necessary, for it is the parent of life."

Had man made the world, he would have made himself immortal, for in the "future" world that he does create, immortality is to be his state. He

---

* Rev. J. White Mailler, " Philosophy of the Bible."

would probably have made a great mistake. Individual drops of water are collected on the brows of
the mountains, they flow down into the valleys and
form rivers, flowing on to the great ocean. By a
silent and imperceptible force, calculated by Leslie
to be two hundred thousand times greater than
that of the combined exertions of the whole human
race, this water raised in vapour, descends in rain,
again forms the river, which with sparkling vivid
vitality flows again to the ocean, and so goes on in
an unbroken circle. The same river flows on in
never ending succession and is thus immortal,
though not one drop of water retains its individuality; but had the river been immortal in man's
sense of immortality, in identity of individual
drops or atoms, the river would have been a
stagnant, stinking, death-diffusing ditch. The
leaves of the trees are born in spring in tender
variegated greens, in summer they take a darker
sameness, and in autumn they change again in hues
all beautiful: and then comes winter, when pierced
by insects, covered with dust, shrivelled by the
frost, they fall off and die, that they may again be
born in spring. Would we change this order of
birth and decay that the *same* leaves might be
everlasting? So with man's coveted immortality,
would we change the present vigorous everlasting
babyhood, childhood, and youth of society, in order
that a comparatively few old people, like the
withered leaves of autumn, might boast that they

had retained their identity from the beginning of the world till now, selfishly keeping out all others from *their* term of existence.

This change of seasons is closely typical of man's existence. In spring everything is young, fresh, vigorous, and green, and all the hilarity and sunshine of early youth belong to it. Summer has its flowers Autumn its fruit, and then comes old age and decay—the sere and yellow leaf—the death of winter. So man has his year—of three score and ten journeys round the sun allotted to him, and then come winter and death and his reappearance in the new growth of spring,—and what does it matter whether the new body be called Dick Snooks as before, or Tom Styles? Happiness depends upon a continuous succession of new sensations; were we organized as we now are, to live much longer than the time allotted to us, our sensations, from being habitual and from the decay of our nervous system, would be too weak to afford us enjoyment, and life would become a burden to us. When time has blunted the feelings, or the objects of them no longer exist, knowledge, so much coveted, is of little use unless it can be, as it now is, infused into new forms capable of all that freshness of feeling in which youth so much excels old age.

With the present arrangement, the great Body of Humanity (considered as an individual), with its Soul, the principle of Sensation, is ever fresh and vigorous and increasing in enjoyment. As yet it is but in its childhood : as its knowledge increases, so will its happiness. Death and Birth, the means of removal and succession, bear the same relation to this body of society, as the system of waste and reproduction do to the human body : the old and useless and decayed material is carried out, and fresh substituted, and thus the frame is renovated and rendered capable of ever increasing happiness. The parallel between the soul of society and that of the individual man is equally complete ; as with respect to the latter, all the aimless studies and useless accomplishments of youth are soon forgotten, while only the knowledge that is serviceable is remembered, so in the great mind of society, the absurd theories and systems that occasionally rear themselves into notice are shortly consigned to oblivion, and all the useful ideas that have existed in the individual minds of the human race, are retained. While our thoughts traverse, as if in personal recollection, the different by-gone ages of society, the minds of all the illustrious men that have lived form part of our own, until we arrive at its infancy, concerning which, as of our own infancy, we can remember nothing. The minds, that is to say, the ideas and feelings of which they were composed, of Socrates, Plato, Epicurus, Galileo, Bacon, Locke, Newton, are thus for ever in existence, and the immortality of the soul is preserved, not in individuals but in the great body of Humanity.

The song of the lark is as sweet to-day as it was
a thousand years ago—what would be gained therefore by its being the same lark ?—but doubtless the
little songster also sighs for immortality and a
place not *in* but beyond the skies. What in man
is worth preserving but his song, and what matters
it in what body that is preserved ? A series or
succession of being seems decidedly the best for
this world, and may be the best for all worlds.
The most that the Natural Theologian is justified
in asserting with reference to a future life is, ' If it
is better, *all things considered*, that I should live
again in another world, I shall be certain to do so ;
if it is not better, all things considered, I do not
wish it.' There need be no forcible rupture of the
known order of God's providence to enable us to
retain an indistinct and troubled dream of previous
existence, the cessation of which existence could be
no more regretted than our non-existence before
we were born. The present recognised order of
things would certainly be better than a reservation
for suffering even of a few: much better indeed
than the infinite suffering of the many. The finite
happiness of all that have ever lived could never
equal the *infinite* suffering of *one*.

To the race, although not to individuals, all
beautiful things are preserved for ever: all that is
really good and profitable is immortal. The lovely
world, although created anew every year, is yet the
same that Adam saw in Paradise. " Life is then

like a beautiful starlight night, in which no long-
seen constellation sets without the rising of
another," and thus generation after generation has
risen and set. And yet for all the elements of
happiness—

> " For love and beauty and delight
> There is no death, nor change,"
> *   *   *   *   *
> " 'Tis *we*, 'tis *ours* are changed ; not they."

It is true—

> " All things that we love and cherish
> Like ourselves, must fade and perish ;
> Such is our rude mortal lot—
> *Love itself would* did they not."
>
> SHELLEY.

We have hitherto considered Death in the light
of a succession of being as opposed to immortality; as
a constant change of the material frames, the recep-
tacles for the time of all alone worthy of continued
existence. We have referred principally to natural
death as it is called, that is, death without violence
—but natural death in all but man does not take
place in the slow process of decay, but in the being
eaten. Life is always preserved at high pressure:
population always pressing on the means of
subsistence. Nature is no respecter of individuals.
Her object seems to be to keep the largest possible
number in the greatest possible strength and vigour
and efficiency for enjoyment. " There is no
exception to the rule," says Darwin, " that every
organic being naturally increases at so high a rate,

that if not destroyed, this earth would soon be covered by the progeny of a single pair." The rate of increase is geometrical. Mr. J. A. Rowell has calculated that from a single specimen of the flesh fly there would proceed in six generations sufficient flies to cover the world to the depth of about a mile and a quarter. Life presses towards existence in a similar way in almost all departments, and the most perfect order and arrangement exist in the mode in which it is kept within due bounds; the good and strong preserved; the weak and bad destroyed. It is most astonishing the systematic provision that prevails for this purpose, and the general ignorance on the subject is if anything still more astonishing. Man would get no " cabbage " if not for the ichneumon fly which destroys the caterpillars that are hatched from the eggs of the common white butterfly. "On the oak," says Dr. Carpenter, "not less than two hundred kinds of caterpillars have been estimated to feed, and the nettle, which scarcely any beast will touch, maintains fifty different species of insects, but for which check it would soon annihilate all the plants in its neighbourhood." Check is placed on check, the death of one superabundant population supporting the life of other descriptions of beings. "After the inhabitants had contrived to extirpate the little crow from Virginia, at an enormous expense, they would gladly have given twice as much to buy back the tribe. A reward of threepence a

dozen was offered in New England for the purple
gracle, which commits great havoc among the crops,
but protects so much more herbage than he destroys,
that the insects when he was gone caused the total
loss of the grass in 1749, and obliged the colonists to
get hay from Pennsylvania and even to import it
from Great Britain. A few years since an Act was
passed by the Chamber of Deputies to prohibit the
destruction of birds in a particular district of
France. They had been recklessly killed off,
and the harvest being swept away in its
first green stage by millions of hungry reapers,
the earth had ceased to yield its increase. Extensive
inroads like these upon the economy of nature
reveal to us its wisdom, and clearly show us that
if one while it is a blessing that particular animals
should eat, at another it is a benefit to the world
that they should be eaten. A flight of rooks
renders services which could not be performed by
all the cultivators of the soil put together, and if
the poor birds are occasionally mischievous they
are richly worthy of their hire. Make the largest
probable allowance for their consumption of a
portion of that crop, the whole of which they
preserve, and they are still immeasurably the
cheapest labourers upon a farm. Pages would be
required to tell all the mistakes which are committed in the blind rage for destruction, and in the
readiness of the lord of creation to believe that
everything which tastes what he tastes is a rival

and a loss. Even wasps, which find no friends, chiefly because they are armed with a sting, which, unlike man, they rarely or ever use unprovoked, are an important aid in keeping certain tribes within bounds." *

As to the ignorant, conceited, and presumptious idea, that the world was made for man alone, we cannot turn our eyes in any direction in which pleasurable sensation is not spread around; every leaf, every blade of grass, the atmosphere, the waters, swarm with creatures in a state of positive happiness, the collective sum of which, perhaps, may greatly exceed that of the human race.

I was much struck with this truth while recently reclining on a bank in a very beautiful grove some two miles in circumference. Its lordly owner and its keepers were absent, and I was probably the only human being there; but the whole area seemed quite complete without man, and only his "madness, pride, impiety" could have supposed it made for him alone. There was not an inch untenanted There was the voice of the pheasant and the jay, of the wood-pigeon and the rook, of the jackdaw and the hawk, and fifty smaller birds : there was the hare, the rabbit, the hedge-hog and the dormouse and shrew, and the sun-beam and the half-shut eye showed the air full of humming life; and the moss on which I lay was full of green and golden bettles, and grass-hoppers

* Quarterly Review, January, 1858.

and long-legged spiders and the thrifty ant. There
was one continued song and hum of enjoyment, and
I could not help thinking how vain and presump-
tuous was man's pretension to monopolise it all.
Here at least the owner was the instrument only
of a happiness far greater than his own, and
probably than of all his dependants. It is true all
were happy in eating up each other, but this
detracts very little from the sum of enjoyment.
" The perch swallows the grub-worm, the pickerel
swallows the perch, and the fisherman swallows the
pickerel ; and so all the chinks in the scale of being
are filled."

" Intimately associated with physical injuries and
pain is the death in which they ultimately result.
This necessary end constitutes to many minds the
chief terror of the incidents which produce it. That
all which lives should be born to die detracts nothing from the wonders of their being. Which would
be the greater marvel, a ship whose timbers should
never rot, or a ship which itself should gradually
decay, but before its lease was out should give
birth to new vessels, which again should bring forth
fresh fleets to be multiplied from age to age in increasing numbers and unimpaired vigour ? This
last is the prodigious method of Providence.
A solitary oak contains within its trunks a power
to generate future forests, which will spread their
giant arms and rear their kingly heads when their
progenitor is returned to the soil from whence it

sprung; while their numerous progeny, from the first-born which rivals the parent-stem to the sprouting acorn which just lifts its leaflets above the earth, will continue to maintain the succeeding line in an unbroken gradation. The system runs through all creation, from man, who is the lord of it, down to the meanest piece of moss that grows upon a wall. In such profusion are the germs of animated things produced, and then cast forth to perish, with no opportunity, from their very excess, to evolve the structure of which each contains the rudiments, that we might think there was prodigality, even to wastefulness, if waste were possible where power is infinite. Without death, far narrower limits must have been put to propagation than prevail at present. The same set of men and animals must have occupied the globe, and myriads of creatures, we of this generation included, could never have tasted the delights of existence. Death therefore may be said to be the parent of life. What would have been the scheme of the Almighty if sin had never entered into the world is altogether beyond our faculties to conjecture. Our knowledge, we find from experience, is limited to observing what actually exists, and it is with admiration that we perceive how the general good is maintained through the general mortality, and each creature is made to contribute both by its life and by its death to the benefit of the rest. The examples are innumerable, and we select a few out of the thousands that might be adduced. There is a class of animalcules called *Infusoria*, because they can be obtained by *infusing* any vegetable or animal substance in water, which, according to Professor Owen, ' are the most minute, and apparently the most insignificant of created beings.' Many of them are so diminutive that a single drop of water may contain five hundred millions of individuals. Nevertheless the varieties in size are such that the difference between the smaller and the greater 'is greater than between a mouse and an elephant,' though even the elephant of the race is invisible to the naked eye. ' They are the most widely diffused, and by far the most numerous of all the forms of organized life '; and whether in fresh water or in salt, 'there is hardly a drop of spray flung from the paddle of a steam boat which does not contain some specimens of the race. They pervade every clime—torrid, frigid and temperate—and extend their reign in the northern latitudes beyond that of the vegetable kingdom. When we consider their incredible numbers, their universal distribution, their insatiable voracity, and that it is the particles of decaying bodies which they are appointed to devour, we must conclude that we are in some degree indebted to these active scavengers for the salubrity of our atmosphere. Nor is this all : they perform a still more important office in preventing the progressive diminution of the present amount of organized matter upon the earth. For when this matter is dissolved or suspended in water, in that state of comminution and decay which immediately precedes its final decomposition into the elementary gases, and its subsequent return from the organic into the inorganic world, these wakeful members of nature's invisible police are everywhere ready to arrest the fugitive organized particles and turn them back into the ascending stream of animal life. Having converted the dead and decomposing particles into their own living tissues, they themselves become the food of larger Infusoria, as, for example, the *Rotifera*, and of numerous other small animals which in their turn are devoured by larger animals, such as fishes; and thus a pabulum, fit for the nourishment of the higher organized beings, is brought back by a short route from the extremities of the realms of organic nature. 'Truly indeed,' says Ehrenberg, 'the microscopic organisms are very inferior in individual energy to lions and elephants, but in their united influences they are far more important than all those animals.' Their own life sustained by the product of death, the Infusoria are destined themselves to perish that they may sustain the frames of the creatures above them, death continuing to support life throughout the graduated scale of existence, until, the circle run, the food once more comes back to the nutriment of animalcules from which it originally proceeded.

H

" The flesh fly species is another indefatigible scavenger, as they increase their weight two hundred-fold in twenty-four hours, and Professor Owen states that there is no exaggeration in the assertion of Linnæus that three flesh flies would devour the carcase of a horse as quickly as would a lion.

" The animalcules supported the dragon-fly, the dragon-fly the newts, the newts the beetle, the beetle the sparrow, and most likely the sparrow some bigger creature before the animal compound was given out to the inexorable maggots, and re-vivified anew in the shape of flies, again to run the destructive round. Nature seems to have taken special pains to maintain in vigour the carnivorous element wherever animal life is congregated to-gether. If the pike is carefully excluded from the fish-pond, he appears there after a time just as though he had smelt out his prey, and made his way to it over earth or through air. The eggs have been carried there on the legs and feathers of the water-fowl, or else been eaten by them, and passed from their bodies undigested. The due balance is maintained in spite of the jealous preserver of fish." *

Thus we find, as Darwin remarks, " that the structure of every organic being is related, in the most essential yet often hidden manner, to that of all other organic beings, with which it comes into

* "Quarterly Review," Jan. 1858.

competition for food or residence, or from which it has to escape, or on which it preys. * * * All that we can do is to keep steadily in mind that each organic being is striving to increase at a geometrical ratio; that each at some period of its life, during some season of the year, during each generation, or at intervals, has to struggle for life,. and to suffer great destruction. When we reflect on this struggle, we may console ourselves with the full belief that the war of nature is not incessant that no fear is felt, that death is generally prompt, and that the vigorous, the healthy, and the happy, survive and multiply." If we do not more justly appreciate the plan of creation, it is owing to the false light that Theology throws upon it; misrepresenting the aim and object of existence, and assigning to man a thoroughly false position in relation to the whole. What Bishop Berkeley says of Metaphysicians is true of Theologians, "They have first raised a dust and then complain they cannot see." Mankind cannot be separated from the rest of creation which must be regarded as one and indivisible. Judged as a whole it is ever progressing; the good, the strong, and the beautiful, daily more predominating. Wherever in the "struggle for existence" and in the ever changing circumstances and conditions to which it gives rise, variations occur favourable to individuals, such improvements, by the law of hereditary descent or "Natural Selection" are retained and transmitted;

and the new and improved specimens having the best chance in the struggle, gradually but necessarily extinguish the old, and take their place. This law of progress—this extinction of the less improved forms of life—this death of the bad to make room for ever better and better, is regarded by Theologians as a cunningly devised scheme of the devil to thwart and blight the objects of creation. Let us hope that we are approaching the dawn of a brighter day, in which the true nature of evil will be recognised and the glory of creation manifest even to our prejudiced, short-sighted, and imperfect vision. With a fuller knowledge of the "Origin, Objects, and Advantages of Evil" will come a clearer perception of the beneficent purposes for which it has been allowed, and more strenuous efforts in the direction of our own welfare towards which it was intended to turn us. In the infancy of our race the causes of all great evils were hidden and mysterious, and were consequently ascribed to supernatural intervention; and were worshipped instead of being sought and removed. Mankind, like a great pig under a burning glass, lay still and squealed instead of getting out of the way. Certain barbarous tribes, from reverential fear, refused even to destroy wild beasts and noxious reptiles, and "plague, pestilence, and famine" were manifestations of divine anger. Now, although the light of science has dissipated these illusions in the physical world, in the mystery of mind and the moral world

they are still as strong as ever; the investigation
of natural causes is neglected, and events are still
ascribed to supernatural ones. But we are
approaching the dawn of a brighter day—although,
according to some, daylight is still far off. As
Buckle says, " The progress of inquiry is becoming
so rapid and so earnest, that I entertain little doubt
that before another *century* has elapsed, the chain
of evidence will be complete, and it will be as rare
to find an historian who denies the undeviating
regularity of the moral world, as it is now to find
a philosopher who denies the regularity of the
material world." *

* History of Civilisation in England, vol. I., p. 21.

CHAPTER VII.

There is still one question on this subject of evil, to the solution of which the present state of our knowledge seems hardly equal, and on which we have still to offer a few suggestions. Considering that happiness is so much dependent upon knowledge and civilization, how is it that society has made such slow progress in knowledge and civilisation? Why is it still in its childhood? Why has moral science, upon which happiness is as dependent as health upon medical science, kept so far in arrear of the other? No man or people can advance alone. It is necessary that the whole earth should be peopled, the object being to ensure the largest sum of enjoyment the world will contain. It is probable that if civilisation had progressed more rapidly, this would not have been effected : mankind would have preferred keeping their numbers within the means of subsistence in a particular country, to going forth into the wilderness of a new world, if instinct rather than reason had not dictated their increase, and had not necessity in consequence obliged them to encounter all the trials and difficulties of new settlers. Such difficulties are not slight; "The immense and apparently insurmountable obstacles which present themselves to the extension of industry on the first cultivation of the earth; the extent of morasses, the thickness of the forests, the ruggedness of the mountains, forbid the hope of success but from the accumulated force of multitudes. In the first attempts to clear the ground, numbers perish from the unhealthiness of the atmosphere, the severity of the labour, the magnitude of the hardships to which they are exposed. From the narratives of the extreme sufferings undergone by the first settlers in distant colonies in our own times, even with the aid of iron instruments and the arts of civilization, we may gather what must have been the condition of the human race in remote and now forgotten periods."*

Another reason why society has advanced so slowly is, that physical comforts must be first secured, before moral and intellectual pleasures can be enjoyed, and necessity was required to drive men forward to the discovery of those arts and sciences upon which the increase of physical comforts depends. We appear to be fast approaching that state in which the powers of production will be so far increased, as to afford leisure for moral and intellectual pleasures to all. To have given man such moral and intellectual desires, at the same time that he was obliged to work eight or

* Alison's Principles of Population, vol. 2, p. 467.

ten hours per day in order to supply his physical wants, must have diminished rather than increased the amount of his enjoyment; wants and desires without the means of gratification being pains.

Again, if either individuals or races rise much above their fellows, they are soon choked in surrounding barbarism. Nations seem also to have their natural periods of decay the same as individuals; they have their youth, maturity, and old age, and then are swept away. " The corrupted communities, and now decayed empires, which have successively risen and fallen during the constant but unobserved progress of civilisation, have been swept away when they had performed their mission in human affairs. There are destroyers provided for the carrion of nations, not less than for the corpses of individuals; pernicious remains are not permitted to taint the moral any more than the natural atmosphere; unseen in ordinary times, the vultures of the North appear in the distance, when their cleansing is required; the Scythian cavalry scent from afar the odour of human corruption, and the punishment of the vices of nations conducts the mighty system of human advancement."†

There is another consideration of great importance to which we cannot attach too much weight, viz., that all knowledge to be available must partake of the character of *experience:* it is

---

* Alison " On Population," vol, 1, p. 80.

probable, therefore, that any quicker mode of revealing knowledge to mankind than the present slow, experimental process, would have been ineffectual. The wisdom of others is of little or no use to ourselves, until experience has made such wisdom peculiarly our own; and the same law applies to society at large.

The present physical perfection of the world is now recognised as the result during countless ages of the same laws at present in operation. Every educated person is sufficiently familiar with geology to know how this has taken place, by the gradual operation of varied physical agencies producing stratum after stratum, with organized beings adapted to the varied conditions of existence in both earth and water, each continuing till another set had arisen apparently more perfectly organized to take its place; and in a continuous succession from very early periods, when beings now totally extinct prevailed, down to a time when some now in existence began to divide the world with them. At last came man, at some comparatively very recent epoch, but there is no evidence at present to fix the date. Science speaks only of slow and gradual changes; there has been ¡no sudden cessation of one order of being and equally sudden commencement of another. We can trace no beginning, no chaos, but law and order and *supreme intelligence* acting through " natural law " throughout.

The earth has thus been very gradually preparing

for its present covering of delicately-framed and
highly-organised sentient life.   Its external coat
is now one net-work of nerves—it feels all over.
"If we admit that the earth being still hot
internally, must have cooled at its surface, and that
this cooling must, in its progress, have caused con-
tortions, dislocations, upheavals of strata ; and
again, that the water charged with matter must
have deposited it ; and that the various crystalized
bodies and metallic veins must have been formed
during certain stages of these formations—it is only
by parity of reason affirmed that the rudiments of
all organic as well as inorganic products and
structures must have been evolved in like manner,
as they were alike included and contained in the
same fused, and therefore once vapourised, or
nebulous, mass.   In that mass all kinds of physical
agents, or the elements of them, thermotic, electric,
chemical, molecular, gravitational, luminiferous, and
by consequence, not less all organic and vital forces,
must have been included.   Out of it in the same
way by equally regular laws in the one case as the
other, must have been evolved all forms of
inorganic and equally of organic existence,—
whether amorphous masses, crystals, cells, monads,
plants, zoophytes, animals, or man,—the *animal*
man ; the *spiritual* man belonging to *another* order
of things, a *spiritual creation.*" * * * "A
rational physico-theology teaches that the succession
of forms of organised life on the globe, up to the

first organisation of all animated nature, were acts of the Divine will, wisdom and power, in precisely the same sense as the revolutions of the double stars and planets, the daily tide, the fall of rain, the ascent of vapour, the action of the sun's light and heat, and all othe natural phenomena, regulated by similar recondite laws, are direct and immediate acts of the same Divine will, wisdom and power." *

"We are led by all analogy to suppose that the Creator operates through a series of *intermediate causes*; and that in consequence, *the origination of fresh species*, could it ever come under our cognizance, would be found to be a *natural*, in contradistinction to a *miraculous* process : although we perceive no indication of any process actually in progress which is likely to issue in such a result." †

"To what natural laws and secondary causes the orderly succession and progression of such organic phenomena may have been committed, we as yet are ignorant. But if without derogation of the Divine Power we may conceive the existence of such ministers, and personify them by the term *nature*, we learn from the past history of our globe that she has advanced with slow and stately steps, guided by the archetypal light, amidst the wreck of worlds, from the first embodiment of the verte-

* Rev. Baden Powell "Unity of Worlds, p. 79; Idem p. 451.
† Sir John Herschell.

brate idea under its old Ichthyic vestment, until it
became arrayed in the glorious garb of the human
form.' *

But, "in regard to man's *spiritual* nature, so far as
that is concerned, it is wholly independent of all
material things, and is therefore relieved from all
possibility of connection, or collision, with any
physical truths or theories." So says Professor Baden
Powell, but this distinction between the animal
and spiritual man is a pure assumption, which the
last sixty years' study of man has entirely dis-
proved. All the mental powers of man, animal and
spiritual, are connected with the brain, and obey
precisely the same law, and of this the Professor
seems to have at least a suspicion, which might very
easily have become a conviction. He says, "*If* any
peculiarity could be shown in man's brain, to confer
powers of *abstraction, moral consciousness*, or the like,
which is deficient in the animal brain, this, in like
manner, would indicate a clear physiological distinction and would bring the case under the category
of *degree of physical organization* or *development*."
There is no *if*,—sixty years ago it was demonstrated
by Gall that such a peculiarity in man's brain did
exist, and this fact ought to have reached the most
advanced men even at Oxford before this. The
existence of man upon this earth is of comparatively
recent date, and he is evidently in his childhood;
the development of his mental growth being slow,

* Professor Owen.

keeping pace with the previous slow growth of the
material world, there is a close analogy throughout. We find man at first very little in advance of
other animals; as they preyed upon one another, he
preyed upon them, and as they often eat their
brothers and sisters, so did he his fellow man, until
he found him too expensive eating, and that it paid
better to set him to work as his slave. As his
numbers increased population began to press upon
his means of subsistence, and he found it easier to
tame animals, and breed and feed them, than to
hunt wild ones; and from a hunter he became a
shepherd. The natural fruits of the earth he found
also very much increased by cultivation, and he
began to sow and reap and settle down upon the
land, and to insist upon vested rights. But the
strong found it easier to steal than to work, and
wars became common; and men organised themselves into communities and countries, and gave up
their liberty to a king or leader, for a common
defence of life and property. Wars were then made
for power and distinction; and to enable men to
live under all these disadvantages and conflicting
circumstances, many mental faculties were called
into activity, and the brain grew and the faculties
increased in strength proportionate to the exercise
they thus received. In mountainous countries,
where the temperature was cold and the means of
subsistence scarce, and it required all the energies
of man's nature, and every faculty to be brought

into exercise to enable him to live ; and in temperate climates, where men could work and the rewards of ndustry were great, the brains grew the largest, and these men have gradually extended their sway over all the rest. Man unlike other animals has a power of profiting by his experience,—of saying what effects follow from known causes, and of thus predicting consequences ; and when his knowledge became too great to be handed down from father to son any longer, it was stored in written records, and *his progress has always been in proportion to his experience, and has been based entirely and solely upon it ; and it is only as knowledge can be thus verified, that is, recorded facts be made to take place over again before his own eyes that experience is of any value. Deductive reason may point to such facts, but they must be tested to be of use.* Individual facts were gradually generalized into laws, and one such law included thousands of facts, of which he had no individual experience. His speculations, metaphysical or theological, upon the nature or essence of the things surrounding him, of either mind or matter, have had little to do with his real progress. At first he supposed a god to preside over every power in nature that was unknown or mysterious to him ; and as he generalized such powers, so he did his gods. A religion based upon such superstition, the produce of the highest minds of the period, might assist a people at its first establish-ment; but when the minds of the people have grown beyond this, it then becomes even a greater impediment from its religious sanction than it was originally a help. Necessity, the mother of invention, and circumstances, call the different mental powers of man into exercise, and they grow with such exercise, and experience, or the Positive Philosophy, as it is called, directs and regulates such powers; and this is the real law of the mind's evolution. While different philosophers have been perfecting their methods, mankind generally everywhere impelled instinctively or intuitively by their faculties—by the law of their minds—have been *acting* upon the Inductive or Baconian philosophy, ordinarily not aided but impeded by method. The faculties naturally take their own method, and most of the discoveries that have been made in science have been made by practical men ignorant of all method. It is quite true that a tortoise in the right path will beat a race-horse in the wrong, and fortunately, however philosophers or the race-horses may wander, nature keeps the tortoise, or the bulk of mankind in the right path. Their wants are constantly craving for their gratification, and accumulated experience points the way.* The Theological and Metaphysical stages through which

* " Man, like other warm-blooded animals, must always have the four prime essentials to life—*fit air, warmth, aliment, and rest after action;* and to obtain the pleasure from using, and to escape the pain from wanting these, are the chief motives to his voluntary action."—Dr. Neil Arnott's " Survey of Human Progress."

the mind passes, as pointed out by Comte, are not the *law*, but merely the history of its evolution. The laws of the moral are as stable as those of the physical world, and apparently as slow in their, operation. It may suit our *pride* to talk of our fallen nature, but history nowhere supports this assumption. The spiritual nature in the savage man is all but rudimentary, and the mass of mankind are still mere animals, acting only in accordance with animal feeling; in the most advanced race and best specimens of other races, layer after layer has been added to the brain until the animal has been lost in the man, and the good, the true and the beautiful predominate, and he is just, respectful, and benevolent. Why the progress of the physical world or of man should have been so slow we cannot say; but the same law of development seems to govern both. We cannot say what ought to be; we can only say what is. That it could have been different—that progress could have been more rapid, is more than we know. All seems the result of fixed law; there is no evidence of what is called *special* Providence, or interference with law, either in Matter or Mind. On this subject, Professor Powell truly says, " To speak of apparent anomalies and interruptions as *special* indications of the Deity, is altogether a mistake. In truth, so far as the anomalous character of any phenomenon can affect the inference of presiding Intelligence at all, it would rather tend to *diminish* and detract from that evidence. But, on the other hand, precisely in proportion as the apparent exception might be explained, and made to vindicate its position in a more comprehensive system of order, so would the evidence be increased and elevated.

"In the present state of knowledge, law and order, physical causation and uniformity of action, are the elevated manifestations of Divinity, Creation, and Providence. Interruptions of such order (if for a moment they could be admitted as such) could only produce a sort of temporary concealment of such manifestations, and involve the beautiful light shed over the natural world, in a passing cloud. * * * A supreme moral cause manifested through law, order, and physical causes, is the confession of science : conflicting operations, abrupt discontinuities, are the idols of ignorance, and if they really prevailed, would so far be to the philosopher only the exponents of chaos and atheism ; the obscurations (as far as it extends) of the sensible manifestation of the Supreme Intelligence." * We know that Professor Powell intends these observations to apply only to the physical world, but we have shown that they are equally applicable to the moral or spiritual world, and that the perfection and even the use of reason itself depend upon the equal supremacy of law and order in the world of mind as of matter.

* Unity of Worlds, p. 157.

Had history been written with a right view of the nature and objects of evil, much light would have been thrown upon the question, as well as upon all those connected with the advancement and slow progress of the race. Even now a universal history of civilisation would dispel much of the darkness which still envelopes the subject. When the common superstitions concerning Evil, shall give place to the above views of its nature and objects; when it shall in all cases be regarded as remedial, and its causes, therefore, inquired into, a much more rapid advance of the race towards the perfection of which it is capable may be expected to take place. Nature will then no longer be judged by her dealings with regard to a single people, nation, or even generation—whom she no more hesitates to cut off, if the general good requires it, than a surgeon does to amputate the limb which threatens the life and welfare of an individual—but with regard to the general good of all her children in all times and places; and the dispensations which to our short-sighted wisdom, frequently appear as unmixed evils, will then prove her to be guided by an unerring and benevolent Power. Although there must still be many difficulties attached to this subject, and the causes of many evils must still remain unexplained, yet to those who trace out final causes, who study the Creator in his works, the mystery of Evil may be sufficiently unravelled to give infinite confidence in

His providence, and faith that farther knowledge will make manifest the benevolent tendency of all creation, and bring home to every heart the all-cheering conviction that " WHATEVER IS, IS RIGHT."

CHAPTER VIII.

THE PRINCIPLES OF MORALITY; MORAL OBLIGATION.

We hear of Moral Obligation, of acting according to conscience, and not according to self-interest, pleasure, appetite, desire; but it is seldom clearly defined in what Moral Obligation consists. Some say it is acting in accordance with the will of God; but then arises the question, what is the will of God? Others say that we are to be governed by an inward monitor, which all possess: but then what is to be the standard by which the indications of this inward monitor are to be judged, since we seldom find two persons in whom its promptings coincide on all subjects. "We are to do so, because it is right," says one; "Because common sense, reason, the fitness of things, the law of nature, justice, the public good, require it," say others. But as Mr. Bentham has ably shown, all these are mere modes of expressing the individual opinion of any one who chooses to dogmatise concerning right and wrong, without assigning any reason for it beyond his own internal conviction.

The science of Morality goes farther than merely to lay down rules of conduct: it has to show the reason for them, and the foundation of the obligation to obey them. The Foundations of Morality can only be discovered by studying the constitution of man and its relation to everything around him. The application of the doctrine of Philosophical Necessity to Virtue and Vice, Praise and Blame, Reward and Punishment, has shown us that, abstractedly, all actions are alike, both with respect to their fitness and unfitness, or with reference to the motives that produce them; that, in *themselves*, they are all equally deserving of praise or blame, reward or punishment, because they are all the produce of causes arising out of natural constitution and circumstances over which the individual has no control; and that, therefore, the only distinction which can be made between actions is with regard to their tendency. Individuals may be estimated by their *motives*, because we cannot help loving that which is amiable and lovable and *generally* produces good; but actions must be viewed as right or wrong, as in accordance with common sense, reason, the fitness of things, the law of nature, justice, the public good, not with reference to anything in themselves, that marks them as such, but according to their tendency— their tendency to produce happiness or misery, pleasure or pain. That it must be as their tendency to produce happiness or misery, has been proved by showing the nature of man's responsibility or *obligation* to act in one way rather than another; as it appears that such accountability is founded upon pain attending some actions, and pleasure others, in proportion as such actions are or are not calculated to promote the welfare of the individual and the happiness of all the sensitive creation. It is to this issue that all the advocates for different standards of morality are obliged to come, if pushed to a conclusion : they are all obliged to acknowledge that the fitness of things means their fitness to produce happiness ; and so of the rest; and that conscientiousness and veneration, which teach us to "do justly and to walk humbly with our God," are virtues inasmuch as they promote our own and the general happiness. All moral rules are derived originally from utility, but the pleasures and pains, or likes and antipathies on which they are based are transmitted to offspring and thus become intuitions—similar to the feelings with which the kitten regards a dog,—it sets up its back and spits at it directly it opens its eyes : the cow also from the same cause, from its having been the custom years ago to bait her forefathers, keeps making imaginery tosses of the dog, whenever she sees one ; and the bull himself is still made furious by the sight of a red colour, although the feeling may have been derived ages ago in the bull fights of Spain. In this way are mixed the tendencies of actions and the feelings with which in a long course of time we intuitively come to regard them, and their original source is thus sometimes lost. What is called the Intuitive School of Moralists, bases its conclusions partly on utility, and partly on such internal convictions, for which no reason can be assigned, except a certain feeling on the subject, and which usually takes the shape of "all men think," "we cannot help feeling," &c. To recognise, however, the obligations of morality is simply to recognise the conditions on which it is desirable men should live, and the authority is enforced by pains and penalties which all are forced to attend to whether the obligations are recognised and acknowledged or not.

It is often said that it is impossible to speak definitely of the objects of creation, that happiness is not a sufficiently worthy object, but that development seems more the end and aim of the Creator than happiness. But what is the use of "development" unless attended by consciousness, and that a pleasurable consciousness? A painful consciousness would be worse than nothing. World on world, in infinite beauty, would be the same as none without beings conscious of their existence, and unless that beauty gave pleasure—a happy consciousness,—it would be useless. Were a universe developed in all possible power and beauty and but one little fly conscious of its existence, that little fly would be of vastly more importance than the universe. Beings might be "developed" in infinite number, size, and power, but of what use would their existence be if they were not happy, or at least a source of happiness?

Pain checks development, and all legitimate development is attended with pleasure, and, in fact, we can see no good in development unless it produces happiness. We cannot see or even understand any other purpose in creation : to be without consciousness is the same as not being ; and consciousness that was neither pleasurable nor painful would be no consciousness, for there is no negation or state of indifference, no sensation, or feeling, or idea, attending either the intellect or sentiments that is not slightly either one or the other. Certainly pain would not be worth living for, and happiness is the only thing left. People speak of pleasure with contempt, because by it is usually meant something carnal and resulting from the lower feelings, but happiness *is simply the aggregate of pleasurable sensations from whatever source derived:* people talk and decry happiness as poor and paltry, as something scarcely worth having, and speak of blessedness as the end to be attained ; but by blessedness they evidently mean a refined kind of happiness, composed principally of the religious and æsthetic feelings. We hear much also in the present day of " Law, Order, and Unity ;" but law, order, and unity, that serve no purpose, are no evidence of wisdom of design.

Though all are ultimately obliged to admit that happiness must be the end and aim of creation, yet a great point of dispute still remains, whether happiness here or hereafter in another world, is the end, and ought to be the aim, of our existence. This question must be decided by the relation which our faculties bear to things around us. We know, from the relation that the lungs bear to water, that we were not intended to live in the water; we know from the relation that the human stomach bears to the different kinds of food, that it was not intended to digest grass, like that of a cow ; from the relation of the eye to the light, we know that we were not intended to live in darkness; so with respect to the relation that the mental faculties bear to things around us, we find that they have direct reference to the present life, and that they would be as useless in a state unlike the present, as the fins of a fish on land or the wings of a bird in the water. So that whatever may be the intention of our Creator with regard to us in a future state, we are certain that he intended us for happiness in this, as happiness is the natural result of the legitimate exercise of all our faculties ; and those faculties, although some few of them are capable of a direction towards a future state of being, have all direct reference to the present world. The obligation, then, that a man is under to act in one way rather than in another is owing to its tendency to happiness or to the avoidance of pain, and Morality may be defined as " the science which teaches men to live together in the most happy manner possible." *

* Helvetius.

CHAPTER IX.

PRINCIPLES OF MORALITY : PAIN AND PLEASURE.

THE ground being so far cleared before us, our line of reasoning is henceforth simple and straightforward, relating only to the question of Pain and Pleasure—Happiness and Misery. These will be found the ultimate springs of all our actions : Pain and Pleasure, which are only other names for desire and aversion, liking and antipathy, being to volition in the sensitive creation what attraction and repulsion are to the motions that go on in the physical world. Man, as we have seen, is equally the agent of Necessity with all other created beings, and this is the law, the first law of his nature, that he should wish for and seek his own happiness; and he is no more capable of avoiding it, or of acting contrary to it, than the atoms of matter can refuse to be guided by the influence which is called attraction. This proposition, however, requires explanation, for it will be immediately denied by many, who, from want of clearly understanding the nature of the law referred to, feel convinced that they are impelled to action by a thousand motives which cannot be said to partake of the character of either pleasure or pain: But those who reason in this way, for the most part think only of mere bodily pleasure and pain. All kinds of feelings emanating from any part of the body; all actions of the mind, whether proceeding from the Intellectual Faculties, the Sentiments, or the Propensities, come under the denomination of Sensations, as before explained; and all sensations are pleasurable or painful, though in a thousand different degrees—at least all that are powerful enough to impel to action. Locke says, " all action has its source in uneasiness ;" at all events all action has a cause. We act either instinctively or from motive. If instinctively, we are impelled directly by some desire, which desire proceeds from the action of some faculty, and each faculty, when indulged in its natural action, is the source of pleasure, and when ungratified, or disagreeably affected, produces pain ; pains and pleasures are thus as numerous in their kind as the faculties. One person will feel pleasure in doing good, another in doing mischief; one in saving money, another in spending it; one will instinctively run away at the slightest cause of alarm, another will as instinctively face it. In all which cases it is not the less a pleasurable or painful sensation that induces each individual so to act, because he does not stay to make a calculation of the balance of pleasures or pains. When we act from motives, and calculation does take place, the will is determined by the greatest apparent good ; good meaning right, duty, &c., which really means pleasure or happiness or the avoidance of pain. The lower animals are impelled immediately to action by pleasures and pains, without even knowing that there are such feelings, $i.e.$, without having any abstract notion of either one or the other, and by far the greater part of our actions are performed in the same way, instinctively, and without any calculation or reference to either pleasure or pain. Some of the most intelligent of the animals, dogs for example, are enabled to make some sort of calculation, and to balance future punishment against present enjoyment, and so also does man in proportion as he becomes enlightened and his feelings are put under the direction of reason. It is here that the moralist can be of use, by enabling us to make a more correct calculation than our unassisted reason could otherwise accomplish ; by showing from experience and from our own constitution and from the constitution of nature, what conduct invariably leads to happiness in the end, and what to misery. The duty of the moralist then is to enable us to make a correct calculation of our pleasures and pains.

If the common objection be urged—Are all men then, eternally calculating pains and pleasures in all their actions ? we answer, no ; they more frequently act instinctively, that is, without calculation ; but the pain or pleasure of the gratification or non-gratification of their wish, or desire, impel them into action. Take, for instance, the most common desire, that of food—appetite. A man, before he eats, does not sit down to calculate the pleasure he shall have in eating, or ‖ the pain he shall suffer if he do not ; but he feels a desire to eat, which desire, if analysed, will be found to consist of a slightly painful or uncomfortable feeling which increases in intensity until it is gratified. All others desires which form the motives to action, are similar in character, but not being equally necessary to the preservation of self, if not gratified the uneasy feeling ceases instead of increasing in intensity.

Are all men, then, moved to action only by the expectation of self-enjoyment, or is it possible to disregard our own individual interests ? Self-enjoyment or individual interest may form no part of our object or aim, and yet it is not the less pain or pleasure that impels us to action. It may be the pleasure of performing what we conceive to be our duty, or the pain following the neglect of it. It may be the pleasure we have in promoting the interests of others, or the pain of seeing them in want of such assistance ; at any rate we cannot be indifferent, whether the end of the action regards ourselves individually or not ; for in a state of indifference there is no motive, nothing to move the will, and we must will before we act. Our choice may lead us willingly to great and continued suffering, but the pains of remorse and self-reproach may be less easy to bear.

Bentham said, " No man ever had, can, or could

have a motive differing from the pursuit of pleasure or the avoidance of pain." "The first law of nature is to seek our own happiness;" and in illustration of this he adds, "Prudence, in common parlance, is the adaptation of means to an end. In the moral field that end is happiness. The subjects on which prudence is to be exercised are ourselves and all besides: ourselves as instrumental, and all besides as instrumental to our own felicity."

"Of what can the sum total of happiness be made up, but of the individual units? What is demanded by prudence and benevolence is required by necessity. Existence itself depends for its continuance on the self-regarding principle. Had Adam cared more for the happiness of Eve than for his own, and Eve, at the same time, more for the happiness of Adam than for her own, Satan might have saved himself the trouble of temptation. Mutual misery would have marred all prospects of bliss, and the death of both have brought to a speedy finale the history of man."*

"But self-regarding prudence is not only a virtue —it is a virtue on which the very existence of the race depends. If I thought more about you than I thought about myself, I should be the blind leading the blind, and we should fall into the ditch together. It is as impossible that your pleasures should be better to me than my own, as that your eye-sight should be better to me than my own. My happiness

* Deontology, vol. 1, p. 18.

and my unhappiness are as much a part of me as any of my faculties or organs, and I might as well profess to feel your toothache more keenly than you do, as to be more interested in your well-being than in my own well-being."

"It will scarcely be denied that every man acts with a view to his own interest—not a correct view, because that would obtain for him the greatest possible portion of felicity; and if every man acting correctly for his own interest, obtained the maximum of obtainable happiness, mankind would reach the millennium of accessible bliss; and the end of morality—the general happiness, be accomplished. To prove that the immoral action is a miscalculation of self-interest; to show how erroneous an estimate the vicious man makes of pains and pleasures, is the purpose of the intelligent moralist. Unless he can do this he does nothing; for, as has been stated above, for a man not to pursue what he deems likely to produce to him the greatest sum of enjoyment, is in the very nature of things impossible.

"Every man is able to form the best estimate of his own pleasures and his own pains. No description of them, no sympathy for them, can be equivalent to their reality. No story of a blow ever produced a bruise; nor was the agony of tooth-drawing ever felt by mere interest excited in the sufferings of a friend under the hands of a dentist. Even were it otherwise, the power of sympathy is nothing till it acts upon self ; a truism, which is almost reducible to the self-identical proposition that a man can feel nothing else but his own feelings. To escape from one's self, to forget one's own interests, to make unrequited sacrifices, and all for duty, are high-sounding phrases, and, to say the truth, as nonsensical as high-sounding. Self-preference is universal and necessary : if destiny be anywhere despotic, it is here. When self is sacrificed, it is self in one shape to self in another shape : and a man can no more cast off regard to his own happiness, meaning the happiness of the moment, then he can cast off his own skin, or jump out of it. And if he could why should he ? What provision could have been made for the happiness of the whole, so successful, so complete, as that which engages every individual of that whole to obtain for himself the greatest possible portion of happiness ? and what amount of happiness to mankind at large could be so great, on the aggregate, as that which is made up of the greatest possible portion obtained by every individual man ? Of the largest number of units, and those units of the largest amount, the largest sum total must be the necessary result."*

The above quotations speak very plainly, and it is absolutely necessary that the principle should be stated as broadly as possible, because there has been and still is, among moral philosophers, considerable

* Deontology, vol. 2, p. 121.

mystification of the subject. The want of proper attention to two facts has mainly caused this obscurity, one of which is, that mankind do not seek happiness or pleasure immediately, but they seek the object of their desires, children, friends' property, and to do what is right and just and kind, and happiness attends upon their gratification : the other, that one class of these desires has the happiness and welfare of others for its object, and it is supposed that in attending to such impulses we disregard ourselves, which is not the case, as we merely sacrifice " self in one form to self in another." To be constantly preaching self-sacrifice is of no avail, for it is only where those feelings predominate that give a pleasure in acting for the good of others, that the good of others will be preferred. An habitual disregard of self and attention to the interests of others, is frequently found, but it is only where there is more pleasure in attending to others than to self. When this is clearly understood, the folly of *preaching* self-sacrifice to the *selfish* will be manifest ; and it will be seen that to further the interests of morality, we must strengthen by cultivation that part of our nature, those moral feelings, that have the good of others for their object : in short, would we have a man pay habitual regard to the welfare of his neighbour, we must address those feelings, and place him in those circumstances that will make it both his pleasure and his interest to do so.

Religion is now ordinarily used for that purpose, and people are told that unless they "love their neighbour as themselves" they will not go to Heaven, but quite the *reverse*. Their conduct in consequence where such teaching acts as a motive, shows at least *how much they love themselves.*

We need not fear the conclusion to which we are constrained to come, that pleasures and pains are the sole springs of action, and that a man necessarily seeks his own happiness, as the law of his being ; in fact, "that he can feel nothing else but his own feelings." The object of the Science of Morality, therefore, is simple ; it is to show what conduct will, on all occasions, best promote our *real* interest; what will produce to mankind the largest sum of enjoyment ; for this only constitutes duty. We shall find that the conduct which produces the greatest happiness to the whole of the sensitive creation, produces the greatest amount of enjoyment to the individual.

We have before asked the question, are men always calculating pains and pleasures ? and we have answered it in the negative, we now ask "*ought* they always to be so doing ?" and again we most emphatically say " No." The laws of morality are such as produce the greatest good to the whole and not always the greatest good to the individual *at the time.* The calculation of consequence must be used therefore only to establish general laws which admit of no appeal—from which there can be no deviation whatever the interest of the individual may appear to be. We act instinctively in obedience to the laws of gravitation, and we have besides certain general laws of motion and mechanics, and so it ought to be in Morals. Mankind might as reasonably be expected to determine, on all occasions, the effect of the varied influences of attraction and repulsion, or to state at once what chemical results would be produced by the combination of different materials, as to be able, without reference to general laws, to decide what conduct would lead to the greatest happiness on the whole. The error most to be guarded against in the carrying out of the greatest happiness principle, according to the utilitarian Philosophy, is, as remarked by Mackintosh, " that of sliding from general to particular consequences; that of trying single actions, instead of dispositions, habits, and rules, by the standard of utility; that of authorizing too great a latitude for discretion and policy in moral conduct; that of readily allowing exceptions in the most important rules; that of too lenient a censure of the use of doubtful means when the end seems to them to be good; and that of believing unphilosophically, as well as dangerously, that there can be any measure or scheme so useful in the world, as the existence of men who would not do a base thing for any public advantage. It was said of Andrew Fletcher, ' he would lose his life to *serve* his country, but would not do a base thing to *save* it.'* These principles have been strongly and legibly marked in our constitution. It is a matter of calculation for the intellect based upon experience and forethought, to tell on all occasions what is right, what is just, respectful, and kind; but there is a principle implanted within us that gives us great pleasure in acting up to it, or great pain if we do not: and it is this feeling that we properly dignify by the name of conscience. The object of morality therefore is to associate what is *right*, calculated in the widest circumstances by the highest minds, with these feelings, so as to generate a habit of mind that shall instinctively and at once, *without calculation*, act up to it. To act, in fact, in accordance with the dictates of conscience, regardless of consequence, whether that lead us direct to the gulf of Curtius, the spiked-barrel of Regulus, the cannon's mouth or the burning stake. In such a *state of mind*, wherever it may in exceptional cases ultimately lead us, is to be found the greatest happiness to the race, and as may be readily proved, to the individual also. Although, therefore, we are moved, and ought to be moved by the pleasures or pains of conscience,— in a rightly constituted nature the strongest feeling of all,—still morality, based upon the greatest happiness principal, is not, as it has been falsely represented by short-sighted or narrow-minded people, a selfish calculation of individual interests,

* Mackintosh's Dissertations, Encyc. Brit., p. 383.

or *in action* a calculation at all, but its universal prayer is—

> " What conscience dictates to be done,
> Or warns me not to do ;
> This teach me more than Hell to shun,
> That more than Heaven pursue."

CHAPTER X.

The object of this Chapter is to shew the connection between the Principles and Practice of Morality rather than the carrying out of those principles into practice; the practice of Morality would require a book in itself. As regards the Practice of Morality, if Law rules in mind as well as in matter, the distinction hitherto set up between the physical and moral laws does not exist, and moral actions have their causes, or invariable antecedents, as well as physical. If Morality then is "the Science which teaches men to live together in the most happy manner possible," if more than this, it includes his well-being altogether, it must take a wider range than has yet been given to it, and it must embrace the physical and mental as well as the moral laws as equally obligatory.

By the study of the physical laws we make ourselves acquainted with the great forces of nature, and according as we use them they either become our servants or overwhelm us in their resistless energy. All material civilisation is based upon the study of Physics, and a man with a weekly income of a pound sterling, is now enabled to the extent of a pound to set other men in all parts of the world to work for him. It is not easy to calculate the number of men that may be thus set in motion on his behalf; there is his tea, sugar, tobacco, —silk for his wife's dress, wool for his own,— the men to take his letters and to print his penny paper—in fact in half the earth they are at work for him for his pound a week. For his rates and taxes, which he so much grudges, he has an army to guard him and to keep all those sources of enjoyment open to him, and judges to see justice done to him, policemen to protect him and his property while he makes this pound a week; roads mended, drained, and lighted for him; bridges kept in repair, &c.; the river is turned in a gentle stream, not as a raging torrent through his house; a church is opened for him for his spiritual needs: and all this may come within this pound a week, so much have the the powers of production been increased by enlisting the forces of nature in our service. By the study of the mental laws we become acquainted with our own constitution. This includes the organic laws, for mind is connected with organisation. On the knowledge of the organic laws health is dependent, and the transmission of a strong mind and body to our children; and upon the ignorance of the laws of the mind is based not only increased mental disease but all those superstitions that at present so much impede the progress of the race. We have banished chance and supernatural agency from physics, but from ignorance of the laws of mind as being equally fixed with those of physics, we have retained them in this department to the great detriment of certain and scientific progress.

The moral laws are supposed only to regulate the intercourse which men have together in society, that they may live together as happily as possible; but it is right, and what is right constitutes the essence of morality,—that we should attend equally to all the natural laws, for unless we do so we cannot be happy ourselves or make others happy. Each set of laws has its own sanctions, its own rewards and punishments, and they all act in harmony. Fire will burn, water will drown the virtuous man no less than the vicious; but upon him whose bodily frame is in a healthy state physical injury is less likely to take serious effect than upon him who has neglected the organic laws; while he whose moral faculties have their proper supremacy, is less liable to incur the risk of such injury, than he whose reason and moral powers are disordered by headlong passions and blind propensities. This subject has been so admirably treated in Mr. George Combe's Constitution of Man that it is unnecessary to pursue it here· When a good and pious man, negligent of the organic laws and of the laws of political economy, falls into ill-health and poverty, it is thought to be a mysterious dispensation of Providence for which provision requires to be made in another and better world. The mass of suffering incident to ignorance and the consequent neglect of the natural laws is incalculable ; plague, epidemic, disease, melancholy, madness, poverty; and these continue to be represented by some of our religious teachers, not as the consequence of our ignorance and transgression of laws with which we ought to be acquainted, but as a necessary part of human nature, consequent upon the transgression of Adam ; inflicted as arbitrary chastisements or trials by God, to be removed only by Him in the same arbitrary manner, prayer being the only proper way to effect their removal. Whereas were they removed by prayer without our first having our attention called to their cause and removing it, it would probably be to our destruction and not our good.

It is our moral duty then to study the nature of everything around us, and · to make ourselves acquainted with the particular constitution it has received from the hand of the Creator, and its relation to our own organization, for whether it will do us good or harm depends upon the adaptation of our conduct to such properties and relations.

It is the province of Moral Science to teach us what our duties are, and of Social Science to place us in circumstances that will best enable us to perform them. Perhaps the most direct means of ascertaining what our duties are,—that is, what are the purposes for which we have been made, is to study the faculties and attributes with which we have been endowed, and thus basing our moral code upon the use of each in the direction for which its nature shows it was evidently intended. I have endeavoured to work out this principle in my "Education of the Feelings and Affections," which will make it unnecessary to pursue the subject at any length here. Morality ought to be at least as certain a science as Chemistry or Medicine; a Moralist ought to be able to speak as certainly as the Chemist or Physician each in his department, of what a person with a definite *mental* constitution ought to do, and in what circumstances he ought to be placed to make him as happy as possible.*

As I have said, my object here is the elucidation of Principles, but I may just mention two or three things in the practice of Morality, that are calculated to work the greatest change for the better in the present state of society, when they come to be clearly recognized as duties. Now they are either overlooked or completely ignored. Thus, no man will consider it right, either with a license or without, to bring children into the world for which he has not a moral certainty of providing properly without the assistance of others. Surely it would be wrong to bring children into the world that we knew would die of starvation; is it not

---

* The bearing of this subject on the Mental Constitution is treated by the Author in his " Science of Man " (Longmans).

also wrong to bring them into the world with the certainty that their support must depend upon other people, either in an exacted poor's rate or any other way ? When a provident person has economised his time and done his work it is quite unjust that he should be set to work again to help to keep a dozen children for another man whose own earnings have never been properly equal to the support of one. Strange as it may seem, the opposite feeling to this almost universally prevails, and prizes are given to agricultural labourers for having families of 12 or 16 children upon twelve shillings a week. Any improvement in the condition of the Working Classes must be based on provident habits ; and all providence, to be effectual, must commence here.

Again, it will not much longer be considered right and fair that when the Capitalist and a hundred Labourers shall work together an equal number of hours with a common object, the Capitalist shall carry off so large a share of the common produce, merely because the present working of the law of supply and demand gives him power to do so. Attention to the " moral check " on population, mentioned above, will stop this abuse and enable the workman by lessening his numbers to make a better bargain for himself.

A more equal and just division of the produce of labour will be a check on the present luxurious mode of living, which is the scandal of the present age; and the upper and middle classes will be obliged to return to nature's more simple pleasures, which are higher, purer, more lasting, and which distinguish man peculiarly as man. Pure air, exercise, healthy appetite, the pursuit of truth, the poetry of nature in beautiful scenery, change of season, the blue sky and clouds and sunsets, the hum and buzz and quietude of enjoyment of insect and animal life, books and the company through them of all the great and good that have departed, how cheap are these, yet how lasting!

It is often thought that vice would be pleasant enough in this world if it were not for the penalties that attend it in another; but this is a great mistake, for every deviation from the moral laws is attended with suffering as certainly, although not so directly and immediately, as in the physical or organic laws, and a person guilty of an immorality will be as surely punished for it as if he were to put his hand into the fire. The instances given above are certainly breaches of the moral law, although, as I have said, not generally recognized and acknowledged, and very much of what is called " evil " in the world is consequent upon them and may be removed upon the removal of the cause. Mankind are scrambling to get all the good they can for themselves individually, and they miss in consequence the higher good to be attained only by arrangements made best to promote the happiness of all. The mysteries of God's Moral Providence are principally owing :—

First, to the non-recognition that all God's laws, physical, moral, and mental, are equally binding upon us.

Second, we compare our condition with that of other people, both real and imaginary, and we consider ourselves entitled to something better than the state and position in which we find ourselves; whereas, if we carry out the doctrine of Necessity to its legitimate consequences, we are really entitled to nothing save a balance of enjoyment, since all our merit is derived.

Third, we have looked upon ourselves as individuals, and have acted too much without reference to the whole, of which we are only a very small part. But what is man, looked at through the doctrine of Philosophical Necessity? A mere link in the chain of causation, connected with innumerable links before his existence, and with the future chain *ad infinitum*, the consequences of his existence being endless ; calling, probably, number- less beings into existence by the same necessary law by which he himself began to be. A mere atom in the mass of sensitive creation, called into existence without any choice on his part, and moved by influences over which he has no more control than an atom of matter over attraction or repulsion, or whatever other laws it may be con- stituted to obey. He, an atom of the great body of mankind, bearing the same relation to it as a single atom of the human body does to the whole : the atom is introduced into the system by the laws of nature ; it passes through the several stages of assimilation, becomes capable of feeling, and again passes away ; so does man from the great body of society. He, however, makes *himself* the centre of time and space, and if one within his little world is removed by death, the whole economy of nature must be inverted to afford him relief ; yet from the *great body of mankind* some hundreds depart and are born every minute. To the eye that views *mankind* and not *man*, it would seem as wise to mourn for the departed,—supposing even that they exist no more, and are to us as before they were born,—as to mourn for those who might have been born, but yet were not.

In the moral government of the world we everywhere find individual happiness made subservient to the general good. Moved on all occasions by necessity, man can merit nothing, and can, in justice, claim nothing but a balance of enjoyment upon the whole of his being. To the very existence of man, as man, general laws are necessary, and the result of these general laws is to produce great variety of conditions with reference to the relative quantity of happiness enjoyed by each creature. Throughout social existence, as we have previously seen, man is made to suffer for the faults of his fellows ; the effects of his neighbour's ignorance or injustice fall upon himself, and by this arrangement the general well-being is secured, by creating the strongest of all motives for each to dispel the clouds of ignorance around him, and to endeavour to carry others forward with himself in the march of improvement.

The principal reason why Morality has not advanced as a science is, that the mental constitution has not been understood, and in ignorance of this, laws for the production of the greatest happiness were empirical and fruitless, as they could have no more foundation in real knowledge than the science of Medicine before the discovery of the circulation of the blood; but as knowledge of the structure and functions of the several organs of the body is essential to minister to their disorders, so an intimate acquainance with the faculties and functions of the mind is requisite to remedy moral disease.

Man is a compound of instincts, and of reason or intellectual faculties for the proper direction of these instincts. The instinct is the incentive to action, and reason the guide to the object of such action. Some of these instincts have reference to our individual welfare. They induce us to cling to life, though excessive pain should for the moment predominate, rendering life for the time being undesirable; they induce us to supply our body with the material necessary for its sustenance; to attach ourselves to those who administer to our pleasures; to accumulate for a future day ; to defend ourselves and repel aggression ; to meet necessary danger ; cautiously to avoid that which has a tendency to injure ; to desire approbation ; to exalt ourselves, and to view things only with reference to self. These are called the selfish feelings. Another class of our instincts leads us to seek for gratification in the welfare of the great body of society ; to desire the happiness of our fellow-creatures ; to treat them with deference and respect ; to do justly ourselves, and to see that justice is done to others. These are termed disinterested feelings, not because they have not as direct a reference to individual happiness as any of the others, but because the happiness derived from their gratification is a consequence and reflection of the happiness of others. We are thus connected by one part of our organization with the earth, and our happiness requires obedience to the physical and organic laws : by the other portion we are connected with the whole mass of sensitive existence, and our happiness equally requires that the laws that connect us with these should be obeyed.

All our faculties are sources of happiness when exercised legitimately, and all have a wide field of action without interfering with the rights or happiness of others, and the object of the moralist is to show how each may be gratified consistently with this limitation. The greatest possible amount of happiness can only be experienced when the disinterested feelings predominate, and in proportion as these take precedence over the rest, does happiness increase ; the reason of which is, that the gratification of the selfish desires decreases with age—it is single and solitary, and confined to one object—while that of the disinterested feelings is boundless in its range, and is composed, not only of the enjoyment which always results from the legitimate exercise of the faculties, but also of the happiness reflected from that of all benefited by such exercise : the former is ever but an unit ; the latter always compound.

Not only is it necessary to morality that those feelings which have the interest of others for their object should have the supremacy, but the intellectual faculties must also be cultivated and enlightened ; for the feelings that prompt us to action are mere blind impulses ; those that have for their object our own individual welfare are as likely to damage as to benefit us, unless guided by reason, and those that have for their object the welfare of our fellow-creatures are as likely to injure them as to increase their enjoyment, unless similarly directed.

As almost all the "evil" in this world originates in passion and perverted feeling, and in error consequent on the limitation of our faculties, and as it is not only necessary to wish to do right, but we must also know what is right, perhaps the highest pursuit of all is the elucidation and spread

K

of truth. We may not all be able to discover new truths, but we may all aid in making what truth there is shine a little brighter. Truthfulness and sincerity therefore must always be reckoned among the first moral duties. It is the one thing needful in this world of shams. So long as merit and demerit are attached to *opinion*, as if we could form what opinions we liked, insincerity is likely greatly to prevail. The best mode of attacking error is by spreading truth, and whatever may be the convictions at which we may arrive, and whatever may be the opinion of society with respect to such convictions, we are bound to state them if called upon. Were each mind thus honestly to declare the faith that it holds, truths that are now treated as errors dangerous to the interests of society, would be at least regarded with respect, out of deference to the talents and character of those that entertain them, and the improvement of our institutions would be more rapid. For though the " world has ever shown but small favour to its teachers ; " though it has ever regarded with an evil and a jealous eye the propounders of new truths, yet the honest expression of all that we believe will be found to be most in accordance with the promotion of our own well-being. We may be neglected and even persecuted by society at large ; yet the sympathy and friendship of the few real lovers of truth, who are capable of appreciating our motives and views, and the internal consciousness arising from the activity of the highest feelings, will more than repay us for all that the world is capable of withholding. Unless this virtue of perfect sincerity be practised, it is impossible that a man's friendships and connexions can be formed upon the only lasting and desirable footing, viz., sympathy of thought and feeling; and though the friends of the man who dares to promulgate and support unpopular truths are necessarily few, yet they are more valuable, and are the source of more happiness than a host bound to him by the ordinary worldly ties, or than the stupid staring and loud huzzas of the multitude.

By expediency we generally mean the adaptation of abstract truths to the present circumstances of the world; giving a body to what has hitherto been a mere spirit; and no spirit can live here without a body, and that adapted to the conditions of its existence. But exceptions to general rules, the dictates of the higher feelings, never can be really expedient, and therefore can never be allowed. Attempting to do good by the habitual disregard of any of the great moral laws is a fatal mistake. The history of the Jesuits is an instructive illustration. The Jesuits' was the holiest of causes —the support of Religion and the Church,—but unfortunately they taught that all means were fair and right in such a cause—they held "that they might do evil that good might come," and what was the consequence? "Before the order had existed a hundred years, it had filled the whole world with memorials of great things done and suffered for the faith. No religious community could produce a list of men so variously distinguished: none had extended its operations over so vast a space; yet in none had there ever been such perfect unity of feeling and action. There was no region of the globe, no walk of speculative or of active life, in which Jesuits were not to be found. They guided the counsels of Kings. They deciphered Latin inscriptions. They observed the motions of Jupiter's satellites. They published whole libraries, controversy, history, treatises on optics, Alcari odes, editions of the fathers, madrigals, catechisms, and lampoons."* But with the admirable energy, disinterestedness, and self-devotion, which were characteristic of the society, great vices were mingled. It was alleged, and not without foundation, that the ardent public spirit which made the Jesuit regardless of his ease, of his liberty, and of his life, made him also regardless of truth and of mercy; that no means which could promote the interest of his religion seemed to him unlawful, and that by the interest of his religion he too often meant the interest of his society. Consequently at the end of this hundred years these principles had brought the whole of the Catholic Church into disrepute, and we find that Tillotson, whose indulgence for various schismatics and heretics brought on

* Macaulay, vol. 2, p. 54.

him the reproach of heterodoxy, told the House of Commons from the pulpit that it was their duty to make effectual provision against the propagation of a religion which demanded from its followers services directly opposed to the first principles of morality. The Jesuits sought power at the expense of truth and mercy, they outraged the fundamental laws by which alone society can be held together, and notwithstanding their training, their talent, and the high objects for which they sought that power, they lived to be powerless, except when working in the dark or under false colours; for in their own characters no one could trust them or place the slightest reliance upon anything they said or did, since with them truth was not sacred and no contract was binding.

A serious mischief is done to the mind by admitting even the supposition that, in any case, the greatest happiness principle will allow of a departure from the general rule of right. Conscience can admit of no appeal; it must be a supreme ruler; for habitual obedience to its dictates is the only means of preventing the mind from being divided against itself, and of keeping it in a healthy state. The Utilitarian Philosophy requires, therefore, to be used with caution. It serves to test the soundness of general rules, and to supply a motive where no such general rules exist: the well-being of society can never be secured by leaving it to every individual to calculate the consequences of each action, but by the obedience of each to those rules that experience has shown generally to tend to happiness. The performance of duty—to do on all occasions what is right, therefore, and not the pursuit of happiness, may be considered as the safest road to happiness; trusting, as we may do implicitly, that if we act in obedience to the moral law, our well-being will be best secured.

The main thing to be sought is the *habitual* predominance of the moral feelings; the maintenance of them in a state in which "the prospect of advantage through unlawful means should never present itself to the mind;" or if it did, that its expulsion should follow instinctively, without any calculation on the subject as to whether the "particular circumstances" do not make it lawful; for he that hesitates is lost. If an action be considered at all doubtful, the thought of it is occasionally entertained, the mind becomes accustomed to the possibility of its performance, and will then generally yield to the first strong temptation. Thus even thoughts at variance with the highest purity of mind should never be permitted to gain entrance, for evil thoughts invariably lead to evil deeds, as minor crimes to greater. So the habitual indulgence of *one* fault lowers the tone of the whole of the moral sentiments, and is incompatible with the higher virtues. It acts physically as well as morally by depriving the moral organs of the nervous energy requisite for their full activity. A certain portion of nervous fluid is generated by the brain, and if this is used by the propensities, it is at the expense of the moral and intellectual organs. *

In the present artificial state of society, where its laws are in so many instances opposed to the laws of nature, every individual act of virtue cannot be supposed to lead directly to happiness. The sacrifice of external advantages required by such an act may even be very great; but we must bear in mind, what moralists too often forget, that it is not in every act of virtue that the reward is to be looked for, but in the general amount of happiness resulting from virtuous dispositions, habits, and feelings; a state of mind which is only attainable by the invariable and constant practice

---

* J. S. Mill says, " Capacity for the nobler feelings is in most natures a very tender plant, easily killed, not only by hostile influences, but by mere want of sustenance ; and in the majority of young persons it speedily dies away if the occupation to which their position in life has devoted them, and the society into which it has thrown them, are not favourable to keeping that higher capacity in exercise. Men lose their high aspirations as they lose their intellectual tastes, because they have not time or opportunity for indulging them ; and they addict themselves to inferior pleasures, not because they deliberately prefer them, but because they are either the only ones to which they have access, or the only ones which they are any longer capable of enjoying. It may be questioned whether any one who has remained equally susceptible to both classes of pleasures, ever knowingly and calmly preferred the lower ; though many, in all ages, have broken down in an ineffectual attempt to combine both."—*Fraser*, Oct, 16, 1861.

of virtue. A man's virtue may be of the negative kind, that is, confined to doing no one any injury; but if he do to no one any good, although he may not actually suffer in consequence, he will lose all the happiness derived from active virtue. His condition will be similar to that of a man born blind, who suffers not positively from the want of sight, never having known what it is to see, but who loses all the advantages derivable from that sense. So the man of low moral manifestation may not be a greater sufferer, but he is susceptible of many degrees less happiness than the highly moral man, in the same way that the brutes are capable of less enjoyment than himself: a pig eats and drinks and sleeps and grunts away his life in a comparatively low kind of enjoyment, and so may he. " If we know a man who is palpably cold-hearted, grasping and selfish, we are authorised to conclude, First, that he is deprived of that delicious sunshine of the soul and all those thrilling sympathies with whatever is noble, beautiful, and holy, which attend the vivacious action of the moral and religious faculties: and, Second, that he is deprived of the reflected influence of the same emotions from the hearts and countenances of the good men around him." * Mackintosh, in speaking of Leibnitz's Ethics, observes, " It entirely escaped his sagacity as it has that of nearly all other moralists, that the coincidence of morality with well-understood

* Combe's Moral Philosophy.

interest in our outward actions, is very far from being the most important part of the question; for these actions flow from habitual dispositions, from affections and sensibilities which determine their nature. There may be, and there are, many immoral acts, which, in the sense in which words are commonly used, are advantageous to the actor. But the whole sagacity and ingenuity of the world may be safely challenged to point out a case in which virtuous dispositions, habits, and feelings, are not conducive in the highest degree to the happiness of the individual; or to maintain that he is not the happiest, whose moral sentiments and affections are such as to prevent the possibility of the prospect of advantage, through unlawful means, presenting itself to his mind. It would indeed have been impossible to prove to Regulus that it was his interest to return to a death of torture in Africa. But what if the proof had been easy? The most thorough conviction on such a point would not have enabled him to set this example, if he had not been supported by his own integrity and generosity, by love of his country and reverence for his pledged faith. What could the conviction add to that greatness of soul, and to these glorious attributes? With such virtues he could not act otherwise than he did. Would a father, affectionately interested in a son's happiness, of very lukewarm feelings of morality, but of good sense enough to weigh gratifications and sufferings exactly, be really desirous that his son should have these virtues in a less degree than Regulus, merely because they might expose him to the fate that Regulus chose? On the coldest calculation he would surely perceive that the high and glowing feelings of such a mind during life, altogether throw into the shade a few hours of agony in leaving it. And, if he himself were so unfortunate that no more generous sentiment arose in his mind to silence such calculations, would it not be a reproach to his understanding not to discover that though in one case out of millions such a character might lead a Regulus to torture, yet, in the common course of nature, it is the source, not only of happiness in life, but of quiet and honour in death? A case so extreme as that of Regulus will not perplex, if we bear in mind, that though we cannot prove the *act* of heroic virtue to be conducive to the interest of the hero, yet we may perceive at once that nothing is so conducive to his interest as to have a mind so formed that it could not shrink from it, but must rather embrace it with gladness and triumph. Men of vigorous health are said sometimes to suffer most in a pestilence. No man was ever so absurd as for that reason to wish that he were more infirm. The distemper might return once in a century. If he were then alive he might escape it; and even if he fell, the balance of advantage would be in most cases greatly on the side of robust health. In estimating beforehand the value of a strong bodily frame, a man of sense would throw the small chance of a rare and short evil entirely out of the account. So must the coldest and most selfish moral calculator, who, if he be sagacious and exact, must pronounce that the inconveniences to which a man may be sometimes exposed by a pure and sound mind, are no reasons for regretting that we do not escape by possessing minds more enfeebled and distempered." *

It may be asked, whether our own happiness be an inducement to morality sufficiently strong? Whether it will be able to produce the self-denial necessary to form a highly moral character? For morality constantly requires the sacrifice of immediate pleasures to greater ones more distant, and of present enjoyment to the good of others. But if our own happiness is not a sufficient inducement to morality, what is? It is true we never *directly* seek our own happiness, but happiness results from the gratification of our desires and affections; we desire the approbation of the public and our own esteem; the love of those with whom we associate: we desire to do what is right; the happiness of others; the love of God; and if stronger motives to action than these can be pointed out, what are they? Are not these the principles of action by which the generality of mankind are influenced? The enjoyments proceeding from the highest

* Mackintosh's Dissertations, p. 338.

feelings of our nature, the love of mankind and of that which is right, are beyond all comparison more animating and durable, as well as more refined and elevated, than those proceeding from selfish or sensual gratifications; and all that can be said, therefore, of him who is called the sufferer for conscience sake, is, that he prefers the higher pleasure to the lower, or the great good in the future to the little good now.

One more essential to the interests of morality we shall mention. It is requisite that the mind should be freed from the degrading notions of the character of the Deity that have been handed down to us from the dark ages of ignorance and superstition, and that it should entertain views more consistent with the Divine Perfections. We must be able to reject, as derogatory to the character of God, whatever is inconsistent with the highest principles of our nature. We must not allow ourselves to suppose that what are Benevolence and Justice to us, are not so to God ; or that He has a love of adulation that we should despise in a human being; that Infinite Benevolence can ordain a balance of misery, or that a balance of misery in this world, and infinite misery in the next, must necessarily be the portion of one part of God's creatures to ensure the welfare of the rest ; or that punishment is vengeance, and that vengeance everlasting; or that a disinterested lover of truth and rectitude will be lost, when

belief *because it is safest* would save him ; that the
Omniscient Deity can propose a plan for the
temporal and eternal interests of His creatures,
which at the same time he knows is inefficient to
the purpose, because he knows it will not be
accepted by them ; that the best and highest
happiness of his creatures here is inconsistent with
their happiness hereafter ; or that the final purposes
of creation are God's honour and glory. No ;
from the mind that has contemplated the perfections of the Almighty in the book of his works,
such degrading notions will be banished, and it will
tremble to impute motives and actions to God that
are inconsistent with the highest virtue even of His
creatures ; though they should be revealed by an
angel from heaven, or by a priesthood claiming for
itself inspiration from the Highest. More consistent is the Atheist than he who allows himself
to entertain such ideas ; more reasonable were it to
believe in no God, than in one possessing such
attributes ! But he who looks deeper into the
ways of Providence, finds a scheme worthy of
Deity, in the production of the largest sum of
enjoyment possible ; finds that He works not by
partial laws, but by such as pervade the whole
sensitive creation, and cannot be resisted by any
supposed freedom of will. He feels the most
implicit confidence in God, finding that there is no
evidence for the existence of any other object but
the good of his creatures ; that pain is necessary

for his preservation, and is as his schoolmaster to instruct him and impel him forward in the race of improvement—that it is intended to correct error, not to punish it. He feels and knows that the laws of God are not changeable, but that he may depend upon them in the calculation of his well-being; and that there is no necessity for us to pray to God that He will alter His laws for us to be happy, but that if we do but study and obey them, our happiness will infallibly follow ; that, as it is the law of his existence that he should desire his own happiness, and morality is the most direct road to it, he must, as he advances in intelligence and sees more clearly this connexion between virtue and happiness, of *necessity* choose the former. To the man who can divest his mind of the degrading superstitions of his childhood, and exercise it upon the great plan of Providence, every cause and effect that he may witness, every truth that he may discover, is a new illustration of the goodness of God. To see Him in His works; to know what He does, and wherefore He does it, is to feel for ever in His presence ; he who thus seeks the Pervading and Creating Spirit of the Universe, sees on every side of him wonders going forward which only God can perform ; each atom obeying the laws of order given to it; each plant elaborately and systemati-cally assuming the form peculiarly its own ; each animal working out the object of its being, and Sensation—Feeling—the great Soul of the world periodically changing its garment, as generation after generation of men, and all living creatures, are organized, vitalized, and again return to their mother Earth to form new combinations. " Is not God's Universe a Symbol of the God-like, is not Immensity a Temple ? Listen, and for organ-music thou wilt ever, as of old, hear the morning stars sing together." *

Sartor Resartus, p. 263.

PART II·

MENTAL SCIENCE.

CHAPTER I.

MATTER.

SUBSTANCES appear naturally to divide themselves into three grand classes : inorganic; organic,
or those which have Life; and those organic
structures which have received another and apparently totally distinct principle, viz., Sensation or
Sensibility.

Inorganic Matter is distinguished by the possession of properties which we call Attraction,
Repulsion, Inertia, that is to say, without *sensation*,
and consequently without *volition*; it possesses
certain tendencies to act in a certain way, which
tendencies are called the laws to which it is
subjected, and which are always uniform. It is to
these tendencies that all the motions going on in
inorganic matter are owing—all the phenomena of
Physics. In relation to such laws, however, when
we say that it is *attraction* that causes all bodies to
tend towards each other, we are not in the least

better instructed with respect to the cause of this tendency, for attraction is only a name invented to express the fact. Newton, therefore, when he showed that the heavenly bodies in revolving round each other obey the same law as the apple in its descent to the earth, did not make us better acquainted with the cause of the motion of either ; although he explained the phenomenon in the only way that it admitted of explanation, by showing that the order in which it takes place is similar to the observed succession of more familiar facts There are also general laws or tendencies which are probably only modifications of those above mentioned. Such are chemical affinities ; which, by variously combining what are supposed to be the different kinds of matter, form all the endless variety of bodies on the face of the globe.

By tracing out and registering the tendencies or laws of matter in the departments of Physics and Chemistry, and by acting in accordance with them, we have been able to turn the powers of nature to our own use and comfort. Such powers now at our command in this country are said to be equal to the joint force of 900 millions of men, or to the inhabitants of the whole globe.*

* Men, stimulated by their natural wants, and using their faculties of mind and body to supply these from around them, have gradually discovered that all the things or objects in nature are but repetitions or multiplications of a few kinds which they conveniently class as being of three kingdoms, called *Animal,*

L

Organized or living matter possesses the same properties and is subjected to the same laws as inorganic; and such laws are so little suspended with regard to organic bodies as to determine the size of both plants and animals all over the world, and ultimately causing old age, decay, and death, or the extinction of life.

Striking as are the phenomena revealed to us in the first named departments of nature, the phenomena of Life are still more so. Two bodies, almost identical to the eye, a stone and a seed, are buried in the ground. In the one there is little or no change; the other expands, bursts, rises from the ground, and makes to itself organs whereby its various functions are performed; the matter of which it is composed is continually changing, throwing off the old and useless material, and converting other matter into its own substance to supply its place; giving to other bodies the power of exercising the same vital energy, *i.e.*, producing forms similar to itself; and then it dies—the vital power leaves the individual existence and is incapable of being further traced by us.

Thus the characteristic of vegetative life is to

Vegetable, and *Mineral:* and further, they have discovered that all the changes or motions incessantly going on among these objects are of but four great kinds, which they have called *Mechanical, Chemical, Vital,* and *Mental.* By study of fit types in these simple classifications, they have acquired such wide knowledge of things and their changing conditions as has enabled them to devise very numerous processes or *arts,* by which they prodigously advance human well-being.

perform the functions of nutrition, respiration circulation, secretion, excretion, and reproduction ; the object of these functions being to produce the changes above mentioned, and thus to preserve the individual existence and the life which supports it.

Two seeds very much alike shall in their growth present altogether opposite appearances, and the *same* power acting upon what appear to us to be similar structures and upon others in which there is very little difference, produces all the varied beauties of the vegetative kingdom. With reference to the primary laws which regulate these differences we are at present little enlightened : one thing, however, appears certain, that however complicated the peculiar laws of life may appear to us to be in the present state of our knowledge, they are fixed and invariable.

Life proceeds only from life ;* no instance having

* We are told by some naturalists that the nervous system does not mark the distinction between the animal and vegetable Kingdom, because there are large classes of animals which have none ; for instance, its existence has not been yet traced in all *infusoria*, in the myriad species of Hydrozoa and Anthozoa, and it is now doubted whether what has hitherto been taken for a nervous system in the Echinodermata has any real existence. But as life appears only to proceed from life, and all sensation to depend upon a nervous system in like manner where we can see clearly, all that we can say is that a nervous system in some cases has yet to le discovered, and with clearer vision and more knowledge it is a fair inference that it will be, for what did we know of the circulation of insects, or of the organ of hearing in the cephalopoda, before John Hunter's time ? We are justified, we think, by analogy in saying that the nervous system in these minute classes has not yet been *clearly demonstrated*, and that is all.

been known of its existence where it has not been transmitted from one organized body to another; in its lowest state of energy it requires to be placed in certain relations to light, heat, and moisture; it depends upon organization. Sensation depends upon life, and all things in inorganic matter, body, and mind, bear a fixed relation to each other, and if this relation be altered in one part the whole is destroyed.

As there is an apparent difference between inert or dead matter and matter which possesses life, so there is an important difference between mere organic life and animal life, or that which has received the additional principle of Sensation. Life and sensation appear to be entirely distinct principles; for although sensation cannot exist without life, yet life may exist altogether independently of sensation.

Life seems to be carried on in the same way in animals as in vegetables. In both, the materials for growth and reproduction of waste particles are supplied by means of the circulation of a fluid through innumerable tubes; the root may be said to be the stomach of the plant, imbibing nutrition from the soil; a system of tubes rising upwards correspond to the lacteals and pulmonary arteries of animals; these are distributed in minute ramifications over the surface of the leaves, which may be termed the lungs of the plant, as here the sap is exposed to the agency of

light and air, and like the blood in animals, under-
goes a change which adapts it to the wants of the
vegetable; this sap then descends through another
system of minute tubes in the inner layer of the
bark, yielding all the juices peculiar to the plant.

There is, however, a difference, and a very
striking one, in the nature of the food proper to
plants and animals; by means of which difference
the vegetable kingdom is made to prepare the way
for the animal. The plant subsists upon inorganic
matter, whilst organic is the necessary food of the
animal. Life in the vegetable converts inorganic
into organic matter. Thus the soil is subservient
to the plant; the plant to the animal; one animal
lower in the scale of sensation to another that is
higher ; and all to the superior capabilities of
enjoyment in man.

Another noticeable difference between plants and
animals, in reference to the organic processes upon
which life depends, is that the former are fixed to
the soil and are therefore always in contact with
their food; whereas in animals which possess a
power of locomotion a different arrangement is
necessary for the supply of nutriment, and these
are, consequently, provided with a receptacle by
which they can carry their food about with them.
To convert this food into a proper supply to replace
the waste particles, other functions are requisite,
more numerous and complicated in the animal than
in the plant.

At the commencement of the scale of organization *i.e.*, where life seems least removed from inorganic matter, the structure is so simple that a single organ seems all that is necessary for the existence of the individual. But the higher the individual in the scale of existence and the more its vital energy. the greater is the multiplication of its organs, the more numerous its functions, and the more elaborate and complex its structure. From the lowest end of the scale to the highest for every different function performed by either plant or animal an additional organ is necessary. The animal performs more functions than the plant, and its structure is, consequently, much more complex; but the organs in both are neither *more* nor *less* than are required for their individual wants.

Life, then, is common to both plants and animals, and is supported in the same way in both; the only difference being complexity of structure in proportion as the functions are more numerous and of a higher order; and the chief distinction between them being that to animals is given sensation, or the power of feeling, in addition to life.

Living and feeling are distinct states, although both existing in one frame. Each state has its own organs and distinct functions, and though sensation is nowhere known to exist without life, yet life continues sometimes to exist when all sensation has ceased or is even extinct. Thus we continue to live when sensation is lost in sleep, and sleep which is rest to the organs of sensation is necessary to the healthy exercise of their functions and even to their very existence. The organs which support life, on the contrary, work without intermission, death being the consequence of their ceasing to act. Could they rest when we are no longer conscious, they would not in all probability wear out so soon, and we should live longer. In cases of apoplexy sensation frequently becomes extinct, at least to all appearance, some days before the merely vital functions cease. In drowning, also, sensation ceases some considerable time before death, and may be again restored if the organic functions have not quite stopped ; so also the stoppage of the heart, or of the circulation of the blood in the brain from pressure, immediately entails unconsciousness ; thus proving the fact that sensation is distinct from life though dependent upon it.

It is difficult to tell when and where the animal life is first added to the organic. So feeble is the energy, so indistinct is the appearance of sensation when it is first added to matter, that naturalists have mistaken what are now known to be animals for plants. The energy of sensation, however, gradually increases as we trace it upwards in the scale of creation, and always with it the enlargement and complexity of the nervous system. The senses and voluntary motion gradually make their appearance in worms, insects, &c., the extra necessary vital functions being at the same time added. We thus ascend the scale through fishes, reptiles, birds, and quadrupeds, the complexity of organs, both nervous and vital, increasing in proportion as sensation and motion become more energetic. Thus the cerebral functions or the diversified powers of thinking and feeling gradually increase until they receive their final development in man, where they produce all the phenomena of Intellect, so far surpassing anything analogous in animals that it requires considerable knowledge of comparative anatomy to refer them to the same source.

"The relation is still stricter between the complexity of apparatus of sensation and the range of feeling than between the complexity of the inferior or organic functions. The greater the number of senses the greater the number of the organs of sense; the more accurate and varied the impressions conveyed by each, the more complex the structure of the instrument by which they are communicated; the more extended the range of the intellectual operations, the larger the bulk of brain, the greater the number of its distinct parts, and the more exquisite their organization. From the point of the animal scale, at which the brain first becomes distinctly visible, up to man, the basis of the organ is the same; but as the range of its functions extends, part after part is superadded, and the structure of each part becomes progressively more and more complex. The evidence of this, afforded by comparative anatomy, is irresistible, and the interest connected with the study of it can scarcely be exceeded." *

"In the nervous system alone we can trace a gradual progress in the provision for the subordination of one animal to another, and of all to man; and are enabled to associate every faculty which gives superiority with some additions to the nervous mass, even from the smallest indication of sensation and will, up to the highest degree of sensibility, judgment, and expression. The brain is observed to be progressively improved in its structure; and, with reference to the spinal marrow and nerves, augmented in volume more and more, until we reach the human brain, each addition being marked by some addition to, or amplification of the power of the animal, until in man we behold it possessing some parts of which animals are destitute, and wanting none which they possess." †

All facts seem to imply that in precisely the same way that life depends upon organization, so sensation or the animal life depends upon a superstructure raised upon this organization, viz., the nervous system. Neither is there a single fact to prove that man is in any way an exception to this rule. His mind and feelings seem to be equally dependent upon his nervous system, and the

* Dr. Southwood Smith's "Philosophy of Health," Chap. I.
† Edinburgh Review, No. 94.

difference between him and other animals, however great, seems owing to the greater complexity
of this system; from which it is evident that
important as this difference may be, there is no
necessity for the introduction of a fourth principle,
as distinct as life from sensation, to account for it.
The functions of parts of the brain which man has
in addition to those possessed by the highest order
of brutes, enable him to communicate his ideas and
to register and generalize his experience, and these
powers constitute his distinguishing characteristic,
without which he would never have risen above the
savage state.

That he is a progressive being is the grand
distinction of man, and the reason of an intelligent
individual of the present age is not so much the
reason of one, as of the whole human race:
everything worthy of being preserved in every
mind that has existed having been handed down to
us, first by oral tradition and then by written
records, making ultimately a greater difference
between a cultivated mind of the present day, and
that of one who has only had the experience of a life
to teach him, than between the latter individual and
one of the higher order of brutes. It is well said
by Dr. Arnott that " a well-informed man of the
present day may be said to possess within the
boundaries of his mind the universe in miniature,
where he can contemplate at pleasure, past events
and the present and the future."

To those who are unaccustomed to trace the origin and growth of ideas through successive ages, and to consider the expansion of mind as the result of the registered experience of all who have preceded us, it is difficult to perceive the resemblance between the wonderful powers of man and those that are developed in a minor degree in the animals. That the mind of man, however, is not an exception to the universal law, which makes the animal life, viz., sensation—thought—consciousness —dependent upon the brain, appears to be incontrovertible if we trace the progression of the mind from childhood to manhood, and the retrogression from manhood to second childhood, as the organs of the brain gradually attain maturity with age, and again with age decay.

Dr. Southwood Smith thus traces this progression and retrogression —" The functions of the organic life are perfect at once. The heart contracts as well, the arteries secrete as well, the respiratory organs work as well, the first moment they begin to act as at any subsequent period. They require no teaching from experience, and they profit nothing from its lessons. On the contrary, the operations of the brain, and the actions of the voluntary muscles, feeble and uncertain at first, acquire strength by slow degrees, and attain their ultimate perfection only at the adult age."

" In the descending series, the animal life fails before the organic, and its nobler powers decay

sooner and more speedily than the subordinate.
First of all the impressions which the organs of
sense convey to the brain become less numerous and
distinct, and consequently the material on which
the mind operates is less abundant and perfect; but
at the same time, the power of working vigorously
with the material it possesses more than proportionally diminishes. Memory fails; analogous
phenomena are less readily and less completely
recalled by the presence of those which should
suggest the entire train; the connecting links are
dimly seen or wholly lost; the brain itself is less
vivid and less coherent; train succeeds train with
preternatural slowness, and the consequence of these
growing imperfections is that at last, induction
becomes unsound just as it was in early youth; and
for the same reason, namely, because there is not in
the mental view an adequate range of individual
phenomena; and the only difference being that the
range comprehended in the view of the old man is
too narrow, because that which he had learnt he has
forgotten; while in the youth it is too narrow,
because that which it is necessary to learn has not
been acquired.

"And with the diminution of intellectual power
the senses continue progressively to fail; the eye
grows more dim, the ear more dull, the sense of
smell less delicate, the sense of touch less acute,
while the sense of taste, immediately subservient
to the organic function of nutrition, is the last to

diminish in intensity and correctness, and wholly fails but with the extinction of the life it serves.

" But the senses are not the only servants of the brain; the voluntary muscles are so equally; but these ministers to the master power, no longer kept in active service, the former no longer employed to convey new, varied, and vivid impressions, the latter no longer employed to execute the commands of new, varied, and intense desires, become successively feebler, slower, and more uncertain in their action. The hand trembles, the step totters, and every movement is tardy and unsteady. And thus, by the loss of one intellectual faculty after another, by the obliteration of sense after sense, by the progressive failure of the power of voluntary motion, in a word, by the declining energy and the ultimate, extinction of the animal life, .man, from the state of maturity, passes a second time through the stage of childhood back to that of infancy. * * * Slow may be the waste of the organic organs; but they do waste, and that waste is not repaired, and consequently their functions languish, and no amount of stimulus is capable of invigorating their failing action. The arteries are rigid and cannot nourish; the veins are relaxed and cannot carry on the mass of blood that oppresses them; the lungs, partly choked up by adventitious matter, and partly incapable of expanding and collapsing by reason of the feeble action of the respiratory apparatus, imperfectly aerate the small quantity of blood that flows through them; the heart, deprived of its wonted nutriment and stimulus, is unable to contract with the energy requisite to propel the vital current; the various organs, no longer supplied with the quantity and quality of material necessary for carrying on their respective processes, cease to act; the machinery stops, and this is death.

"And now the processes of life at an end, the body falls within the dominion of the powers which preside universally over matter; the tie that linked all its parts together, holding them in union and keeping them in action, in direct opposition to those powers dissolved, it feels and obeys the new attractions to which it has become subject; particle after particle that stood in beautiful order, fall from their place; the wonderful structures they composed melt away; the very substances of which those structures were built are resolved into their primitive elements; these elements, set at liberty, enter into new combinations and become constituent parts of new beings; those new beings in their turn, perish; from their death springs life, and so the change goes on in an everlasting circle."

As the elements of which the body has been composed "enter into new combinations and become constituent parts of new beings," so, even with reference to this world, may it be truly said that the mind does not perish, but that the essential parts of it descend to our children, or in the shape of written documents—registered experience, help to form the minds of hundreds of the human race.

CHAPTER II.

In the previous chapter we have seen how nature, in the vast variety of her movements, seems systematically to approach towards one object, the production of Sensation or Sensibility or Consciousness. The laws of inorganic matter prepare the way for organic, for plants and vegetables possessing life; the vegetable kingdom prepares the way for the animal, and upon the vital functions of animals is dependent the nervous system which it seems to be the object of all the other complicated processes to produce, and with which Sensation or feeling is as intimately connected, as Attraction with inorganic matter, or Life with organic.

The world appears to have been created with the view of containing the largest possible amount of sentient existence. Not only organized structures possessing life, but beings endowed with sensation teem on every side of us ; the wide-spreading ocean, the earth, the air, are full of them ; each possessing a constitution adapted to the sphere in which it moves. There appears to be no situation where vegetation or the effects of vegetation exist that does not support some kind of animal life : stagnant water and noxious marshes, decaying vegetable and animal matter, all swarm with sentient beings, and what is death to the more perfectly organized beings, is the source of life to others lower in the scale. Distinct worlds of sensation seem to exist, in the water, in the air, in the earth, as well as on the earth, all possessing a wonderful adaptation of structure to their place in creation. How beautiful, for instance, is the world of insects, fitted as these are, in their various transformations, to inhabit the different elements. How complicated is their structure, bodily and mental, enabling them to live in a world of their own, inaccessible to the obtuser senses of man. They hear and see and feel and smell and taste what is too subtle for his perception : they have music and a language that he cannot understand : they sport in all the colours of the rainbow, and delight in their own gay clothing. The variety of structure in the organs of the senses, in the wings, legs stings, ovipositors, mouths, and internal machinery for the supply of waste, of these little creatures, is among the great wonders of comparative anatomy. Not less wonderful is the perfection with which such internal machinery, in beings so frail and low in the scale of existence, performs its work ; turning death into life, putrefaction into the most beautiful and variegated structure, producing the lamp of the glow-worm, the sting of the bee, and the venom that maddens the sluggish ox   No less

M

admirable and appropriate is the structure of every
living creature, from the tribes of infusoria upwards, each possessing the powers of sensation,
and consequently intelligence, in the degree that
is requisite for its happiness and maintenance in
creation.

The most highly organised being is Man, and the
aggregate of all his sensations, whether proceeding
from external or internal impressions, we denomi-
nate his mind. The mind, therefore, is intimately
connected with the brain and nervous system, and
all the functions of the body are important only as
they promote the healthy action of the brain, for it
is sensation alone that makes life of any value.
The due regulation of such functions is essential
therefore, to the proper action of the mind.

It is represented by some who fear the supposed
results of what is called materialism, that the brain
is merely the instrument that the mind makes use
of in its connexion with the body. On the other
hand it is said " Mind is the functional power of
the living brain." " As I cannot conceive _Life_ any
more than the power of attraction," says Dr.
Elliotson, " unless possessed by matter, so I cannot
conceive _mind_ unless possessed by a brain, or by
some nervous organ, whatever name we may
choose to give it, endowed with life. I speak of
terrestrial or animal mind; with angelic and divine
natures we have nothing to do, and of them we
know, in the same respects, nothing. Observation

shows that superiority of mind in the animal creation
is exactly commensurate with superiority of brain ;
that activity of brain and of mind are coequal;
and that, as long as the brain is endowed with life,
and remains uninjured, it, like all other organs,
can perform its functions, and mind continues; but,
as in all other organs, when its life ceases, its power
to perform its function ceases, and the mind ceases ;
when disease or mechanical injury affects it, the
mind is affected—inflammation of the stomach
causes vomiting, of the brain delirium; a blow
upon the head stuns; if originally constituted
defective, the mind is defective ; if fully developed,
and properly acted on, the mind is vigorous ;
accordingly as it varies with age, in quality and
bulk, is the mind also varied—the mind of a child
is weak and very excitable; of the adult, vigorous
and firm ; and of the old man, weak and dull,
exactly like the body ; and the character of the
mind of an individual agrees with the character of
his body, being equally excitable, languid, or torpid,
evidently because the brain is of the same character
as the rest of the body to which it belongs ;—the
female mind exceeds the male in excitability as
much as her body : the qualities of the mind are
also heriditary, which they could not be, unless they
were, like our other qualities, corporeal conditions ;
and the mind is often disordered upon the dis-
appearance of a bodily complaint, just as other
organs, besides the brain, are affected under similar

circumstances,—the retrocession of an eruption may affect the lungs, causing asthma ; the bowels, causing interitis ; or the brain, causing insanity,— phthisis and insanity sometimes alternate with each other, just like affections of other organs ; the laws of the mind are precisely those of the functions of all other organs,—a certain degree of excitement strengthens it, too much exhausts it ; physical agents affect it, and some specifically, as is the case with other functions, for example, narcotics. The argument of Bishop Butler that the soul is immortal and independent of matter because in fatal diseases the mind often remains vigorous to the last, is perfectly groundless, for any function will remain vigorous to the last, if the organ which performs it is not the seat of disease, nor much connected by sympathy, or in other modes with the organ which is the seat of the disease,—the stomach often calls regularly for food, and digests it vigorously, while the lungs are almost completely consumed by ulceration. All the cases that are adduced to prove the little dependence of the mind upon the brain, are adduced in opposition to the myriads of others that daily occur in the usual course of nature, and are evidently regarded as extraordinary by those who bring them forward. An exact parallel to each may be found in the affections of every other organ, and each admits of so easy an explanation, that it may be truly said, "Exceptio probat regulum." *

* "Human Physiology," p. 32.

But whatever may be the way in which Sensation is connected with the nervous system, it does not at all affect the reasoning founded upon the fact of that connexion. We do not call attraction a function of matter, but we never find matter existing without attraction—so we never find Life without organization, or Sensation without a nervous system.

The world is sustained and governed by "forces" of which we really know nothing, although we hide our ignorance under high-sounding names, such as Attraction, Repulsion, Chemical, Electrical, Vital, Mental, &c. When we say a thing takes place by the force of attraction, we think we have explained it, but it is no such thing; we have merely named a certain group of phenomena occurring in a certain order, and which occur uniformly or invariably in that order. We know nothing of the "force" of attraction in itself—it is only known to us in its effects; we have no powers which enable us to lift the veil and look beyond.*

* The theory of "force" is that it is equally indestructible with matter. Like matter, it may change its forms in a thousand ways, but it cannot be lessened or annihilated. Light and heat are forces, and heat may become what is called latent, but it is not the less present and at work, although for a time hidden from us. If we may theorise on the formation of worlds, and on this "interchange of forces," we may suppose that when the stars or planets, from their original nebulous state, took a more solid form, there would be a great evolution of heat, which force would gradually take other shapes, such as attraction, light, electricity, chemical affinity, life and nervous force, and feeling or mind. We hear much of the power of mind over matter, and

Apart from what it *does* we have no knowledge of

it is popularly supposed that it is the soul that sets the body in motion; but the force that moves the steam-engine and that which moves the body are precisely similar and generated in a similar way. Thus Dr. Arnott says:—

"James Watt, when devising his great engine, knew well that the rapid combination of the oxygen of atmospheric air with the combustible fuel in the furnace, produced the heat and force of the engine ; but he did not know that in living bodies there is going on, only more slowly, a similar combination of the oxygen of the air with the like combustible matter in the food, as this circulates after digestion in the form of blood through the lungs, which combination produces the warmth and force of the living animal. The chief resemblances of the two objects are exhibited strikingly in the following table of comparison, where, in two adjoining columns, are set forth nearly the same things and actions,, with difference only in names :—

The steam - engine in action takes—	*The animal body in life takes—*
1. Fuel, viz., coal and wood, both being old or dry vegetable matter, and both combustil le.	1. Food, viz., recent or fresh vegetable matter and flesh, both being of kindred composition and both combustible.
2. Water.	2. Drink (essentially water).
3. Air.	3. Breath (common air).
And produces –	*And produces—*
4. Steady boiling heat of 212 degrees by quick combustion.	4. Steady animal heat of 98 degrees by slow combustion.
5. Smoke from the chimney, or air loaded with carbonic acid and vapour.	5, Foul breath from the windpipe, or air loaded with carbonic acid and vapour.
6. Ashes, part of the fuel which does not burn.	6. Animal refuse, part of the food which does not burn.
7. Motive force, of simple alternate push and pull in the piston, which, acting through levers, joints, bands, &c., does work of endless variety.	7. Motive force, of simple alternate contraction and relaxation in the muscles, which, acting through the levers, joints, tendons, &c., of the limbs, does work of endless variety.

it, and we separate it from other forces by any

8. A deficiency of fuel, water, or air, first disturbs, and then stops the motion.	8. A deficiency of food, drink, or breath, first disturbs, and then stops the motion and the life.
9. Local damage from violence in a machine is repaired by the maker.	9. Local hurt or disease in a living body is repaired or cured by the action of internal vital powers given by the Creator."

—" A Survey of Human Progress," p. 158.

This generation of force it is which makes the inactivity of solitary confinement and ennui so painful, and which makes employment necessary.

"Generally speaking, the average amount of daily food necessary for healthy men is estimated at 12 oz. of beef, 20 oz. of bread, with about ½ oz. of butter. These articles contain a force capable, if applied by a machine, of raising fourteen (?) million pounds weight to a height of one foot ; that is, the oxidation of the elements contained in them would give rise to an amount of heat equivalent to that effect. But in the human body, though it far surpasses all machines in economy of force, the utmost amount of power attainable from them is not more than equivalent to three and a-half millions of pounds raised to the height of a foot ; and an average day's labour does not exceed two millions of pounds thus raised. The difference is mainly due, doubtless, to the number of internal actions which are carried on in the living body ; such as the circulation, the movements of respiration, and the production of animal heat. These consume a great part of the force of the food, and leave only a remainder to be disposed of in muscular exertion."—*Cornhill Magazine,* September, 1861.

The action of the cerebellum is the most expensive of all forces, and if this begins too early it seriously impairs the growth of the body ; if it is too large and active in after life it very much decreases the muscular energy.

We require a new system of hygiene in which "force" shall be properly and proportionately distributed. The thinking powers probably absorb a larger portion than the vital, and the vital than the merely muscular. A due balance is required

dissimilarity in its action.   Mind as a force should

between the feelings and the activities—between bodily labour and head work.

The force generated or the energy of the locomotive organs in the animal is supposed to depend upon the quantity of red globules which carry the oxygen, the union of the oxygen and carbon taking place in the general circulation, and not, as is usually supposed, in the lungs only, in respiration ; the lungs not being hotter than the rest of the body.   On the other hand, it is well known that increased respiration consequent on exercise generates an increase of heat, so that it is probable that the union goes on in both.

The original mind of George 'Stephenson was among the first to perceive these truths.   He said of the power propelling his locomotives, that it was the light of the sun bottled up in the earth for tens of thousands of years—"light, absorbed by plants and vegetables, being necessary for the condensation of carbon during their growth, if it be not carbon in another form,— and now, after being buried in the earth for long ages in fields of coal, that latent light is again brought forth and liberated—made to work, as in that locomotive, for great human purposes."— "The Life of George Stephenson," by Samuel Smiles, p. 475.

Thoughts and feelings are now supposed to be the immediate correlates of the vital forces, and the vital of the physical.   The quantity or intensity of consciousness or feeling is determined by the constituents of the blood, as is familiarly seen in the action of alcohol, opium, and hashish upon the mind.

Herbert Spencer says—" Various classes of facts thus unite to prove that the law of metamorphosis, which holds among the physical forces, holds equally between them and the mental forces.   Those modes of the Unknowable which we call motion, heat, light, chemical affinity, &c., are alike transformable into each other, and into those modes of the Unknowable which we distinguish as sensation, emotion, thought : these, in their turns, being directly or indirectly, re-transformable into the original shapes.   That no idea or feeling arises, save as a result of some physical force expended in producing it, is fast becoming a common-place of science ; and whoever duly weighs the evidence will see, that nothing but an overwhelming bias in favour of a pre-conceived theory, can explain its non-acceptance.   How this be treated in the same way, for we know nothing of it apart from what it does, and we can define it only by the appearances it puts forth, that is, by its effects. The Irishman's directions for making a cannon, were to " take a round hole and pour metal round it." Now this is the process the meta-physicians have been pursuing in the construction of their psychological systems;—they have been studying the nature of the force—of the spirit—by a process called " reflection of consciousness " instead of its conditions and manifestations, and their practical progress has been in proportion. Dr. Gall was the first to follow the right method. He observed mental manifestations and character-istics, that is, Mind in its effects only. At school he observed that the boys most famous for verbal memory had very prominent eyes: he also observed that there were large and prominent eves without this mental characteristic He afterwards dis-covered that in the case where it was connected with verbal memory and a facility of learning

metamorphosis takes place—how a force existing as motion, heat, or light, can become a mode of consciousness—how it is possible for aerial vibrations to generate the sensation we call sound, or for the forces liberated by chemical changes in the brain to give rise to emotion—these are mysteries which it is impossible to fathom. But they are not profounder mysteries than the trans-formations of the physical forces into each other. They are not more completely beyond our comprehension than the natures of Mind and Matter. They have simply the same insolubility as all other ultimate questions. We can learn nothing more than that here is one of the uniformities in the order of phenomena." —" First Principles," p. 280.

languages the prominence o the eye was owing to
the large size of a convolution of the brain at the
back of it, which pushed it outwards and a little
downwards, and thus enabled him to distinguish it
from a mere large and prominent eyeball. He
conceived that if there was an external sign of one
mental faculty there might be of others, and he set
himself henceforth to observe. He heard of people
celebrated as mathematicians, for mental calculation,
for drawing, music, &c., and he examined and took
casts of their heads. He found that a faculty for
drawing was much too general, for many who had
a very correct appreciation of form had little of
size, and where the idea of form and size was
correct there was none of relative proportion. He
found many also with colour blindness—that is, who
could not distinguish one colour from another, or
particular colours from others. He found in all
these cases particular parts of the brain more or
less developed, and by comparing one brain with
another he ascertained which part was connected
with particular mental faculties. So that by this
means of investigation he did not discover
faculties of perception', conception, memory,
imagination, and judgment, as the metaphysicians
had done, and which are merely modes of action of
all the faculties; but he discovered faculties of
form, size, weight, colour, order, number, time,
tune, &c. He found similar differences between
the brave and the timid, the firm and the yielding,

the cruel and the humane, the hopeful and the
desponding, the rogue and the honest, the open and
the secretive, and wherever he heard of any mental
peculiarity, any great virtue or deficiency, there he
directed his observation ; and we are told that
" abandoning every theory and preconceived
opinion, Dr. Gall gave himself up entirely to the
observation of nature. Being a friend of Dr.
Nord, Physician to a Lunatic Asylum in Vienna,
he had opportunities, of which he availed himself,
of making observations on the insane. He visited
prisons, and resorted to schools ; he was introduced
to the courts of princes, to colleges, and to courts
of justice ; and wherever he heard of an individual
distinguished in any particular way, either by
remarkable endowment or deficiency, he observed
and studied the development of his head. In this
manner, by an almost imperceptible induction, he
at last considered himself warranted in believing
that particular mental powers are indicated by
particular configurations of the head."* In this
way commenced the purely inductive mode of
studying the mind : he did not sit down and reflect
upon his consciousness—upon the various trains of
thought and feeling that passed through *his own*
mind, but he looked at mind objectively as it
displayed itself in others, showing what it could do
from what it had done. In fact, it was the *order of
nature* only in this department as in every other

* Combe's System of Phrenology, p. 69, 4th Edition.

that he set himself to observe The mode of investigation has been assiduously followed by others, and thence has arisen a tolerably complete list of the primitive mental facultics, and a system of mental philosophy which furnishes so far a key to most of the disputes upon the subject which have occupied so much of the time of ancient philosophers and modern metaphysicians.

Dr. Gall did not confine his observations to man, but turned his attention to animals also, and found their intellectual faculties and what are called their instincts—that is, their peculiar habits and propensities, dependent upon their nervous systems, differing from man only in the degree and completeness of development. He says—" The integral parts of the brain augment in number and development, as we pass from a less perfect to a more perfect animal, till we arrive at the brain of man, who, in the anterior-superior and the superior region of the frontal bone, possesses several parts of which other animals are deprived, and by means of which he is endowed with the most eminent qualities and faculties, with reason, and the feeling of religion and the existence of God."

All facts tend to prove that mind in man and in the lower animals is marked by a difference only of degree ; the self-protecting, the self-regarding, the social, the perceptive faculties are common to both, and in both they are alike connected with organization. The mind of animals is what each requires for its peculiar position, and we find them combative, passionate, proud, vain, cunning, acquisitive, affectionate towards their wives, children, and friends, and possessing some of the intellectual powers in a higher degree than man. We have no wish to lower man in the scale of creation. and there is certainly great superiority in the human mind over the brute ; but the airs of superiority which he gives himself, as if there were no relationship, are based upon pure assumption. Such airs are often superlatively ridiculous in those who think themselves the highest specimens of their race, as well as in the lowest. We may respect the noble brute, but to respect the human brute is impossible !

Phrenologists then have laid down as certain knowledge on the subject that the brain (in either sense as functional or as the medium of manifestation) is the organ of mind ; that it is not a single organ, but consists of a number of parts, performing distinct functions, comprising all the different propensities, feelings, and faculties which distinguish one animal from another, and all others from man.

They have not only demonstrated that each mental faculty is connected with a particular part of the brain, but also that the power and intensity which each faculty is capable of manifesting is in proportion to the *health, quality,* and *size* of the part. Also that such health, quality, and size, depend upon hereditary tendencies as well as upon the health and strength of the vital functions and the general appearance of the person.

The power of manifestation of the mental faculties is found to increase with exercise, and to decrease with disuse.

Phrenologists have also shown that the size of the organs of the brain is indicated by the shape of the head ; the health and quality are not so obvious, but may generally be determined.

A faculty is admitted as primitive ; that is, as the function of a single organ, and not compounded of several united by a principle of association ;

" Which exists in one kind of animal and not in another ;

" Which varies in the two sexes of the same species ;

" Which is not proportionate to the other faculties of the same individual ;

" Which does not manifest itself simultaneously with the other faculties ; that is, which appears or disappears earlier or later in life than other faculties ;

" Which may act or rest singly ;

" Which is propagated in a distinct manner from parents to children ;

" Which may singly preserve its proper state of health or disease."—G. Combe's System of Phrenology, p. 140, 4th Edit.

* It is not my intention in this work to enter into the merit of Phrenology as an Art ; I merely adopt its Psychology as based upon its accepted method of investigation.

CHAPTER IV.

IT is an acknowledged truism, " What can we reason but from what we know ;" but had mankind given due weight and importance to this mere truism and have settled the not unimportant question, " What can we really know ?" it would have saved them from the endless controversies concerning the nature of matter and of mind, materialism and immaterialism, that have occupied metaphysicians from the remotest ages until now. Had they seen the necessity of establishing first principles in Metaphysics, as in Physics, and of laying down a clear chart of the mental faculties, their powers, relations, and modes of action, it would, even as the spirit upon the face of the waters, have reduced the chaos of their systems to order and utility.

Such a chart, óf the necessity for which Locke forcibly expressed his conviction, but which neither he nor any one of those who have adopted his mode of investigation has been able to supply, has been furnished by the new philosophy of Phrenology, which has succeeded in pointing out the fundamental powers of the human mind, not by *mere* reflection on consciousness, but by a method strictly inductive.

According to this system, then, we find that we have been endowed with certain propensities and sentiments on which our happiness has been made to depend, for their exercise is attended with highly pleasurable sensations, the aggregate of which constitutes happiness. These faculties or feelings bear certain relations of love and antipathy to external things ; we can trace no reason from the nature of things themselves why one object should excite love or antipathy more than another ; but such a relation has been established between us and them to answer a certain purpose. Another set of faculties has been added to these, bearing that relation to the external world which shall best enable man to bring his feelings into activity, direct them to their proper ends, and thus insure that happiness which is the object of his being.

We can know nothing, therefore, but that which results from the relation established between our intellectual faculties, and what we intuitively believe to be an external world.

Each intellectual faculty has received a particular constitution, in consequence of which it is susceptible of a form of intelligence or mode of thought peculiar to itself ; but there is no reason that we can discover why it should produce one kind of ideas more than another, except that it has been so constituted with relation to its external cause for a particular purpose.

The intellectual faculties are of two kinds, those

which are acted upon by external causes, through the medium of the senses, and the ideas belonging to which, therefore, are modified by the sense; and those faculties that act upon these ideas when so furnished by the first class. They have been very properly divided into ideas of Simple and Relative Perception.

All the knowledge, therefore, that we acquire of an external world is of its action through the medium of the senses upon only a few of the mental faculties, and which action of the perceptive faculties alone would be quite insufficient to give us the idea of Nature as we now conceive of it. The world, as it appears to us, is created in our own minds by the action of the faculties of Relative Perception and of Reflection upon the comparatively few ideas furnished by the faculties of Simple Perception.

Our ideas of things result from the relation that has been established between the object or cause, the sense, and the three classes of intellectual faculties, and it has been the want of knowledge of this fact, and of what belongs to each of these departments, which has caused most of the differences, controversies, and obscurities of metaphysicians. One class has argued for the real existence of an external world exactly as it appears to us; another has maintained that the world only exists in part as it appears to us: and a third that it is solely and entirely a creation of the mind.

Much has yet to be learned in this department of Psychology, but enough is already known to show what degree of truth or error exists in the old systems, and it may not be uninteresting to examine briefly what light our more exact knowledge throws upon the Metaphysicians.

HOBBES tells us that the thoughts of man, singly, are a *representation* or *appearance* of some quality or other accident of a body without us which is commonly called an *object.* Which object worketh on the eyes, ears, and other parts of a man's body; and by diversity of working, produceth diversity of appearance.

The original of them all is that which we call sense, for there is no conception in a man's mind which hath not at first, totally or by parts, been begotten upon the organs of sense. The rest are derived from that original.

Ideas are but apparitions unto us of the *motion, agitation, or alteration which the object worketh in the brain,* or spirits, or some internal substance of the head.

Hobbes is the precursor or founder of the School which held that to *think* is to *feel.*

There is nothing in the above to which the Phrenologist can take exception. By the sense he evidently means sensation, and we do not see that he can be charged with holding the dogma, "Nihil est in intellectu, quod non prius fuerit in sensu," for he says that "there is no conception in a man's mind which hath not at first, totally or *by parts*, been *begotten* upon the organs of sense;" as the Phrenologist holds that such conceptions are formed by the faculties of Reflection and Relative Perception acting upon those of Simple Perception, which are derived directly from the sense. Hobbes is said to have *confounded* thought with feeling; but thought *is* feeling: an idea is a feeling or sensation, slight or feeble in proportion to the relatively small size of the portion of the brain with which it is in connection. When the 'intellectual faculties are very large and much used, so great is the feeling of enjoyment in their exercise, that it amounts almost to an intellectual passion. Hobbes is also said to be a materialist, but we are not aware that he confounded an idea with its cause or the object, and as we know nothing of the essence of either, it is impossible to say wherein they differ.

LOCKE held that ideas are derived from two sources, Sensation and Reflection; he might more properly have said that most of our ideas are derived from five sources,—the object, the sense, and the three classes of mental faculties, Simple and Relative Perception, and Reflection.

He laid it down as a first principle, that the mind perceived only forms and qualities, and that our idea of matter was derived from reflection, as we could not but conceive otherwise than that there was a substratum or subject to which these qualities belonged. Now we perceive substance as directly through Individuality as we do its primary qualities of solidity, extension, &c.; and we perceive its primary qualities no more directly than we do what he calls its secondary of colour, &c. Locke was opposed to the doctrine of innate ideas, that is, of truths independent of experience, but by innate ideas in a phrenological sense is meant not the mind's own ideas, but its own modes of thought which it impresses upon the objects of our experience.

BERKELEY. " When Berkeley denied the existence of matter, he meant by ' matter ' that unknown *substratum*, the existence of which Locke had declared to be a necessary *inference* from our knowledge of qualities, but the nature of which must always be altogether hidden from us. Philosophers had assumed the existence of Substance, *i.e.* of a *noumenon* lying underneath all *phenomena*— a·substratum supporting all qualities—a *something* to which all accidents *inhere*. This unknown substance Berkeley rejects. "I am not for changing things into ideas' he says, ' but rather ideas into things; since those *immediate objects of perception*, which according to you are only *appearances of things*, I take to be the real things themselves." " Berkeley therefore, in denying the existence of matter, sided with common sense. He thought, with the vulgar, that matter was that of which his senses informed him ; not an occult something of which he could have no information. The table he saw before him certainly existed: it was hard, polished, coloured, of a certain figure, and cost some guineas. But there was no *phantom table* lying underneath the *apparent table*—there was no invisible substance supporting that table. What he perceived was a table and nothing more ; what he perceived it to be, he would believe it to be, and nothing more. His starting point was thus what the plain dictates of his senses, and the senses of all men, furnished."*

Berkeley believed in what we all necessarily believe, in the ideas furnished by individuality, by which we as directly *perceive* substance, as we do qualities by the faculties of form, size, weight, colour, &c. Berkeley was right so far, but wrong in the inferences he drew from his original induction.

IDEALISM. According to Locke the only reason for inferring the existence of Matter is the necessity *for some synthesis of attributes*. Berkeley assumed this synthesis to be a purely *mental one;* but as Individuality perceives matter as *directly* as we perceive attributes, no such synthesis is required, and both are wrong. " The objects of knowledge are ideas ; " it is true we are only conscious or have knowledge of ideas, but reflection on that consciousness tells us that the ideas are not purely subjective, but are compounded equally of the object or cause, the sense, and the subject or

* Lewes's Bio. Hist. of Philosophy, pp. 463, 466.

intellect. We cannot resolve an idea so compounded into its elements; "it is God's synthesis, and man cannot undo it;" but it is only by assuming such idea to be simple or purely subjective, and thus confounding it with its cause, —the objective with the subjective, the ego with the non-ego—that Idealism can exist. Ideas are found without any immediate cause without ourselves, as in dreams, visions, &c., and are therefore said to be purely subjective, but such ideas, however vividly repeated, must have been received originally from *without*. Now although ideas can only be known to us in this compound state, and although we have no power to analyse them, yet it is very possible to conceive that both subjective and objective may exist separately. We cannot but suppose that the causes of our ideas, whatever they may be, may continue to exist without our perceiving them. Ideas, based upon our forms of intelligence, may cease to exist, but the world may continue and create an entirely different set of ideas in the minds of beings differently constituted. Appearances *may* be *the production of the mind* to which they appear, (Idealism,) or they may be the pure *presentation* of the things themselves (Realism); we have no faculties that tell us anything of the *purely* subjective or the *purely* objective, and the supposed differences between Realism and Idealism are vain distinctions, based upon pure assumptions.

HUME. "Locke had shown that all our

knowledge was dependent upon experience. Berkeley had shown that we had *no* experience of an external world, independent of perception; nor could we have any such experience. He pronounced matter to be a figment. Hume took up the line where Berkeley had cast it, and flung it once more into the deep sea, endeavouring to fathom the mysteries of being. Probing deeper in the direction Berkeley had taken, he found that not only was Matter a figment, Mind was a figment also. If the occult substratum, which men had inferred to explain material phenomena, could be denied, because not founded on experience; so also, said Hume, must we deny the occult substratum (mind) which men have inferred to explain mental phenomena. All that we have any experience of, is impressions and ideas. The substance *of* which these are said to be impressions, is ocult—is a mere inference; the substance *in* which these impressions are supposed to be, is equally occult—is a mere inference. Matter is but a collection of impressions. Mind is but a succession of impressions and ideas."*

As we have seen, we have a mental faculty whose function it is to give us our idea of matter; but we have none that I am aware of which gives us the idea of mind as distinct from "the succession of impressions and ideas." We are conscious of perceptions; the external cause of them we call matter, the internal or subjective, we call mind;

* Bio. Hist. Philo., p. 480.

the aggregate of the external we call the world,
the aggregate of the internal the mind.   The form
of thought peculiar to Individuality probably
originates the belief in the individuality of both, but
whether in *reality* it belongs to either we do not
know.   Individuality may no more belong to mind,
composed as it is of separate ideas and sensations,
than to what we call the world; or it may belong
to each only in the same sense; each separate
simple idea or sensation, and each separate simple
substance being alone individual.   Whatever we
may be supposed to know of matter in consequence
of our direct perception of it through Individuality,
and of its qualities through the other perceptive
faculties, we certainly know nothing of mind but
as the aggregate of all our ideas and sensations;
and as Hume says " mind is but a succession of
impressions and ideas."   Hume held that there is
not, in any single instance of cause and effect, anything which can suggest the idea of power or
necessary connection.   Our belief in power he
ascribes to habit.   Now precisely as Individuality
gives the idea of substance does Causality
give the idea of power.   Eventuality takes
cognizance of the succession of phenomena,
—of mere antecedence and sequence; but
consequence, or our perception of power in
every causation, is derived from Causality.   Our
faculties thus tell us of substance and of power;
whether they tell us truly or not we cannot say,

but we necessarily believe them. We have treated of this belief and of power more at large farther on.

KANT. Knowledge derived from objects or causes without us we call knowledge derived from experience. Kant affirmed that besides this experience we had innate ideas not derived from without, which were necessarily true, because we could not conceive them otherwise. These ideas he held to be superior to those derived from experience because they were universal and necessary, while those derived from experience were contingent; but as he believed the realities of things to transcend or to be above the range of our faculties, his philosophy was called Transcendental.

We conceive that Kant has not succeeded in proving that we have any ideas not derived from the sources we have already indicated, or if he has he certainly has failed to show that such "intuitions" are absolutely or even necessarily more true than the truths derived from exeprience.

Time, Space, and Causality, Kant holds to be innate ideas, and to have no objective reality : we have already shown whence such ideas are derived. The celebrated *categories* are Kant's mode of arriving by Reflection on consciousness at the list of Intellectual Faculties or modes of thought which Gall arrived at by observation, and they correspond to his faculties of Simple and Relative Perception and Reasoning Powers. Kant's distinction between the Understanding or Judgment, and Reason, we have seen that phrenology confirms. Each faculty judges of its own objects, as form of form, colour of colour, &c,, and in this sense animals have judgment, which is sometimes mistaken for reason : but reason is a higher power and generalizes such judgments, and traces the laws of cause and effect.

" God, the Soul, and the World, Kant holds to be the three ideas of Reason, the laws of its operation, the *pure forms* of its existence. They are to it what space and time are to Sensibility, and what the categories are to Understanding " These ideas are considered to be wholly independent of experience, and we have still to show that this is an error, and to trace the derivation to the source of all our other ideas—experience. Kant also holds that all belief, that is, all fundamental belief on which all reasoning is necessarily founded is instinctive or intuitive. In this he was quite right, as we shall endeavour hereafter to make evident. The system of Fichte, Shelling, and Hegel are open to similar criticisms, but as substantially such criticisms would be a mere repetition of what we have already laid down, it is needless to go into them.

The great question at issue was, and still is,— Have we, or have we not any ideas which are absolutely, objectively true ? It is generally supposed and affirmed that " nothing is known to us as it is," that is, *per se*, but only as it appears to us, or as it affects *us* ;—but if we cannot know

noumena, only phemomena—if we do not know
what things really are in themselves, is it not
equally unphilosophical to deny, as to affirm,
anything with respect to them ? Whether, therefore, our faculties give us real knowledge and
things are in reality what they seem to us ; whether
their intimations are absolutely as well as relatively
true as far as they go, and appear the same to all
intelligences, and the same to creature as Creator,
is what we really know nothing about. Absolute
truth like Eternity may belong only to the One,
and may be even impossible to all finite intelligence.
Lewes says in his examination of the " Common
Sense " philosophy, " No one doubts that we believe
in the existence of an external world. Idealism
never questions the fact. The only doubt is,
whether that belief be objectively as well as
subjectively true. To say that the belief in
objective existence is a Fundamental Law, is simply
saying that *we are so constituted* that we are forced
to attribute external reality to our sensations. As
well say we are so constituted that fire applied to
our bodies will give us pain. We *are* so constituted.
What then ? Does this advance us one step ? Not
one. We have still to seek some proof of the *laws
of our constitution* being the measure of the *laws
of other existences*—still to seek how what is true of
the subjective must necessarily be true of the
objective." *

Bio. Hist. of Philo., 2nd Ed., 7. 522.*

But after all, this difference between objective and subjective may be a delusion—a riddle which *in the nature of things* is insoluble; for what is truth? What is real knowledge? Must not the idea of a thing and the thing itself be *always* something distinct? Can any intelligence, however high know more than how it is affected by things external? It is true we can give no "positive" answers to these questions, and we must rest satisfied with probabilities only, and it certainly does seem most *probable* that things really are what they seem to us. That our knowledge, at least as far as it goes, *is* necessary and universal. That there *is* such a thing as space, that there is a universe of suns and systems and a world in which are real rivers and trees, and light and shade, and men and animals, and all that constitutes beauty and utility; and in fact, we will not say that what is subjectively true is objectively true also, but that subjective and objective are indissoluble.* But fortunately our real interests are not left dependent upon probabilities. It is of little consequence to us how other beings may be affected by their world

* "One may say that the creation grows conscious of itself in man. What a glaring and absurd contradiction do our Byronic poets fall into, when they praise nature at the expense of man! What is nature till man is there to feel and understand? What are suns and stars, mountains and the ocean, without the human eye? What that is that lies behind the eye—marvellous brain, or something more—I do not precisely know; but I know this, that it both receives from the eye and gives to the eye. What if I am indeed no other than this fine bodily instrument made

or by ours. Man's intellectual faculties may supply him only with relative truth, but he has his own field of *absolute* truth and that is the region not of ideas, but of *pleasures* and *pains*. Absolute certainty is attainable here, for *no* "Intelligence" high or low, can confound one with the other, and our intellectual faculties are sufficient to guide us in the pursuit of one and the avoidance of the other, and that is all in which they could be useful to us, and possibly, therefore, all for which they were ever intended. Locke, who appears to us the most sensible of all our metaphysicians, seems fully to comprehend this, and in his researches stops here—He says, "How short soever our knowledge may be of a universal or perfect comprehension of whatever is, it yet secures our great concernments, that we have light enough to lead us to the knowlege of our Maker and the sight of our own duties." And again, "as to myself, I think God has given me assurance enough as to the existence of things without me; since by their different application I can produce in myself both pleasure and pain, which is one great concernment of my present state" He

sensitive to a thousand impulses—what if I am indeed this 'living lyre,' swept over by every wind, and tremulous to every ray of light—living lyre conscious of its own melody? I am still nothing less than that wondrous instrument that has converted *motion* into melody—the *thing* into a *thought*. Or, to change my metaphor, I am that sensitive mirror in which the reflected world becomes a conscious world, and knows itself as the creation of God."—Thorndale on the Conflict of Opinions, p. 359.

continues, "for our faculties being not suited to the full extent of being, nor to a perfect, clear, comprehensive knowledge of things free from all doubt and scruple, but to the preservation of us, in whom they are, and accommodated to the use of life ; they serve our purpose well enough, if they will but give us certain notice of those things which are convenient to us." If then our faculties furnish us with all such knowledge as can be useful to us, we can afford to remain *sceptical* as to their correctness or power in departments in which they could be of no use. Pleasure and Pain are to voluntary motion what attraction and repulsion are to inorganic matter, and the Science of Morality is to the analysis of Pleasure and Pain what the Science of Chemistry is to the different substances that compose this globe.

CHAPTER V.

" All belief, it is evident, must be either direct or indirect. It is direct when a proposition, without regard to any former proposition expressed or understood, is admitted as soon as it is expressed in words, or as soon as it arises silently in the mind. Such are all the order of truths which have been denominated, on this account, first truths. The belief is indirect when the force of the proposition, to which assent is given, is admitted only in consequence of the previous admission of some former proposition with which it is felt to be intimately connected, and the statement in words, or the internal development of these relative propositions in the order in which their relation to the primary proposition is felt, is all that constitutes reasoning. The indirect belief which attends the result of reasoning, even in the proudest demonstration, is thus only another form of some first truth which was believed directly and independently of reasoning; and, without this primary and intuitive assent, the demonstration itself in all its beautiful precision and regularity would be as powerless and futile as the most incoherent verbal wrangling."

" Without some principles of immediate belief,

then, it is manifest, that we could have no belief whatever; for we believe one proposition, because we discover its relation to some other proposition which is itself, perhaps, related, in like manner, to some other proposition formerly admitted, but which, carried back as far as it may, through the longest series of ratiocination, must ultimately come to some primary proposition, which we admit from the evidence contained in itself, or, to speak more accurately, which we believe from the mere impossibility of disbelieving it. All reasoning, then, the most sceptical, be it remarked, as well as the most dogmatical, must proceed on some principles which are taken for granted, not because we infer them by logical deduction, for this very inference must then itself be founded on some other principle, assumed without proof, but because the admission of these first principles is a necessary part of our intellectual constitution."*

That *belief* or *faith* is something more than a mere intellectual perception there can be little doubt, and I have previously endeavoured to point out the particular part of the mental constitution to which it belongs. It must be regarded not as a mere perception, but as a sentiment dependent for its direction, like conscientiousness or benevolence

* Brown's Phil. of the Human Mind, Lecture 13, p. 78.
"The whole is greater than a part: How exceedingly true! Nature abhors a vacuum! How exceedingly false and caluminous. Nothing can act but where it is: with all my heart; but *where* is it?"—Sartor Resartus, p. 52.

upon the intellectual faculties. Like the other
feelings, it is a blind instinct, and as conscientiousness, or the disposition to do right, cannot of itself
dictate what is right, so the instinctive tendency to
believe, equally requires the guiding and restraining
hand of reason. Faith, Hope, and Charity, are
virtues only when properly directed, the first to
truth, the second to reasonable expectation, and the
third to the real interests of mankind.

But what are these *first truths* which Dr. Brown
says are believed directly and independently of
reason, and from which all other belief results?
We find little difference in opinion between mathematicians, and it is because they first agree upon
the grounds of reasoning; they lay down certain
principles or axioms founded upon their own
definitions, and these stand with them in the place
of *first truths.* For instance, "A point is that
which hath no parts, or which hath no magnitude."
"A line is length without breadth." "Let it be
granted that a straight line may be drawn from
any one point to any other point," that is, *from* that
which has no parts and no magnitude, *to* that
which has no parts and no magnitude : we may
readily grant this when it has been discovered
where that is. Proceeding in this way any kind of
propositions may be proved. And yet, as Dr.
Brown shows, it is the only way in which we can
reason at all. From the want of such admitted

o

grounds of reasoning in Mental Science, meta-physicians have invariably arrived at different conclusions.

Phrenologists have discovered the connexion between the primitive faculties of the mind and certain parts of the brain, and by constantly repeated observations, have pointed out the relation between external objects and certain organs, and between other organs and these, so that the exact mode of manifestation of most of the fundamental powers of the mind is now known. The indications that such faculties give us, the modes of thought or intelligence peculiar to each, whether real or ideal, must be received as first truths, upon which all reasoning is founded. Belief attends the action of each faculty, and cannot be separated from it. The most sceptical, if they express doubt in words, express belief in practice.

Thus, an object is presented to the senses, a tree, for example; we are impressed with ideas of its form, size, colour, and impenetrablility, or power of resistance, and we believe it to possess all these qualities ; and Individuality gives them unity and substance ; so that we believe not in a separate form, size, colour, &c., but in an individual tree to which all these qualities are attached. The idea of substance, including that of extension and relative position, gives us the idea of space, and we believe that space exists, although our reasoning faculties tell us that that to which we have given the name is only an idea, a sensation, a kind of feeling.

Again, Eventuality notices the circulation of the sap in the tree, the budding forth of the leaves, the ripening of the fruit, and so on, and Time gives the idea of succession in such phenomena; and we believe in both action and time. Causality notices the connexion of the sap with the root, and of the root with the earth, and we believe that there is a real dependence and connexion, one upon the other— a real power in the earth to sustain the tree. If we possessed only the knowing faculties, we should perceive the earth and the tree and believe in them as existences, but Causality gives the idea of something more, of the relation that they bear to one another, and we believe that the tree could not exist without the earth, or, at least, that the earth causes the growth of the tree.

Comparison observes the situation necessary for the growth of the tree; that if the tree be placed in the earth, without the root, it will not grow; and takes note of all other conditions necessary to the continuance of its being, so as to be able to apply such knowledge to other situations; and we believe that the differences and resemblances, of which Comparison gives us the ideas, exist.

Causality also traces the connexion between these ideas and the brain, between the brain and the external sense, and between the sense and something acting upon it, and we cannot but believe that a real connexion exists between these sequences, one producing another; hence we believe in the actual existence of a something external, which something we call a tree. The idea of a tree, its properties and relations, are associated together in one idea in the mind, so that we are never conscious of it without the belief that it has a cause, that cause being the last link that we trace in the chain of sequences, and regarded consequently as an external existence.

Our reason is sufficient to show us that the greater part of those things in which we believe, are the produce of our own minds only: thus, number, space, time, action, motion, relation, the ideas of which are not formed by the senses, may be no more the real properties of substances than the names by which we designate them, which names themselves are supposed by the ignorant to be as much inherent parts of the substance named, as we are apt to suppose its relations to be.

So we believe in substance as perceived by Individuality, and in power as perceived by Causality. With respect to the latter, seeing that one event always follows another, we regard the latter as the cause of the former. As, also, we find nothing existing by itself, but everything in the relation of antecedent and consequent, we become impressed with the belief that this relation is a necessary one, and invariably look for an antecedent or cause.

" We see in nature one event followed by another. The fall of a spark on gunpowder, for example, followed by the deflagration of the gunpowder, and by a *peculiar tendency of our constitution*, which we must take for granted, whatever be our theory of power, we believe, that, as long as all the circumstances continue the same, the sequence of events will continue the same; that the deflagration of gunpowder, for example, will be the invariable consequence of the fall of a spark on it; in other words, we believe the gunpowder to be susceptible of deflagration on the application of a spark, and a spark to have the power of deflagrating gunpowder.

" Power is significant not of anything different from the invariable antecedent itself, but of the mere invariableness of the order of its appearance in reference to some invariable consequent; the invariable antecedent being denominated a cause, the invariable consequent an effect. To say that water has the power of dissolving salt, and to say that salt will always melt when water is poured upon it, is to say precisely the same thing; there is nothing in one proposition which is not exactly, and to the same extent, enumerated in the other.

" To know the powers of nature, is, then, nothing more than to know what antecedents are and will be invariably followed by what consequents; for this invariableness, and not any distinct existence, is all that the shorter term, power, in any case expresses."*

It is true that this is all that we know of the powers of nature, but it is not all that we believe, for from the action of the primitive power of the mind, Causality, an idea of force or power is derived, and we believe, and must believe, as implicitly in its existence as in the reality of anything the idea of which we receive through the senses. Thus, " If a cannon be fired, and the shot knock down a wall, Individuality and some other perceptive faculties observe only the existence of the powder. Eventuality perceives the fire applied to it, the explosion, the fall of the building, as events following in succession ; but it forms no idea of power in the gunpowder, when ignited, to produce the effect. When Causality, on the other hand, is joined with Eventuality in contemplating these phenomena, the impression of *power* or *efficiency* in the exploding gunpowder, to produce the effect, arises spontaneously in the mind, and Causality produces an intuitive belief in the existence of this efficiency, just because it is constituted to do so."†

It is true Causality gives the impression of power or efficiency, but without another mental faculty no belief would attend it. Wonder, as we have endeavoured to show before, creates belief as it invests all our ideas with a feeling of reality.

* Brown's Philosophy of the Human Mind, Lecture 6.
† George Combe.

It does more; it gives to this idea of *power* a personality; it dresses it in all the clothing that the other faculties furnish; adds to it unity, infinity, ascribes to it the tendency or design of all causation, and transforms it into a God, infinite in power and goodness.

Thus DIRECT BELIEF, that is—"where a proposition, without regard to any former proposition expressed or understood, is admitted as soon as it is expressed in words, or as soon as it rises silently into the mind," is founded and must attend upon the action of each of the primitive intellectual faculties; the indications that they give of the existence and relations of the external world being the First Truths upon which all reasoning must be based.

Belief in Testimony is merely belief in ideas furnished by Causality, that is, the action of the primitive faculty of Causality gives us a perception of a relation existing in a train of sequences, and our belief is in proportion as that relation seems sustained and unbroken. "For what is Testimony? It is itself an event. When we believe anything, then, in consequence of testimony, we only believe one event in consequence of another. But this is the general account of our belief in events. It is the union of the ideas of an antecedent and a consequent by a strong association."*

Belief in Propositions, or indirect belief, is

* Mill, vol. 1, p. 290.

founded upon a perception of relation between such propositions, and the knowledge previously furnished by the primitive faculties of the mind upon which direct belief depends. Such is the belief in God.

TRUTH.—Truth to man. is merely the record of his feelings and impressions. But what is the proof that this is true? There is no proof : we must take it for granted : we intuitively believe it, and we cannot for any *practical* purpose believe otherwise. The present condition of *self* is all of which we can speak with absolute certainty. The existence of an external world, with its properties, connexions and dependencies : with everything relating to past, present, or future ; and consequently our own identity, must all be taken for granted; the only evidence of their truth being that we feel with reference to them as we say that we do.

The evidence of Truth will, therefore, be different to every individual mind ; neither can that which is truth to one mind be strictly said to be truth to any other; as no two minds are exactly organized alike, and no two minds are ever, therefore, affected exactly in the same way. We have seen that our ideas depend equally upon the object or cause, the sense, and the subject or intellectual faculty ; and although the object and sense may be the same, yet the intellectual faculties differing, as they do more or less in all men, the perception of the object differs. We may readily conceive of an intelligence with faculties so differently constituted from our own, that all which we call truth should to it appear falsehood. Matter might appear to such a mind to have different properties, different relations, different dependencies. In minds constituted in other respects like our own, the addition of a single faculty might be sufficient to alter the whole appearance of nature. It is unphilosophical, therefore to suppose that the causes of ideas in us are necessarily what they appear to be; all that we can affirm respecting them is that they affect us in a certain manner; and the description of the mode in which we are affected is that which constitutes truth to us.

The "first truths" or fundamental principles upon which all reasoning is based being different in all men, our surprise need not be excited when we find that the line of argument that appears irresistible to one, utterly fails to convince another; and that two individuals seldom arrive exactly at the same conclusions. Thus, one sees only coincidence where another traces causation, and is enabled to employ the same causes to produce the same effects in different circumstances. And yet is it not the commonly received opinion that all men naturally are equally capable of judging; and are not men frequently the most dogmatical on those subjects which they are the least capable of understanding, and the most eager to refute those arguments the force of which nature has given them no faculties to appreciate? This may be accounted for by the fact that each person instinctively believes that which he himself perceives, whether his perceptions be correct or not: and the greater part of such belief is formed at a period during which our perceptions are likely to be incorrect from their incompleteness. Belief also being instinctive, is as readily extended to the *ideal* as to the *real*, to fancied relations of cause and effect as to true ones. Thus, when the judgment is not sufficiently strong to examine correctly the grounds upon which belief is founded, prejudice will come to its aid and cause a man to maintain his point in spite of reason, and even contrary to it. But since all men think and feel and believe differently, what is to be the test of truth? We can have no other than experience. The record of the mode in which the majority of men are affected by the external world must be considered truth with respect to it. That which appears blue to the majority, must be said to be blue, although to some few who possess a peculiar development of the faculty that perceives colour, it may appear to be green or pink.

With regard to the truth of those propositions upon which experience does not directly bear,—the existence of a Deity, for example,—the only test can be the relation of such propositions to those of which experience does inform us. And here it is

that mankind fall into controversy and error; for
while all agree with respect to those truths of
which direct experience affords everyday proof, the
evidence for those truths which require to be
searched out by the reasoning powers, must appear
valid or otherwise, as those reasoning powers are
more or less efficient ; so that what seems
indubitably true to one may be considered im-
probable or even absurd by another who is more
capable of sifting evidence. To all thus acquainted
with the diversified powers of the mind, dogmatism
is not only wrong, but exceedingly absurd. All
that the philosopher can do is to say what he sees,
and invite other people to look and see if they can
see it also.

That which Mr. Combe relates of a few
individuals, will be found to apply to all mankind,
viz., "That there is a tendency to believe *without
examination;* and that an effort of philosophy is
necessary to resist belief, instead of evidence being
requisite to produce it." The natural tendency of
all minds is to credulity and not to scepticism, and
it is necessary that it should be so, for " faith
removes mountains." Ignorance believes, but
philosophy doubts and examines. Of that which
constitutes the belief of the great mass of mankind,
one half at least may be shown to be erroneous.
They believe in things and beings for the existence
of which there is not the slightest evidence, and
their minds are filled with imaginary relations of

cause and effect, which the experience of a life is insufficient to disprove or correct.

To searchers after truth, then, it is absolutely necessary that nothing be admitted which is not either a first truth, or founded upon a first truth. A single proposition believed without sufficient evidence is dangerous to all truth; it becomes with us a first truth, upon which we build all kinds of erroneous conclusions. If we attempt to go beyond that to which our faculties are limited, if we attempt to reason independently of those first truths which it is the province of each faculty to furnish, we immediately fall into absurdities and contradictions.

For instance, the term "infinite," used so much by theologians, is usually employed to designate that which is unlimited, boundless, to which nothing can be added or taken away. But this definition consists of words without meaning, for our faculties give us no knowledge of that which is boundless; and in reasoning upon it we necessarily plunge into obscurity. Thus, concerning "infinite" space, if this planetary system were to be deducted from the universe, we cannot suppose that the universe would be less infinite than it was before; therefore, a part is as great as the whole.

So of Infinite Duration or Immortality, as applied to beings who have begun to be: in consequence of this beginning of existence they can never be said to live for more than *half an Eternity*;

therefore that which is infinite is capable of being halved.

Again, the doctrine of Infinite Divisibility implies the same absurdity and contradiction. "Everything," as Hume says, "capable of being infinitely divided contains an infinite number of parts; otherwise the division would be stopped short by the indivisible parts, which we should immediately arrive at. Finite extension must, in this case, suppose an infinite number of parts."

Upon speculative points like these, theory upon theory has been formed, and mankind have been engaged in perpetual controversy, and will be so to the end of time, unless, by a close analysis of the powers of the mind, showing the relation that has been established between us and the external world, the boundary of our possible knowledge be determined. With the help of an analysis like this, which will acquaint us with each intellectual faculty and its function, we shall be in no danger of wasting our powers in the vain attempt to overstep this boundary: we shall possess a standard by which first truths may be determined—the want of which has led to the unwise extension of them by one party, and the equally unwise limitation of them by others, producing thereby endless errors and uncertainty respecting that science which of all others ought to be the most certain, as in it are involved the highest interests of mankind.

BELIEF IN DEITY.—The belief in supreme power

we find nearly universal in all countries yet known to us; and this Power has been "in every clime adored" as far back as written records extend. In the first ages of the world the powers of nature were deified and worshipped under every variety of form, with attributes borrowed always from man's own nature, fashioned according to the laws of his own intelligence and the degree of civilization then prevailing. Every cause that was hidden, every antecedence not evident to the senses, a spiritual Being was created to supply; the earth was peopled with fairies and genii, and'there were gods of the winds, of the sea, and of the air. As man increased in intelligence, his gods diminished in number, and as his knowlege enabled him to generalise the powers of nature, he attached them to one supreme source, the Great Cause of all.

This is only in accordance with the laws of the human mind; Wonder or Faith gives the sense of reality; and wherever this sense of reality exists, there is an irresistible tendency to invest it with the forms of our own intelligence. In this manner our sensations and ideas are to us realities, and although they are known to us as a train of separate thoughts only, yet we invest them with the form of intelligence peculiar to Individuality, and we have the idea and speak of the mind of man as simple and indivisible—as one individual mind. We even individualize all things that exist, and call it the universe. So we individualize the separate impressions of power or efficiency derivable from every separate cause, and thus form the idea of God as *one*, as a personality. But it is evident that this is to invest the Great Cause of all with an attribute derived from our particular form of intelligence, and we may as much err in ascribing to Him unity or personality as if we were to depict Him under our own particular bodily shape.

But if it be irrational to measure the infinite by powers that have relation only to the finite; to invest the Deity with our own forms of thought, our own modes of intelligence; it is, if anything, more inconsistent to ascribe to Him feelings which belong to man, and which have been given to enable him to perform his part upon this earth. Necessarily believing in a God, however, we have formed Him after our own image, not unfrequently ascribing to Him some of the lowest of our feelings in their greatest abuse. We have no faculties that can make us acquainted with God as He is, or with his mode of existence, and we only degrade Him by reducing Him to our level.

What then do we know? Almost nothing: for "who by searching can find out God?" It is a great mystery before which we must be content to bow down in awe and reverence. The "forces" or powers of nature we have seen to be indestructible. they are transmitted, they may change their form, and all the varied effects we see may be, and probably are, the result of one original force set in motion at the beginning. But when we speak of beginnings, we immediately feel that we are out of our depth. "There is no efficient cause, or anything that exerts an agency in the dominion of nature. A cause is a thing uncaused; if produced, it must resign its title, and be ranked as an effect; consequently there cannot be a string of causes in nature: one only is so, and all the rest are only passive results."*

It is impossible to get away from this reasoning. Man's powers, mental, as well as bodily, are derived. The one only cause we call God.† But the "force" in nature is not a blind force, it is intelligent. The proof of intelligence is that it moves towards a given end or purpose: we judge of the nature of that intelligence by the object or worthiness of that purpose; the object of morality is universal happiness or good, and in proportion as the intelligence in nature tends towards that end do we

* Rev. J. W. Mailler, "Philosophy of the Bible," p. 39.

† "Sweep away the illusion of time; glance, if you have eyes, from the near moving cause to its far distant mover. The stroke that came transmitted through a whole galaxy of elastic balls, was it less a stroke than if the last ball only had been struck and sent flying? Oh, could I (with the time-annihilating Hat) transport thee direct from the beginnings to the endings, how were thy eyesight unsealed and thy heart set flaming in the light-sea of celestial wonder! Then sawest thou that this fair universe, were it in the meanest province thereof, is in very deed the star-domed City of God; that through every star, through every grass blade, and most through every living soul, the glory of a present God still beams. But Nature, which is the Time vesture of God, and reveals Him to the wise, hides Him from the foolish."—Sartor Resartus, p. 274.

say it is a *moral* intelligence and *not* a mere *primum mobile.*

We see a man working towards definite aims and we infer individual intelligence like our own, which on examination we find to be ruled by general laws ; we see also all nature working towards definite aims, and we quite as logically infer general intelligence acting on the *body* of the universe, as our intelligence does on our bodies, and governing *by* general laws, if not like men governed by them.

Many thinkers, such as Hume, Kant, Shelley, and Holyoake, have maintained that a Great First Cause is an assumption, and hold it to be quite as logical and reasonable to suppose that causes have always had their efficiency as that they ever had a beginning. It may be so, for we know nothing about beginnings, but that there is a presiding Intelligence it is very difficult to doubt. The Atheist, however, does not think so; he assumes that there is an inherent power in each cause which has *always* existed and that in the infinite concourse and commingling of atoms in infinite time and space, the present order of things has arisen ; every thing inharmonious having a natural and necessary tendency to destroy itself, and only that which is good and harmonious being permanent or having power to continue in existence at all.

But we have something besides power—we have beauty—the garment of God : how do we account

P

for this ? It is true the great forces in nature are the aggregate of infinitely small ones; it is the animalcules, the corals, the imperceptible power that raises the water from the deep, that work the great changes in the world; but whence come the flowers ? " Methinks, if there were no other proofs of God's goodness, the flowers would supply them in abundance. Answer it to thyself, poor soul that doubtest of his love. * * Why has he made these flowers ? Why does he send to thee these *little* joys, as gentle and unnoticed often as a mother's kiss upon a sleeping child ? There is not, it would seem, a conceivable reason to be given for the existence of flowers (at least for their beauty and perfume), other than the intention to provide for man a pure and most delicate pleasure. Geologists tell us that in the epochs there are few traces of flowers; such as were being small and probably of the secondary colours, mere vessels for the ripening of the seeds. Only when the human era approached, the order of the rosacae appeared, the fruit trees with their luxurious burdens, and all our brightest and sweetest flowers, till the wilderness rejoiced and blossomed as the rose. Thus as the coal and the iron, and the stone, were laid up in the dawn of time for our use to-day, so the flowers sprout up over the earth for our delight, and to deck the cradle God had prepared for his child.* This is very prettily put, but it·contains the old

* Miss F. P. Cobbe, Fraser, 1861.

leaven of man's supremacy at the expense of the rest of creation. If in the epochs there were no flowers, so were there no insects. Flowers seem more by right to belong to the insect world, than to man.

It is singular how the *à posteriori* reasoning on Deity agrees with the *à priori* of Spinoza and others. According to Spinoza "There is but one infinite Substance, and that is God. Whatever is, is in God; and without Him nothing can be conceived. He is the universal Being of which all things are the manifestations. He is the sole Substance, Mode cannot exist. God, viewed under the attributes of Infinite Substance, is the *natura naturans*—viewed as a manifestation, as the Modes under which his attributes appear, He is the *natura naturata*. He is the cause of all things, and that immanently, but not transiently. He has two infinite attributes — Extension and Thought. Extension is visible Thought; and Thought is invisible Extension : they are the Objective and Subjective of which God is the Identity. Every *thing* is a mode of God's attribute of Extension ; every *thought*, wish, or feeling, a mode of his attribute of Thought. That Extension and Thought are not Substances, as Descartes maintained, is obvious from this : that they are not conceived *per se*, but *per aliud*. Something is extended : what is ? Not the extension itself, but something prior to it, viz., Substance. Substance is uncreated, but creates by the internal necessity of its nature. There may be many existing things, but only one existence; many forms, but only one Substance. God is the 'idea immanens'—the One and All.   God is not the material universe, but the universe is one or part of His infinite Attribute of Extension: He is the *identity* of the natura naturans and the natura naturata."

It is a mere verbal resemblance, therefore, this of Spinozaism to Atheism. The following from Schelling's "Philosophische Schriften," accurately draws the distinction between Pantheism and Atheism :—" God is that which exists in itself, and is comprehended from itself alone; the finite is that which is necessarily in another, and can only be comprehended from that other. Things therefore are not only in degree, or through their limitations different from God, but *toto genera*. Whatever their relation to God on other points, they are absolutely divided from him on this: that they exist in another and he is self-existent and original. From this difference it is manifest that all individual finite things taken together cannot constitute God, since that which is in its nature *derived*, cannot be one with its original, any more than the single points of a circumference, taken together, can constitute the circumference, which as a whole, is of a necessity prior to them in idea." " These are but the innumerable individual eyes with which the Infinite World Spirit beholds himself."

Schiller says "Nature is an infinitely divided God," and again, "The Divine One has dispersed itself into numberless sensible substances, as a white beam of light is decomposed by the prism into seven coloured rays. And a divine being would be evolved from the union of all those substances, as the seven coloured rays dissolve again into the clear light-beam. The existing form of Nature is the optic glass, and all the activities of spirit are only an infinite colour-play of that simple divine ray. Should it ever please the Almighty to shatter the prism, then the barrier betwixt himself and the world would fall to ruin; all spirits would disappear into one infinite spirit, all accords would melt into one harmony, all streams would rest in one ocean. The attraction of the elements gave to nature its material form. The attraction of spirits multiplied and continued to infinity, must finally lead to the abolition of the separation, or (may I utter it) create God. Such an attraction is Love."*

Fichte says, all "appearance," whatsoever we see in the world, is but as a vesture of the "Divine Idea of the world," for "that which lies at the bottom of appearing."

Emerson in his Essay on "Compensation" says, "Everything in nature contains all the powers of nature; everything is made of one hidden stuff. The true doctrine of Omnipresence is, that God reappears with all his parts in every moss and cob-

* Philosophical Letter, p. 40.

web; thus the universe is alive."

In one thing only all the most advanced minds agree—viz., that it is as impossible to disconnect God from the material living universe, as it is to disconnect the Soul from the corporeal living body; still we know nothing "Positively;" the great mystery is still veiled. A very clever writer on the Nebular Hypothesis, in the Westminster, (July, 1858), observes, "It remains only to point out that while the genesis of the solar system, and of countless other systems like it, is thus rendered comprehensible, the ultimate mystery continues as great as ever. The problem of existence is not solved : it is simply removed farther back. The nebular hypothesis throws no light upon the origin of diffused matter; and diffused matter as much needs accounting for as concrete matter. The genesis of an atom is not easier to conceive than the genesis of a planet. Nay, indeed, so far from making the Universe less wonderful than before, it makes it more wonderful. Creation by manufacture is a much lower thing than creation by evolution. A man can put together a machine ; but he cannot make a machine develop itself. The ingenious artisan, able as some have been, so far to imitate vitality as to produce a mechanical pianoforte-player, may in some sort conceive how, by greater skill, a complete man might be artificially produced; but he is totally unable to conceive how such a complex organism gradually arises out of a minute structureless germ. That our harmonious universe once existed potentially as formless diffused matter, and has slowly grown into its present organised state, is a far more astonishing fact than would have been its formation after the artificial method vulgarly supposed. The nebular hypothesis implies a First Cause, as much transcending the mechanical God of Paley, as this does the fetish of the savage." The doctrine of the later Stoics was that the entire body of matter unfolded itself from a principle of life as inherent in its constitution as the property of vegetation in the seed: it advanced from inorganic to organic, and thence through a series of ages to the highest intelligence in man. We cannot say we see how this theory differs from the above, or from the modern " theory of Development," and although it certainly appears most in accordance with all modern discoveries in Geological science, yet we cannot say with the writer in the Westminster, that it appears to us to show more power, or to excite more wonder that intelligence should be millions of years evolving than days in creating; the same general laws of Deity, and the same direct operation would appear to be at work in both cases. Anaxagoras says (500 B.C.), " In the beginning there was the Infinite, composed of homœomeriœ, or elementary seeds of infinite variety. But the mass of elements were as yet unmixed. What was to mix them ? What power caused them to become arranged in one harmonious all-embracing system ? This power he declared to be Intelligence, the moving force of the universe. He, on the one hand, had rejected Fate, as an empty name ; on the other, he rejected Chance, as being no more than the Cause, unperceived by human reasoning."* The most advanced theories of the present day appear to go little beyond this guess of Anaxagoras's more than 2,000 years ago.

BELIEF IN REVELATION.—We have shown that each man's own judgment is, and must be to himself, the standard of truth; that what appears to him to be true, is, for the time at least, truth to him. This is simply making reason the test of all truth, and it may be interesting to inquire whether we have, or can have, any higher standard. There are many who say "the revealed word of God" is the standard of truth, and we are called upon to "submit our reason to revelation." But this fundamental principle of priestcraft is an error, and we never are or can be called upon to submit our reason to anyone or anything. Reason was given to man for his guidance, and it must be supreme in everything. Admitting fully that "the revealed declarations of God" are the highest standard of truth, it is "reason that has to determine where such "revealed declarations" are to be found, and not only so, but to interpret them afterwards, and there is

* Lewes's Biographical History of Philosophy, p. 66.

no *possible* means of determining that to be Revelation which is *opposed* to reason. There has been much useless discussion as to the possibility of working miracles, for granting to the fullest extent their possibility, what do they prove? It has usually been considered sufficient evidence that men were "sent of God" if they had this power of working miracles. But supernatural power contains no evidence in itself of whence such power is derived. There may be a hundred sources from which such powers might be derived besides the One Supreme. There may be a hundred intelligences between us and Deity, with power little short of the highest, and such may not *necessarily* wish our good or have no interest in deceiving us. The fact is, we have no means whatever of discriminating between the power of God and the devil, but by the tendency of such power; that is, the purpose for which it is used; and our reason is the only means of determining this tendency. The Jews accused Christ of working miracles by the aid of Beelzebub, and if we know it was not so, it is from the tendency of that teaching which the miracles were wrought to confirm. Baxter says all creeds come directly from the devil. How are we to discriminate between angels of light and darkness, supposing the wings and the horns and hoofs are myths? Who is to say what are the powers and intelligence of either? and if the existence of such "principalities

and powers " be admitted, who is to say what "revelations," let them be accompanied by whatever
signs and wonders they may, necessarily come
from God ? Can we be too cautious not to accept
anything, from whatever apparent source derived,
that may appear to derogate from His character ?
and have we not the right to say in *all* such
cases to all unknown powers and intelligences,
"Jesus I know and Paul I know, but who are
ye ? " No, there can be no sufficient *external*
evidence of a Revelation ; it must be *internal;* as
Christ says, "If any man will *do* his will, he
shall know of the doctrine whether it be of God,"
and this is the only test. Power is and can be
no evidence of anything but itself, and each
separate fact can only be proved by its own
evidence. Experience, that is, conformity to the
"order of nature," is the *only* test of truth. Mankind have always worshipped power and they still
continue to do so, but there is no necessary connection between power and truth, or between
power and goodness, and as we know nothing of
the moral tendencies of created intelligences not of
this world, we are called upon all the more to be
true to the light of *reason* which *our* Creator has
implanted within us. If the powers of Good and
Evil—we speak with all reverence—are as equally
divided as the common belief supposes, how is it
possible to distinguish between them otherwise ?
It is quite impossible to accept any power, or reve-

lation, or inspiration, as coming from God that is not in harmony with His creation, and with our highest feelings,—for those were implanted in us by our Maker. New acts of really *divine* power must always be in harmony with the old, for it is impossible that *any authority* can establish anything at variance with natural truth : that is, with the laws of God as inscribed in the Book of Nature. Consequently we find enlightened Protestants of the present day quietly abandoning whatever may run counter to this reason and moral sentiment, to the established facts of science, or to the daily experience of human nature, just as the infallibility of the Pope was given up ages ago. It follows, that no miracle, or supernatural power merely, could prove the doctrine of a future state, for, as we have said, the doctrine could be *proved* only by its own evidence, viz., experience that people do live again after this life ; and the only miraculous attestation of such a doctrine that could be accepted as *proof*, would be to introduce us to those who have gone before us. Mere power, then, in any shape, cannot attest a Revelation ; after all it must be the accordance of such Revelation with the known order of God's providence, and *reason* only can show what that order is. Reason also can alone test the various claims to "Inspiration" which are advanced for the sacred writings of all nations, and Revelation and Inspiration being recognised, reason only can interpret them and

determine their *true meaning*.   Reason is thus the
supreme arbiter here as in everything else, and the
Protestant principle of the right of private judgment requires to be carried much farther than it
has hitherto been,—and if we are not called upon
to surrender our judgment to anything on earth,
still less are we called upon to do so for anything
beyond the earth, because we are still less able to
determine its claim upon our faith.   God has not
left us without a sufficient test of what may come
from Himself, but this test is and can only be the
too often much despised Reason.

CHAPTER VI.

CONSCIOUSNESS, IDENTITY, ASSOCIATION.

With reference to the truths called "first truths," although they must be placed at the foundation of all *practical* reasoning and belief, they are merely instinctive indications given us for our guidance under the circumstances in which we are placed upon this earth, informing us of the temporal relation between external things and beings possessing our particular organization : and as we have faculties that test the evidence of the senses, so the evidence of one intellectual faculty, or class of faculties, may be tested by others in the same mind. These instinctive indications may primarily be classed under the heads of Consciousness, Identity, and Association.

Matter is known to us only as the cause of certain sensations which we call by various names, as solidity, extension, &c., but whether this cause be material or immaterial, substance or mere force, we have no means of determining. The Mind is only the aggregate of all the sensations of which a being is conscious; individuality and unity being given to it by a form of our own intelligence.

By Consciousness we mean Sentience or Feeling, as distinguished from the absence of feeling.

Plants show a kind of sensibility, but, as far as we know at present, they have no feeling. Consciousness includes every kind and degree of feeling, from that of the first protoplastic monad to man. It is dependent upon Life, and increases in power and intensity in proportion to the enlargement and complexity of the nervous system. With increased size of brain we have varied functions, with strength of feeling in proportion to size and quality, until in man we have all the variety of sense, thought, intellect, emotion, and propensity, all of which are modes of sentience or feeling, and constitute our Consciousness. It is a mere truism, therefore, to say that our individual consciousness is all we know or can know; for all other things are known to us only as they appear in our Consciousness, which appearance, so far as we know, tells us nothing of the reality. A thing (object) cannot be like a thought. All that we know of what is outside ourselves (*i.e.*, our own consciousness), even of its very existence, is only more or less probable inference. With reference to such things we cannot say " I know ; " only " I believe ; " we *know* only how we are affected by their different modes of manifestation. Furthermore our Consciousness tells us nothing of its own essential nature, and therefore we cannot say how it differs essentially from anything else; and all systems *based* upon such supposed differences (between Matter and Spirit, material and immaterial, &c.)

are in reality baseless. We do not know whether our thoughts are material or immaterial; we know only the thoughts. Consciousness is the medium through which all other things must be viewed by us, and no doubt it is a very limited medium. There may be thousands of things around us that do not appear there, either directly or by their effects. What we call Spirit does not appear directly in our Consciousness, but only indirectly by its effects. It is perceptible to us in no other way. There is much of what is now called the Spirit-world that may yet grow into direct consciousness by our getting organs by which we can perceive it. To what extent our Consciousness tells us the truth we do not know, although we are obliged to trust it for all practical purposes. It appears to me to be a special medium through which we view things for a special purpose. All feelings resolve themselves into either pleasure or pain; to be perceptible they must be either one or the other; and so far only, probably, are they entirely reliable; all else is more or less illusion and delusion.

SELF CONSCIOUSNESS is Reflection on Consciousness. It is one part of the mind taking cognizance of the other. A man feels, and knows that he feels; he analyses the nature of the feeling. This is not the case with animals. It is this difference between Consciousness and Self-Consciousness that has so mystified and muddled the subject, and led to such a diversity of opinion upon it. Reflection on Consciousness only is called knowledge. A simple act of consciousness is a Perception without a Percipient: it is only from Reflection on Consciousness that we get a Percipient.

With respect to Unity of Consciousness, although there are two hemispheres to the brain, and although there must be a great variety of thoughts and feelings going on in the brain at once, yet consciousness is single, a chain or succession of thoughts and feelings which appear to us but as one. In what way these varied thoughts and feelings are so combined as to form one thread, we do not exactly know. Some think we have an organ of Consciousness, but such a varied succession of feelings could not proceed from one organ. The unity of Consciousness is probably owing to our being able to reflect upon, to attend to, only one feeling at a time. It is perhaps the function of what Phrenologists call the organ of Concentrativeness that gives this power of association and attention. This organ is especially deficient in some special cases of madness, where the patient has little or no power of combining ideas. May it not be the function of this part of the brain to draw all the varied threads of consciousness together and present them as a single thread? Each successive idea or feeling is thus a compound one, compounded of *all* the feelings present at that time. Michelet tells us of the " spider that from the extremity of its body (formed of four screw plates or tubercles which can be drawn in and out like telescopes) ejects by its movement a very little cloud, that increases in size from minute to minute. This cloud is composed of threads of an infinite tenuity ; each tubercle secretes a thousand, and the four—by combining together their four thousand threads—make the unique and tolerably strong thread of which the web is woven." * Our single thread of consciousness may probably be woven in the same way. " When people speak of the eager gluttony of the spider " —says Michelet—" they forget that it must either eat a double quantity or soon perish ; it must eat to recruit its body, and eat to renew its thread.' The thread of our consciousness is equally dependent on the supply of food.

Some people think that it is the special function of the Mind to produce, not only this Unity of Consciousness at any given moment, but also the unity we ascribe to all our thoughts and feelings. No doubt such a sense of unity is a function of the mind. This assumed unity has, however, no real existence. Mind is a mere abstraction, standing for the aggregate of all our thoughts and feelings ; and it has no existence apart from the succession of thoughts and feelings which constitute our Consciousness. There is not Mind *and* Consciousness. Each separate thought and feeling is a separate entity, each having its portion of the Divine

* The Insect, p. 215.   Q

Existence, just as each separate "organic unit" of the body has its own separate life and soul: the sense of individuality and unity being given by a form of our own intelligence.

What we term Perception, Conception, Memory, Imagination, Judgment, are only diversified sensations, different in their degree of intensity and in their character to the feelings resulting from the action of the Propensities and Sentiments, but still mere sensations, We are not justified in designating the mind as the *cause* of sensations; for of cause we know nothing but as the invariable antecedent, and the invariable antecedent of these sensations is, so far as we have yet discovered, the action of the brain. Nor are we justified in saying that the Mind is material, because that would be equivalent to saying that Sensation is material, which would be to make the cause and effect the same. All facts, however, justify us in saying that Sensation is caused by that which we call material, in the only sense in which we·can use the term cause.

The Senses are merely the medium of communication with the brain. The Mental Faculties are the Intellectual Faculties and the Feelings. The Intellectual are those that perceive existence — Individuality, Form, Size, Weight, and Colouring; those which perceive the relations of external objects — Locality, Order, Number, Eventuality, Time, Tune, and Language; and the Reflective Faculties of Comparison, Causality, and Congruity, which compare, judge, discriminate, and perceive congruity or purpose.

The Feelings are the Self-protecting, the Self-regarding, the Social, the Moral, the Æsthetic, and the Religious. Memory is the result of the changes which thinking and feeling make upon the brain or upon its modes of action; these are deeper in early life; and in old age, when the brain is less susceptible to such impressions we often recur to these early memories. Instinct is memory transmitted through organisation to offspring. The mark of a cut made upon the body is repeated however often the particles that form the body may be changed, so Memory repeats the past, but it is only a faint repetition; the consciousness of twenty years ago is no more the same than a cut on the body, made twenty years ago, is the same in appearance a when first made.

"Consciousness," says Mr. Combe, "means the knowledge which the mind has of its own existence and operations."* In this sense, Consciousness belongs to man alone; for though the brutes possess feelings and ideas—though they are endowed with perception, conception. memory, and a kind of judgment, yet there is not the slightest evidence that they are conscious of such states of mind; they seem to experience mere trains of sensations, and to be impelled by them to action, without having any idea of their existence.

* System of Phrenology, p. 647.

The question has often and naturally arisen, how is it that with a plurality of organs, and each of them double, Consciousness is invariably single; so that we are never conscious of more than one feeling or idea at the same time.

The answer is simple, viz., that however great may be the variety of feelings and ideas occurring in the mind simultaneously, they make but one *sensation*. A compound sensation it may be called, because composed of other sensations which may be distinguished separately when occurring consecutively, but not the less a simple and indivisible sensation at the moment of our being conscious of it; in the same way that a musical chord is not the less a single sound, because the notes of which it is composed may be struck successively, each producing a separate sound.

But it has been objected, that the mind has, in fact, the power of taking cognizance at the same moment, of the component parts of its compound sensations; for instance, that when, in a band of music, the different instruments combined make but one sound, a practised ear will listen to two or three of the instruments separately; but if this process of listening be carefully analysed, it will be found that the ear merely follows the different instruments one after another, so rapidly, that the idea of succession is lost, and the separate acts of attention appear simultaneous.

The notion of the simplicity and indivisibility of

the mind itself seems to have originated from the observation of this law of our nature, viz., that more than one feeling or idea cannot exist simultaneously in the same mind, but, of whatever organs they may be the produce, they blend and make but one sensation.

IDENTITY. It has been previously explained that all our knowledge must be derived from the instinctive indications of our Intellectual Faculties, which indications must be admitted as first truths in reasoning on all practical subjects, although they may not be intended to inform us of the real nature of things, but merely of the relation established between ourselves and the external world. Some of our faculties, our reasoning powers, for instance, are capable of passing judgment upon the other organs as to whether their indications be correct or not, and they suffice, in several instances, to show that what some of our faculties would represent to us as real existences, have no place but in our own minds.

It seems to be necessary to our present mode of existence, not only that we should have the power of individualizing, but that we should be able to attach a certain idea of *sameness* to individual existences, so that what appeared to be an individual yesterday seems to be that self-same individual, and no other, to-day, and will continue to be so. Without this sense of Identity, the world would seem but an assemblage of flitting phantoms, and all would be confusion and chaos; but that it is merely a feeling given to us for wise purposes, there being nothing answering to it in reality, our *reasoning powers would render probable.* Philosophically speaking, nothing with which we are acquainted remains the same for two seconds together. The same river flows on for ever, yet the same water never passes the same spot, and no one has ever really been twice on the same stream. The atoms of which bodies are composed are in strict union with the atmosphere, and are continually blending their particles with everything around them. Organized bodies are perpetually changing their structure by the vital processes of waste and reproduction; and if the mind continued the same for any perceptible time, we should lose all consciousness of its existence; for it is only by its successive changes that it is cognizable to us at all. No idea or feeling of the mind can ever be said really to be repeated, for whatever may be the character of memory, it never presents ideas, in every respect, as they at first occurred; either they differ in intensity or in their association with other ideas. So that, in fact, at no two perceptible periods of an individual's existence is the mind strictly the same.

What is it that constitutes the sameness between the infant and the old man—between a person when possessing sound health and vigorous intellect, and when weakened in mind and body by disease?

How is it, that although we perceive the process of change continually going on in ourselves throughout our whole system, so that from one important period of our lives to another we seem to be altered beings; yet still the feeling of Identity clings to us? Whence we know not—unless we believe it to proceed from a principle of our nature; to be the result of an intuitive or instinctive action of faculties, indications of which must always be admitted as the grounds of all practical reasoning, and taken for granted as *they cannot be tested.*

The "I," or SENSE of IDENTITY or PERSONALITY is mainly dependent upon memory. The delusion with respect to our Mind, that it is something in itself apart, and more than the aggregate of our thoughts and feelings, is fostered by the sense of Identity or Personality, but there is not Consciousness and the "I." The "I" is only a unit in the sequence of our consciousness. A feeling, the instant when it exists, is not recognised as ours. We have a feeling which gives the belief in the external world as really existing as we perceive it; and we have a feeling which refers our consciousness to ourselves and gives the belief in Identity, although neither body nor mind are ever *the same.* The body is constantly passing from the inorganic to the organic world and *vice versâ;* the mind also is constantly passing from what we call physical to mental force, and *vice versâ.* It is the mysterious power we call Life—a selecting and assimilating power, dominated by the organism which enables this to take place, and which properly constitutes Identity.   As long as Life continues, the creature may be said to be the same, however varied the form.   The egg, the grub, the pupa, and the butterfly are the same being. When Life departs and the individual is no longer bound together by this mysterious tie, the Identity is destroyed.   The essential Identity underlying both body and mind is Life—the same Life.   Life, Force, Spirit, are identical.   Our powers, both bodily and mental, are most of them derived from ancestors, hereditarily transmitted in the vast chain from the monad to the man, the memory of their previous existence having been lost; but not altogether so, for, as Wordsworth says :—

> Our birth is but a sleep and a forgetting :
> The Soul that rises with us, our life's star
>   Hath elsewhere had its setting
>   And cometh from afar.
>   And not in utter nakedness,
> But trailing clouds of Glory do we come
>   From God who is our home.

Ours is the " Future State " of the long chain of Being that has preceded us.

It is clear, however, that whatever our reasoning powers may tell us with respect to the instinctive action of our faculties, we still must put implicit faith in their indications, and since it is necessary for us to believe that there are individual existences, and that they possess identity, it is not put within the power of the strongest intellect to shake this belief in practice, whatever it may do in theory.

ASSOCIATION. Much has been commonly attri buted to Association, which an intimate knowledge of the primitive faculties of the mind proves, in no way, to belong to it. Feelings, Propensities, and Sentiments have been supposed to be formed by it. The observation of the fact that the Intellectual Faculties are necessary for the guidance of the feelings, for their direction in action, may have generated this error. Our thoughts have also been supposed to follow each other in an established order, and metaphysicians have endeavoured to base education upon general laws of such associations. But so great is the diversity in minds that such general laws may never be discovered, and the causes that determine a train of thought, a succession of ideas in one individual, can seldom, if ever, be applicable to another. But though the importance of the principle of Association has been, in some cases, misunderstood, it cannot be over-estimated. We have seen that it is upon a very narrow stratum of ideas that the external world, as it appears to us, is built; the ideas derived directly from the senses, such as sounds, smells, tastes, and touch, and from the organs of some of the perceptive faculties, are probably all that the other mental faculties have to act upon to create within us the whole order and beauty of nature, or the whole picture of the world as it appears to us.   Any defect in the power of association of ideas would disturb the whole of this harmony.

But it is the association of feelings with ideas to which the highest importance attaches.   The propensities and sentiments being mere blind impulses, and depending upon the intellectual faculties for their proper direction, every variety of erroneous association between the intellect and feelings is formed in early life, before the reason has been taught, cr is capable of judging for itself of the correctness of the connexion.   Such associations are common to all the feelings, and until they can be broken, tend on all occasions to mislead the judgment.   One of the most common illustrations, and one familiar to every one, is the association so frequently formed between darkness and danger. Stories of ghosts and other frightful absurdities are related to children, until they fear to be left alone in the dark.   As they grow older they may reason very correctly upon the groundlessness of such fears, but darkness does not the less excite their feeling of Cautiousness.   So strong is the association in some cases, that there are instances on record of physically and morally brave persons who, after being in twenty battles without being conscious of fear, have yet dreaded to be left in the dark.   There is a great variety of objects to which the same feeling may be as erroneously attached, and there are few persons who have not some antipathies, compounded of hatred and fear, that have no better foundation. "Some persons have what is called an antipathy to a spider, a toad, or a cat. These feelings generally originate in some early fright. The idea of danger has been, on some occasions, intensely excited along with the touch or sight of the animal, and hence the association so strongly formed that it cannot be dissolved. The sensation, in spite of them, excites the idea and produces the uneasiness which the idea imparts."*

False associations with the feeling of Conscientiousness are still more injurious in their tendency. This feeling gives us no knowledge of what is right or wrong, but merely approves the right, and gives the disposition to act in accordance, when it is known to us what is right. In early childhood, before the judgment is active, it must be associated with what the tone of society approves; and whether the standard of morality be high or low, it is not the less difficult to break the association in after-life, and to make us *feel* that to be wrong, which we have been early taught to regard as right.

This law of the mind has been the great prop of superstition in all countries and ages; for the religious feelings, like all the others, are capable of any direction. The feeling of Veneration, which

* Mill, vol. 1, p. 75.

There can be little doubt that such erroneous associations do not always originate with the individual, but that the state of the brain, on which they depend, is transmissible to offspring.

gives the disposition to venerate and respect, to worship and adore whatever we may be taught to consider worthy of such sentiments, may be associated equally in the infant mind, with a wooden idol, the sun, the moon, an animal, a prophet, a saint, a crucifix, or the God of the universe. Accordingly, there is scarcely anything that some superstition has not made to usurp the place of the Most High in the minds of the ignorant and deluded. " He in whom Veneration is powerful," says Mr. Combe, " and to whom the image of a saint has been from infancy presented as an object to be venerated, experiences an instantaneous and involuntary emotion of veneration every time the image is presented to him, or a conception of it formed; because it is now the sign which excites in him that emotion, altogether independently of reflection. Until we can break this association, and prevent the conception of the image from operating as a sign to excite the faculty of Veneration, we shall never succeed in bringing his understanding to examine the real attributes of the object itself, and to perceive its want of every quality that ought justly to be venerated." The same law applying, not only to the image of a saint, but to all creeds and dogmas, each sect of religionists have always shown themselves anxious to take advantage of it, by impressing the minds of the young with the doctrines of their particular persuasion, and associating their religious feelings with them, before the feebly-developed reasoning power is capable of forming a judgment for itself. Veneration, Hope, and Wonder, jointly compose the religious feelings, and in this way, may be made to take any direction; that is, a child may be taught to worship anything, however unworthy; to hope for anything, however unreasonable; and to believe anything, however monstrously absurd. Such associations, once formed, are not easily broken, and until they are, a person is disqualified from forming a philosophical examination of the grounds of his belief. Who does not see that such is the mode in which religious belief is generally propagated in all countries; that people are made to *feel* and not to *reason* upon the subject, and that such feelings constitute with each nation, whether Chinese, Hindoo, Mahometan, or Christian, the *internal evidence* for each particular religion, whether true or false? Feeling, therefore, can never be adduced as a proof of the truth of any religion; since this *internal evidence* is professed alike by the advocates of each nation's particular creed,

The law of association also explains another mental phenomenon, viz., sudden conversion, as it commonly takes place. A strong religious impression has been produced in childhood; the religious feelings, with Cautiousness, have been associated with particular creeds, with particular interpretations and passages of Scripture, but circumstances have, for a time, overcome those impressions, and such feelings have given place to others. The animal propensities have probably assumed the ascendancy; but the early association has not been broken, any more than the association of fear with darkness is broken because forgotten in the day-time. An allusion to the formerly-cherished creed—a passage of Scripture—a single word — is often sufficient to bring back these early impressions with redoubled force; and alternate fits of sorrow and remorse for former backslidings, and of joy from the natural rebound of the feelings from a state of deep depression, are the consequence. In most cases, however, the discarded worldly propensities will at times regain the ascendancy, which accounts for the frequent sinning and repenting during such states of feeling.

They who are ignorant of the natural mode of action of the mental powers, suppose that there is something supernatural in such phenomena; but it will be found, upon investigation, that all cases of "conversion" and "religious experiences," are strictly in accordance with the general laws of mind, and have no title to be classed amongst things miraculous. This knowledge of the mental constitution seems to be absolutely necessary to rescue some minds, and those, too, naturally strong ones, from the depths of superstition, and to dis-possess them of the belief that they are the instruments of divine and spiritual influences. Thus, in cases where the religious feelings have been cultivated to the exclusion of others, and where means have been taken to keep them predominant by the continued and invariable repetition of devotional exercises, by "coming out of the world," and by constant attendance upon public religious services — the judgment, meanwhile, being systematically excluded from having any share in their regulation — the high enjoyment resulting from the natural exercise of such feelings is imagined to be of a supernatural character. And when these feelings, proceeding principally from Veneration, Hope, and Wonder, are internally active, without any apparent external stimulant; when strong faith, brilliant hopes of eternal felicity, and a feeling of self-abasement take possession of the mind, it is not to be wondered at that the conviction is irresistible that such aspirations proceed from more than natural causes, and that the Spirit of the Most High possesses the heart. And so, in truth, it does, and ever does; but God "acts not by partial, but by general laws."

It is thus that each religion has its "internal evidences," which, being planted in the inmost recesses of the heart, render any external evidence unnecessary; and, in fact, are capable of resisting it, and of supporting any amount of positive contradictions and absurdities.

"The name given to the intellectual ideas which enter into the composition of religion is THEOLOGY. It means the notions which we form concerning the Being to whom, or the objects to which, reverential' and devotional emotions should be directed.

> ' Lo the poor Indian ! whose untutored mind
> Sees God in clouds, or hears Him in the wind.'

This is the theology of the Indian. The Hindoos and the Mahommedans have embodied their theology—in other words, their notions concerning the objects to be reverenced and worshipped—in books. The emotional faculties of the people being trained to reverence, as Divine revelations, the narratives and dogmas which these books contain, the compound becomes in their minds religion. Hence, an individual may be highly religious, and know nothing of theology beyond the narratives and dogmas which have been entwined with his religious emotions from his infancy : while another may be a profound theologian, acquainted with the original languages of Scripture, skilled in all the controversies which have taken place concerning the authors by whom its different parts were written, the time and order of their appearance, their title to the attribute of inspiration, and the true meaning of their texts, yet not be religious. In point of fact, experience shows that, in many instances, the more an individual knows of these subjects, the less religious, in the common acceptation of the word, he becomes — *i.e.*, his reverence for the special dogmas and observances, which in his youth he was trained to regard with religious awe, diminishes,

"The difference between religion and theology, which I have here endeavoured to indicate, may be farther illustrated by comparing them to the warp and woof of a web. The weaver fixes in his loom, first, long threads stretching out directly from his own position, and these are called the warp. Then he puts thread upon a shuttle, which he ever and anon casts between the long threads, and these cross threads are called the woof. The web or cloth is composed of two series of threads closely pressed together. Now, in our present problem, the native sentiment of reverence and devotion may be likened to the warp. It is the foundation or first element of the web. The theological ideas may be considered as the cross thread or woof. As the shuttle adds the woof to the warp to make the cloth, the intellect adds theology, or particular notions about God, to the emotion, and the two combined constitute what we commonly call religion. The Hindoo religion is the primitive pure emotion, with such intellectual ideas as the priests of the country have been able to weave into it. The Mahommedan and Christian religions may be described in similar terms; and thus it is that the composite web of reverential emotion and

R

intellectual ideas which each nation has formed for itself, is called its religion. The compound nature of this web is not usually perceived by its votaries. The Hindoo regards his sacred web as altogether pure religion; and the Mahommedans, and the Christian, of whatever sect, do the same.

" The primitive emotion, when energetic and excited, is so overpowering, that it carries the whole mind captive. When it acts blindly, it dethrones reason, stifles conscience, and enlists every passion to vindicate the honour and glory of the Being whom it has been trained to reverence. When the woof of error has been added in infancy, and the web of superstition formed, every thread—that is to say, every notion concerning God, and his priests, and man's duty to both—becomes sacred in the eyes of the devotee, and stirs the emotion into a glow of rapture if gratified, and of pain, accompanied by indignation and fury, if offended. In this state of mind, barbarous nations plunder and slay in honour and to the glory of their gods.

" In Christian nations, analogous phenomena appear. We all profess to draw our religion from the Bible; but in Scotland, one woof is woven into the warp, in England another, in Ireland a third, in Germany a fourth, in Russia a fifth, and so on."*

* Science and Religion, by G. Combe, p. 18.

CHAPTER VII.

Many important deductions result from our knowledge of the connexion between the Mind and Brain: and many facts there are now on record that point to general principles yet to be discovered, which, in all probability, are of equal, if not of much greater moment than those with which we are now acquainted.

One of the most important of the practical principles derivable from the knowledge of this connexion is, that all the physical laws that tend to increase the health of the body generally, and of the brain as a part of its organization, must tend also to increase the health and strength of the mind. It is found, by experience, that, as the muscles of the body become larger and stronger by use, so the brain increases in activity and size by judicious exercise—and with it the mental powers. The brain also grows or acquires firmness, health or strength, *unconsciously*, that is, without conscious exercise, both in sleep and when awake, and the processes of thought in which we have been previously engaged unconsciously attain clearness and strength, and when after rest—when a subject even has been laid aside for weeks or even months, we find ourselves advanced in it and thinking easier.*　So also the feelings take a bent or direction not known until new circumstances call into conscious manifestation the new condition the organ has acquired. †

It requires a definite amount of force to be supplied to the brain to produce consciousness; when there is less than a given quantity it does not take place.　There is only a certain amount of force supplied by the food, and when this is greatly employed elsewhere, as for instance, in

* " It has often happened to me," says Sir Benjamin Brodie, " to have been occupied by a particular subject of inquiry—to have accumulated a store of facts connected with it, but to have been able to proceed no further.　Then, after an interval of time, without any addition to my stock of knowledge, I have found the obscurity and confusion in which the subject was originally enveloped to have cleared away, the facts seemed all to have settled themselves in their right places, and their mutual relations to have been apparent, although I have *not been sensible* of having made any distinct effort for that purpose." —Psychological Inquiries, by Sir B. C. Brodie.

† " That our feelings towards persons and objects may undergo most important changes without our being in the least degree aware, until we have our attention directed to our own mental state, of the alteration which has taken place in them, a very common but very characteristic example of this kind of action is afforded by the powerful attachment which often grows up between individuals of opposite sexes, without either being aware of the fact ; the full strength of this attachment being only revealed to the consciousness of each when circumstances threaten a separation, and when each becomes cognizant of the feelings entertained by the other.　*　*　We continually speak of the ' feelings ' which we *unconsciously* entertain towards

the all-important action of assimilation, or putting
in the new matter, the brain has a deficient supply,
and unconsciousness or sleep intervenes. Habit
mainly regulates when this shall take place. Also
in dreams, the force that has been engaged elsewhere returns to the brain at irregular times
and in varied quantities, lighting up different
parts of the brain, and therefore of our consciousness irregularly, and in this way arises the
extraordinary discrepancies of our dreams. Thus
we feel no fear in the midst of the greatest danger,
cautiousness is asleep, &c., &c. Sometimes more
than the usual power is supplied to the Intellect,
and we are cleverer when asleep than awake. It
is a singular thing that almost all my own
nightmare dreams are difficulties in travelling,
which I myself never experienced ; but my
father, a very shy man, travelled a great deal
in early life, and was just the person to feel
these difficulties, and no doubt has transmitted
this aptitude of brain to me.

another, and of our not becoming aware of them until some
circumstances call them into activity ; so that it would seem
as if the material organ of these feelings tends *to form itself* in
accordance with the impressions which are habitually made
upon it, and that we are as completely unaware of the changes
which may have taken place in it, as we are of those by which
passing events are registered in our minds (in the memory),
until some circumstance calls forth the conscious manifestation,
which is the 'reflex' of the new condition which the organ
has acquired."— Dr. Carpenter's Human Physiology, pp. 609-10,
5th edit.

Peculiar dispositions, aptitudes, and tendencies of the mind, as well as general bodily constitution, are transmitted from parents to offspring.

It is also known that activity and power of mind depend greatly upon quality of brain. Some are capable of great mental endurance, whilst others sink under the slightest exertion; some are active, others slow: all of which differences are dependent, not so much upon organization, as upon quality of brain. It has not yet been discovered what it is that causes these varieties..

Of the action of the mind upon the body, and the body upon the mind, and of the causes and modes of this mutual influence, many very curious facts have been registered, but our present knowledge is insufficient to enable us to generalize them and turn them to much practical account.

Nervous energy, however generated, or from whatever source derived, seems equally essential to thinking and feeling as to digestion; for whenever it is drawn off to assist in digestion, or other mere bodily offices, the power of thinking and feeling is proportionally decreased. Deep study and digestion mutually impede each other. So, if the nervous energy is spent in bodily exercise, great mental activity is impossible. A certain portion only of nervous fluid, or whatever else it is, is generated, and if used in one direction cannot be used in another.

Thus the activity of one mental organ is quieted

by calling another into exercise; so also deep study or great activity of the anterior lobe of the brain decreases the energy of that portion of it connected with the feelings, and the undue indulgence of a propensity weakens and frequently prevents the proper predominance of the moral feelings.

There are cases in which this nervous energy appears to be deranged, as in epilepsy; or in which it seems to be increased almost without limit, as in the paroxysms of passion or madness, or in the temporary excitement occasioned by the use of stimulating drinks; during which time persons naturally weak seem to acquire a supernatural strength, so as often to require the force of several strong men to restrain them.

Each organ of Propensity and Sentiment appears to exercise its peculiar influence upon the body, and to have its particular set of muscles attached to it. This influence produces what is called the natural language of the faculty; appearing when it is strongly marked, not only on the countenance, but throughout the whole person. Who is not more or less acquainted with the impress of Benevolence, of Veneration, Firmness, Conscientiousness, Hope, Wonder, Self-Esteem, Love of Approbation, Combativeness, Cautiousness? This natural language of the faculties gives rise to a great variety of important mental phenomena; for each feeling has not only a strong influence over most of the bodily functions, but is also, when manifested in this way, intelligible to others, and has the power of calling into activity the same feeling in them : thus harshness produces harshness, and kindness kindness; it is in this way that good or bad feelings may be stimulated, and this kind of sympathy become an important element in moral training. There is a manifest difference in the influence of the speaker who feels forcibly what he is expressing. and who therefore throws the natural language of that feeling into his manner, and the one who delivers the same speech heartlessly, and without feeling his subject.

" True sympathy," says Mr. Combe, " arises from the natural language of any active feeling exciting the same feeling in another, *antecedently to any knowledge of what excited it in the person principally concerned;* and this is sufficient to account for the origin of panics in battles and in mobs, and for the electric rapidity with which passions of every kind pervade and agitate the minds of assembled multitudes." The epidemical mental diseases that sometimes pervade particular countries and districts, manifesting themselves by suicide, tumults, riots, acts of violence, and fanaticism, may be accounted for partly in this way and partly by nervous disease, bordering on madness, caused by mental excitement and religious emotion. Imitation, Mental Imitation, Veneration, Hope, Wonder, Cautiousness, when called into violent and continued action under abnormal conditions, produce the most unlooked for and extraordinary effects. Thus we have the Crusades, and more extraordinary still, — the Children's Crusade in 1212. The Plague or Black Death, which between the years 1347 and 1350, carried off in Europe full 25,000,000 of people, produced the Brotherhood of Flagellants; in Germany, the St. Vitus's Dancing Mania; and in Italy the same effect was said to have been produced by the bite of the tartantula, a large spider. The St. Vitus's Dance was attended by a religious element; in the tarantism this element was wholly wanting. This mania continued through the 15th and into the early part of the 16th century, and we are told that it frequently happened, as with sceptical spiritualists of the present day, that unconcerned and mocking spectators were drawn into the vortex by an irresistible impulse; — thus a Bishop of Foligno allowed himself to be bitten by a tarantula, professing himself utterly sceptical, but the usual symptoms soon began to show themselves, and he, like the others, was obliged to dance to obtain relief; so also were many others of the clergy, who altogether disapproved of dancing; music and dancing being the sole means of cure. The Revivals in America and Ireland are similar phenomena, and the Shakers, Jumpers, Barkers, Spiritualists, are no doubt, in some degree aided more or less by imposture, similarly affected. Women, from their more excitable temperaments, are the soonest affected, and the mania always increases with the accession of numbers.*

The nerves connected with the brain are everywhere distributed over the body with the minutest care, and are also intimately connected with each other throughout the whole system. Every impression occurring at the extremity of the system is instantaneously propagated to its centre; and for every action of the mind there is a corresponding action outwards in the organs intended to administer to its gratification. If this intimate connexion

* A writer in "Fraser," writing on Mental Epidemics, says—"Fanaticism, credulity, fear, sympathy, have combined to spread the infection; the element of imposture has seldom been wholly wanting. From the united operation of these agents disease has extensively resulted; disease, partly physical, partly mental, depriving the patient, for a time at least, of all power of self-control, and propagating itself by the very sight of its symptoms. Hysteria, and the kindred affections, are as certainly present in the most recent of these demonstrations as in the most ancient. Physiological laws have undergone no change. Dr. Hecker remarks—' Demonomaniacs' convulsions, somnambulism, catalepsy, emotional disorders of every kind, are manifested at the present day in all places where fanatical sects pursue their practices, with quite as much importance as at any other times, only in more limited circles. In these cases it is easy to observe that in the great majority of the lookers-on, nearly the same excitement is evinced as in any previous century; and those morbid phenomena are very commonly regarded as the revelations of a most hallowed inspiration, and even as miracles, when they are often nothing more than the physical consequences of a nervous irritant. Practical psychology seems in many circles not yet to have got out of its infancy.' Especially it may be added, the pathology of *religious* emotions deserves deeper study than it has perhaps ever yet received.' —Fraser, April, 1862, p. 500.

and communication be interfered with, either by being checked or suspended, some particular form of disease is the consequence. It is with respect to these kinds of diseases that miraculous cures are often said to be performed; for any strong mental emotion that shall send the nervous current through the system with more than ordinary force, will frequently restore the nervous communication that has been impeded, and cure the disease consequent upon it. Implicit belief, or faith, itself a strong feeling, is necessary to call the other faculties into the simultaneous action required to produce a strong mental emotion; faith, therefore, is the first thing necessary; nothing can be done in such cases without it. If we observe even the ordinary effects of the mind upon the body, we must feel convinced that the combined action of some of our strongest feelings, in such extraordinary cases, is sufficient to produce the so-called miraculous cures on record. We see how readily tears or blushing are produced by the slightest mental emotion: we witness the ordinary effects of grief in deranging the system, and the opposite effect of joy and a happy state of mind in promoting a cure. In fact, no emotion takes place in the mind without some temporary effect upon the bodily system; which ordinarily passes unobserved from the want of the recognition of the strict communication that exists between the mind and the body.

Amongst the most extraordinary of the phenomena connected with this subject are undoubtedly "sleep-waking" and "sleep-walking." Under the influence of somnambulism, people are said to read and write with their eyes shut, and in the dark, and to do other wonderful things. This is accounted for on the supposition that one sense, under particular circumstances, may be so excited and become so exalted, as to supply the place of another. Thus Dr. Carpenter, speaking of what Mr. Braid calls hypnotism, says:—"The exaltation of the muscular sense, by which various actions that ordinarily require the guidance of vision, are directed independently of it, is a phenomenon common to the mesmeric, with various other forms of artificial as well as natural somnambulism." He has repeatedly seen, he says, Mr. Braid's hypnotized subjects write with the most perfect regularity, when an opaque screen was interposed between their eyes and the paper, the lines being equidistant and parallel; and it is not uncommon for the writer to carry back his pencil or pen to dot an *i,* or cross a *t,* or make some other correction in a letter or word. Mr. B. had one patient, who would thus go back and correct with accuracy the writing on the whole sheet of note paper; but if the paper was moved from the position it had previously occupied on the table, all the corrections were on the *wrong* points of the paper as regards the *actual* place of the writing, though on the *right* points as regarded its previous place. Sometimes, however, he would take a fresh departure, by feeling for the upper left-hand corner of the paper; and all his corrections were then made in their proper positions, notwithstanding the displacement of the paper.

In the phenomena classed under the head of electro-biology, the will of one person appears to become completely under the control of another.

Many of the phenomena of Animal Magnetism, or Mesmerism, are attested by such high authority as to leave no room for doubt as to their general truth. We quote the following page from Dr. Elliotson : — "'Among all the phenomena,' says Professor Dugald Stewart, 'to which the subject of imitation has led our attention, none are, perhaps, so wonderful as those which have been recently brought to light, in consequence of the philosophical inquiries occasioned by the medical pretensions of Mesmer and his associates. That these pretensions involved much of ignorance, or of imposture, or both, in their author, has, I think, been fully demonstrated in the very able report of the French academicians ; but does it follow from this that the *facts* witnessed and authenticated by those academicians should share in the disgrace incurred by the empirics who disguised or mis-represented them ? For my own part, it appears to me that the general conclusions established by Mesmer's practice, with respect to the physical effects of the principle of imagination (more par-

ticularly in cases where they co-operated together)
are incomparably more curious than if he had
actually demonstrated the existence of his boasted
science; nor can I see any good reason why a
physician, who admits the efficacy of the *moral*
agents employed by Mesmer, should, in the exercise
of his profession, scruple to copy whatever processes are necessary for subjecting them to his
command, any more than he should hesitate about
employing a new physical agent, such as electricity
or galvanism.' "

"The result of Gall's investigation was this:—
'Neither we nor any other dispassionate observers,
who have been present at the famous experiments
of which such wonderful accounts have been given,
have witnessed anything supernatural or contrary
to nature: we ought therefore to abandon the
belief of the metamorphosis of nerves (the performance of the function of one nerve by another)
to those who are better organised for the marvellous
than ourselves. . . . . . How often in
intoxication, hysterical and hypochondriacal attacks, convulsions, fever, insanity, under violent
emotions, after long fasting, through the effect
of such poisons as opium, hemlock, bella-donna,
are we not, in some measure, transformed into
perfectly different beings, for instance, into poets,
actors, &c.?' 'Just as in dreaming the thoughts
frequently have more delicacy, and the sensations
are more acute, and we can hear and answer; just

as in ordinary somnambulism we can rise, walk,
see with our eyes open, touch with the hands, &c.'
'We acknowledge a fluid which has a special affinity
with the nervous system, which can emanate from
an individual, pass into another, and accumulate, in
virtue of particular affinities, more in certain parts
than in others.' 'We admit the existence of a fluid,
the subtraction of which lessens, and the accumulation of which augments, the power of the nerves;
which places one part of the nervous system in
repose, and heightens the activity of another;
which, therefore, may produce an artificial somnambulism.' "

" A rigid mathematician, La Place, observes, that
' of all the instruments which we can employ, in
order to enable us to discover the imperceptible
agents of nature, the nerves are the most sensible,
especially when their sensibility is exalted by
particular causes. It is by means of them that we
have discovered the slight electricity which is
developed by the contact of two heterogeneous
metals. The singular phenomena which result
from the extreme sensibility of the nerves in
particular individuals have given birth to various
opinions relative to the existence of a new
agent, which has been denominated animal magnetism, to the action of the common magnetism,
to the influence of the sun and moon in some
nervous affections, and, lastly, to the impressions
which may be experienced from the proximity of

the metals, or of a running water. It is natural to suppose that the action of these causes is very feeble, and that it may easily be disturbed by accidental circumstances; but because, in some cases, it has not been manifested at all, we are not to conclude it has no existence. We are so far from being acquainted with all the agents of nature, and their different modes of action, that it would be quite unphilosophical to deny the existence of the phenomena, merely because they are inexplicable in the present state of our knowledge.'"

"Cuvier fully admits Mesmerism :—'We must confess that it is very difficult, in the experiments which have for their object the action which the nervous system of two different individuals can exercise, one upon another, to distinguish the effect of the imagination of the individual upon whom the experiment is tried, from the physical result produced by the person who acts upon him. The effects, however, on persons ignorant of the agency, and upon individuals whom the operation itself has deprived of consciousness, and those which animals present, do not permit us to doubt that the proximity of two animated bodies in certain positions, combined with certain movements, have a real effect, independently of all participation of the fancy. It appears also clearly that these effects arise from some nervous communication which is established between their nervous systems.'

" I have no hesitation in declaring my conviction that the facts of Mesmerism which I admit, because they are not contrary to established morbid phenomena, result from a specific power. Even if they are sometimes unreal and feigned, and, when real, are sometimes the result of emotion,—of imagination, to use common language; but that they may be real and independent of all imagination, I have seen quite sufficient to convince me. . . . . To ascribe the phenomena which I have witnessed to emotion and fancy, to suppose collusion and deception would be absurd. They must be ascribed to a peculiar power; to a power acting, I have no doubt, constantly in all living things, vegetable and animal, but shown in a peculiar manner by the processes of Mesmerism. I have witnessed its power at least three times a week for two months; and should despise myself if I hesitated to declare my decided conviction of the truth of Mesmerism, I am willing to believe that a sleep-waker may prophesy morbid changes in himself with accuracy, as the boy mentioned by Gall predicted the termination of his fit if his friends would lead him into the garden, and the girl mentioned by Lord Monboddo, predicted the cessation of her disease with equal accuracy. . . . . But I have never witnessed more than what, it is certain, takes places in health and disease. I have seen persons sent to sleep, I have felt and

S

heard others declare they had tingling, and heard some declare they had various other sensations and pains, I have seen twitchings, convulsions, and spastic contractions of muscles, loss of power of muscle, and the most profound coma; and I have seen these evidently and instantly removed by the process. I have seen one sense restored in the coma by the process, so that the person was insensible in taste, smell, sight, and yet heard and answered questions well. I have seen paroxysms of sleep-waking and ecstatic delirium, which had been originally induced by its disturbance of a system already epileptic, put an end to evidently, and in general quickly, by Mesmerism. But I have not witnessed persons seeing through walls or paste-board, nor tasting or smelling with the epigastrium or fingers; nor speaking or understanding languages they had never learnt; nor telling the circumstances past, present, and to come, of persons they had never heard of before. . . . No marvel has yet presented itself in my experience: nor has any good been yet effected in the diseases of my patients; but the perfect coma induced in some of them would be an inestimable blessing in the case of a surgical operation, which I am positive might have been performed without the slightest sensation on some of the female patients, exactly as took place at the Hotel-Dieu, where a cancerous breast was removed in Mesmeric coma from a poor woman, without her knowledge. I have no doubt that I shall in time see all the established phenomena of sleep-waking,—writing, reading, and doing endless things, even better than in the waking state. But, before I see, I cannot believe more.*

Most physiologists are now prepared to admit with Dr. Carpenter, 1st, A state of complete insensibility, during which severe surgical operations may be performed without the consciousness of the patient. 2nd. Artificial somnambulism, with manifestation of the ordinary power of mind, but with no recollection in the waking state of what has passed. 3rd. Exaltation of the senses during such somnambulism, so that the somnambule perceives what in his natural condition he could not. 4th. Action during such somnambulism on the muscular apparatus, so as to produce, for example, artificial catalepsy; and 5th. Curative effects. Dr. Carpenter, however, has not yet seen sufficient evidence for belief in the higher phenomena of clairvoyance. Others, however, go much farther; thus, Walther, the Professor at Landshut, quoted by Gall, "for a description of the stages of Mesmerism, in the highest of which (clairvoyance,)

* Elliotson's Human Physiology, p. 677, et seq.

Hospitals for the cure of disease by Mesmerism have been established under Dr. Elliotson's guidance and direction.

time and space no longer present obstacles to the penetration of the magnetised, — who sees as distinctly into the interior of the magnetiser's body as into his own,—the reason of which is, that all the nervous system is an identity and a totality—a pure transparence without cloud, an infinite expansion without bounds or obstacles. Such is universal sense; and as in the waking state the soul is more closely and intimately united with the body, and natural sleep is a more intimate communication of our soul with the universal soul of the world; so in magnetic sleep our soul is united in the most intimate manner with the soul of the world and with the body, and with the latter not by means of the nervous system only, but immediately in all its parts and members, so that life is no longer a particularity, but original life.' "*

Dr. W. Gregory thus summarizes his belief in his Letters on Animal Magnetism :—" I think we may regard it as established; first, that one individual may exercise a certain influence on another, even at a distance; secondly, that one individual may acquire a control over the motions sensations, memory, emotions, and volition of another, both by suggestion, in the conscious, impressible state, and in the magnetic sleep, with or without suggestion; thirdly, that the magnetic sleep is a very peculiar state, with a distinct and

* Elliotson's Human Physiology, p. 674.

separate consciousness; fourthly, that in this state
the subject often possesses a new power of perception,
the nature of which is unknown, but by means of
which he can see objects or persons, near or distant,
without the use of the external organs of vision;
fifthly, that he very often possesses a very high
degree of sympathy with others, so as to be able
to read their thoughts; sixthly, that by these
powers of clairvoyance and sympathy, he can sometimes perceive and describe, not only present, but
past, and even future events; seventhly, that he
can often perceive and describe the bodily state
of himself or others; eighthly, that he may fall
into trance and extasis, the period of which he
often predicts accurately; ninthly, that every one
of these phenomena has occurred, and frequently
occurs, spontaneously, which I hold to be the
fundamental fact of the whole enquiry, Somnambulism, Clairvoyance, Sympathy, Trance, Extasis,
Insensibility to pain, and Prevision, having often
been recorded as natural occurrences. Tenthly,
that not only the human body, but inanimate
objects, such as magnets, crystals, metals, &c., &c.,
exert on sensitive persons an influence, identical,
so far as it is known, with that which produces
Animal Magnetism; that such an influence really
exists, because it may act without a shadow of
suggestion, and may be transferred to water and
other bodies; and lastly, that it is only by studying
the character of this influence, as we should that

of any other, such as Electricity or Light, that we can hope to throw light on these obscure subjects."

The last proposition refers to the discoveries of Baron Reichenbach, who has shown by a great number of experiments, that there exists in all bodies, and throughout the universe, a peculiar principle, analogous to magnetism, electricity, light, and heat, yet distinct from them all, to which he gives the name of *odyle*. It is most manifest in powerful magnets; next in crystals, and exists in the human body, the sun, moon, stars. heat, electricity, chemical action, and, in fact, the whole material universe. Those who are most sensitive to this influence are persons of feeble health, especially somnambulists; but it is found that about one-third of individuals, taken promiscuously, and many in good health, are sensible of it; and it was by a series of observations on persons of all classes and conditions for years, that the facts have been elicited.

Baron Reichenbach says, "There is nothing in these observations," which he had just detailed, "that, after the contents of the preceding treatises, can surprise us; but they are certainly a fine additional confirmation of what has been stated in regard to the sun and moon, and also of the fact that the whole material universe, even beyond our earth, acts on us with the very same kind of influence which resides in all terrestrial objects;

and lastly, it shows that we stand in a connection of mutual influence, hitherto unsuspected, with the universe; so that in fact the stars are not altogether devoid of action on our sublunary, perhaps even on our practical world, and on the mental processes of some heads."

That Mesmerism *may* be true in all its stages, we think can scarcely be disputed by those who have followed us in our investigation into the present extent of our knowledge of both mind and matter. The phenomena alluded to in this chapter, relating both to animal magnetism and to sympathy, in its various modes of manifestation, seem all to emanate from one source, and to point to some nervous agent, some general power or force, or perhaps some fluid, which, if it exist at all, must perform a most important part in the human constitution; the discovery of which will be a vast step gained towards the knowledge of all the influences that affect and rule over the mind of man.

If we allow ourselves to enter the field of speculation there is much to be said. I have heard of great wonders, upon testimony the most respectable, but I have witnessed nothing more than what may be accounted for from the heightened action of the sense, or of the mental faculty; sight and hearing greatly increased, and the abnormal, not the normal condition of the mind, in action. We do not know of what the natural faculties are capable, if greatly enlarged or greatly excited. The large size of the organ of number will enable an idiot to calculate mentally what another can scarcely do with the slate, and the large size of the mathematical faculties in Sir Isaac Newton enabled him to anticipate results that took hours to work out in the regular way. The building instinct of animals seems to result from some peculiar constitution of the organ of constructiveness. Cats and dogs can find their way home across hundreds of miles of country, without any assistance from the finger posts, being able to do so apparently from the peculiar or exceptional action of the same organ of Locality which enables man to find his way with facility in proportion to the size of the organ. There is nothing probably more wonderful in Mesmerism than the faculty manifested by the carrier pigeon; it is taken hundreds of miles away, and then released; it ascends into the air, makes two or three turns, and then flies *straight* home again. Some of the phenomena of Mesmerism, if true, would seem to annihilate the ordinary modes of thought in time and space, enabling us to know the past, and bringing us into an immediate contiguity with the absent as with the present. Might not this be through the action of some rudimentary organ, intended for service in some very advanced state of the world's civilization, and which being more largely developed in some individuals than in others, is abnormally excited by the aid of Mesmerism, and casts its shadow before: or, might it not be by the odylic force, which makes what we call solid matter, perfectly transparent to sensitives? As the heavenly bodies in their immeasurable distance act upon our brains, not only through the force of light, but through the odylic force, may not our brains also act, and be acted upon, by other brains at a distance? Electricity unites two batteries, and almost as quick as thought carries a message across the Atlantic. Why may not the more subtle force of odyle unite two brains? The electric battery of the brain carries its mandates instantaneously through the nerve wires to all parts of the body: why should they stop there? I believe there are many facts to show that they do not, but they want generalizing. Many phenomena would seem to indicate that the partition-wall of individuality, which separates the mind of man from that of mankind, can be broken down, and we may become all-knowing and intelligent, as regards all that has ever formed part of the knowledge of the race. But deductions from the phenomena connected with this subject must, for the present, be regarded as mere speculations.

As to the phenomena of what is called "Spiritualism," people of well-known character and undoubted powers of intelligence and habits of philosophical observation, tell us that after six or eight years' careful investigation in private families, and after sitting in many hundreds of " circles," they are obliged to come to the conviction that the phenomena are genuine, and that there are both forces and intelligences which do not come at present within any recognised law. Of course, there is much deception, and still more self-delusion, mixed up with the subject; but it seems almost impossible not to come to the conclusion that there is a residue of truth. The question then is, whence come these phenomena ? From whom, or what, are they derived ? Here there is a great difference of opinion, the great majority, as has ever been the case since the world began where the causes are hidden, ascribing them to spiritual agency. We are supposed to prove, every time when by an act of the will we move a limb, that spirit moves matter. Now, we know nothing of the nature or essence of "force," and we may call it "spirit" if we like ; but we do know that precisely the same force that moves the steam-engine, moves the body, and that this force is generated by the union of carbon and oxygen and the consequent evolution of heat. Whatever may have been the *origin* of all motion, *this* force is unattended with intelligence ; but late investigations have *proved* that vital forces are correlated from physical, and mental from vital ; and further investigation of the correlation of forces may show whence the particular force is derived that is displayed in these so-called spiritual manifestations. "Each manifestation of force can be interpreted only as the effect of some antecedent force: no matter whether it be an inorganic action, an animal movement, a thought, or a feeling. Either this must be conceded or else it must be asserted that our successive states of consciousness are self-created. Either mental energies, as well as bodily ones, are quantitatively correlated to certain energies expended in their production, and to certain other energies which they initiate : or else nothing must become something, or something must become nothing."* It is probably to this correlation that we must look for the force displayed in these extraordinary phenomena : but whence the intelligence? This, further investigation, I think, will prove to be merely the reflex and reflection of our own embodied intelligence, as manifested in the abnormal conditions of mind to which I have alluded in this chapter. The conditions requisite for its manifestation are precisely those attending the preter-natural states of mind attending mesmeric action, such as clairvoyance, electro-biology, &c., &c., in which given constitutions and temperaments are necessary, and the failures consequently are more numerous than the successes. The mind acts through the brain and the senses ordinarily are necessary to set the brain in motion ; but that it may be acted upon

* Herbert Spencer.

directly by some other force, and without the aid of the senses, appears to be now an established fact ; also, the nervous force, not generated but eliminated by the brain, and guided by the will, moves the body; but of what nature is this force ? We know it is the correlate of physical forces, but what other "form" it may take, or how far and to what extent it can act upon other things and other brains, and consequently other intelligences, outside the body, is not yet known ; but that it has such power to act, I think is more than probable. Very much lies beyond the ken of ordinary sense and vision, and our five senses are rather clumsy instruments to deal with the imponderables. The microscope shows a material world within them, and a sensitive nervous system not only sees what is not apparent to ordinary sense, but appears even to break down the boundary of sense, and to reveal a world beyond.

There is quite a new world lying open for our investigation in this direction, and its pursuit is not calculated, *ultimately,* to lead us back into the bonds of superstition, but forward in the path of Cerebral Physiology and the true Science of Mind.

It might fairly have been expected that the light of Science and general Education would have dispelled for ever the darkness of superstition and fanaticism, but this cannot take place till the Science of Mind is much advanced, so as to lay bare the true causes of the spiritual emotions which generate, or lie at the root of, such states of mind.

SUMMARY AND CONCLUSION.

THE freedom of will, and of action, with which we suppose ourselves to be endowed, is a delusion. For ages men believed the sun to go round the earth, because it seemed to do so. A similar delusion is at the base of our Ethical system, because we *seem* free. Whence, then, the source of the delusion ? Our apparent freedom consists in the absence of all physical restraint, and in our power therefore to do as we please; but what we please to do depends upon our mental constitution and the circumstances in which we are placed. The forces of nature which culminate in mind, re-act on nature, as an intelligent power, and thus the hand of necessity is hidden, but it is not the less there, acting with undeviating regularity and resistless force. It is true that the " liberty" seems infinite, and action inexhaustibly various ; yet the limitation is complete, and the mighty controlling power ever present, although unseen and unnoticed, and pressing with the lightness of a feather.

Nothing, then, under the circumstances, could have happened but that which did happen,; and the actions of men, under precisely the same circumstances, must always issue in precisely the same results. We may dismiss then the past, with all its vain regrets, and we must learn to judge of our position by what it really is and may be, and not by what we vainly suppose it might have been ; for nothing is more certain than that we could not have acted differently in any act of our lives, with the state of mind and circumstances then existing. Half the misery in life arises from not seeing and knowing this, and from the feeling that we *could* have done otherwise, might have done otherwise, and ought to have done otherwise ; and half the crime results from the feeling of revenge, based on the same error.

"Let the dead past then bury its dead," for the past could not have been different, and comes not back again; the present, the future, only are in our power; for the experience of the past—the consequences of our actions,—alters both the mind and circumstances, and makes a different result possible.

Hence the doctrine of Philosophical Necessity, or the Law of Consequences, becomes of the highest importance, — teaching as it does, that for every consequence, or effect, there is an antecedent cause, which is always equal, under like circumstances, to produce the same effect, and can produce no other ;—thus making us, as we attain the knowledge of such causes, masters over our own condition for good or ill.

The various superstitions fostered in the minds
of the ignorant, in all ages and countries, have
taken their rise in the misunderstanding of this
law. Spiritual agents of every imaginable kind,
Gods of the Woods and Streams, of Earth and
Air, Genii, Fairies, Angels, Devils, Immaterial Souls,
have all been brought forward to account for effects
whose causes lay remote from ordinary sight; while
each of these agents has been gifted with a *free-will*,
or power of acting, or not, under similar circumstances; so that the uniformity of the laws
of nature has been lost sight of, or has been
unknown. All uncivilized nations, and even such
as have attained considerable knowledge, reter all
natural effects inexplicable to themselves, to the
power of spirits or demons. No rational means
are therefore taken to secure the blessings, or avert
the ills, which come and go at the caprice of these
mysterious powers; but charms and offerings,
sacrifices and prayers, are used to appease their
wrath, or propitiate their favour.

Good and evil have been represented as depending upon the influence of the Stars, of Fate, of
Original Sin—upon the conflicting power of Satan
with that of the Spirit of God—rather than as the
natural and necessary consequences of our own
conduct. It has been overlooked that our Creator,
in giving us Reason, or a capability of foreseeing
consequences, has given us power over both good
and evil, and that such a gift would have been

rendered comparatively useless, if not fatal, if He had permitted the established course of nature—upon which the exercise of reason is dependent—to be interfered with by influences obeying no fixed law, or none, at least, upon which man could calculate.

Since about the year 1700 no one has been burnt for witchcraft in our enlightened country; but the Devil, according to the most favoured creed, is still supposed to be powerful among us. The true character of evil is disguised, and in our popular religious instruction natural effects are attributed to anything but their real and efficient causes. Our moral and religious teachings are still largely mixed with the superstitions of the dark ages, instead of having for their object to make known the "Law of the Lord"—the Physical, the Organic, the Moral Law,—with the natural pains and pleasures connected with it. May we not hope, however, that the time approaches when God shall be known in His works, and a Spirit of Evil no longer be supposed to divide the sovereignty of the earth with Him; when Chance, already dismissed from the physical, shall be banished from the moral world; when especial influences, no longer expected in the one, will not be looked for in the other?

Herein consists the difference between "Necessity" and Fatalism. The fatalist believes that everything

T

is written in the book of fate, and must happen **as**
there written, and it is useless therefore taking **any**
steps to avoid it ; thus paralysing all effort : on the
other hand, the necessarian believes that for every
effect there is a cause, which is equal at all times
to produce the result desiderated, and that, therefore, the knowledge and use of these causes put
fate in his own hands.   It is true that what is
written in the book of fate must come to pass;
since that is no more than saying that what will
happen will happen ; but if we were permitted to
read this book, we should find that the difference
of faith in the fatalist and necessarian was itself
the efficient cause of an entirely different fate to
each believer.

But the necessarian must still use motives ; and
as in practice he must praise and blame and love
and hate as others do, this, it is said, is the same
thing as if he continued to believe in free will.
It is true he must still use motives, but he knows
that if he. does not use efficient ones, he cannot
succeed ; whereas the believer in free-will thinks
it always a chance whether he shall succeed or **not**,
and if he blames any one, it is generally any one
but himself, to whom the fault properly belongs.

Responsibility can have no reference to the **past**,
which could not have been otherwise, **and** cannot
be recalled ; it consists only in the natural and
necessary consequences of our actions.   These consequences are the same, and the responsibility is **the**

same, therefore, whether a man is a free agent or not. The consequences, that is, the pain or punishment is the same, whether we are pushed into the fire, fall in, or put ourselves in voluntarily, the object of the suffering being our own good—to keep us from being burnt.

Punishment, therefore, must be regarded only as the means to an end, and, except for our good, is unjust and unnecessary. Retributive justice, as it has been wrongly called, is simply revenge, and as an element in our penal codes has always done more harm than good, as the action of our revised codes, from which it is omitted, abundantly testifies.

Sin is based upon the erroneous supposition that we could have acted otherwise than we did: and since all punishment is for our good, forgiveness of sins would be an injury.

Evil is the natural and necessary limitation of our faculties, and our consequent liability to error; and pain, which we call evil, is its corrective. It is our Guardian and Guide, our Schoolmaster, our Stimulus to Action and to all those efforts by which the strong and good are preserved and the weak and bad destroyed, and by which the world goes ever on to better and better.

All experience, it is said, proves man to be a free agent, which means simply that he has the power to do as he pleases. But his actions, or what he pleases to do, result from his natural character and the circumstances in which he is placed. It is clear, then, that what we have to do is to improve the character, and to make a wise disposal of all the circumstances that influence it. Locke says, " As far as man has power to think or not to think, to move or not to move, according to the preferences or direction of his own mind, so far is a man free." Since, then, the only " freedom " we have is limited to action in accordance with our natural powers and capacities, our aim must be to develop fully these powers and capacities, and to remove all impediments, external and internal, to their free and complete action. There must be no external compulsion from physical impediment, or internal compulsion from defect in the mind itself; no obstacle to the full exercise of our natural powers both of body and mind. Education in its full meaning is the developing and perfecting of all these powers.

We in England have not much to complain of in the way of external compulsion, and to this fact there is not only *our own* testimony. M. Scherer lately (May, 1862) observed in the *Temps*:— " England is the classic land of liberty ; and for this reason it is a holy land—a land which more than one exile has turned to with gratitude. We do not now speak of political institutions, but of civil liberty, of the respect for the rights of all, of independence of exertion, of the space left open for individual action, of the mildness of the laws, of the fewness of regulations. Elsewhere regulations are the rule ; elsewhere liberty exists only where it is expressly stipulated ; but in England it is liberty which is everywhere, and always supposed. Elsewhere, civil life is encircled by a network, invisible but inextricable, of restrictions; but in England every man speaks, teaches, prints, meets, associates, builds, travels, exercises his calling in industry and commerce, fills the professions, carries out all his designs, without hindrance from anything whatever but the equal right of his neighbour."

J. S. Mill, in his work on Liberty, justly contends that " one very simple principle is entitled to govern absolutely the dealings of society with the individual, in the way of compulsion or control, whether the means used be physical force in the form of legal penalties, or the moral coercion of public opinion. That principle is, that the sole end for which mankind are warranted, individually or collectively, in interfering with the liberty of action of any of their number, is self-protection. That the only purpose for which power can be rightfully exercised over any member of a civilised community, against his will, is to prevent harm to others. His own good, either physical or moral, is not a sufficient warrant." We have nearly arrived at this in England.

As to our mental freedom, that is another thing : very little has yet been done towards perfecting our ˙ natural powers, or bringing them into harmonious action. Our natural powers, both bodily and mental, we derive from our parents; much therefore depends upon race, upon breeding. Now the art of breeding has been carried of late years to a most extraordinary perfection among animals. The most exquisite hot-house plant does not more surpass its original weed than some animals now surpass their ancestors in symmetry and grace. Short of turning one species into another, the breeder can do anything with his material. The scientific application of physiological principles has revolutionised the whole system. But at present this has been confined to the brute creation ; all attention to natural law has been ignored in the breeding of the human being; and yet more depends upon the original constitution than upon the training or education afterwards. Mental power and capacity depend upon the nervous system, and very little more than the direction of that power and capacity upon education ; and the perfection of brain and nervous systems, and even mental aptitudes are transmitted from parent to offspring, and are dependent upon the physiological principles that have revolutionised our Cattle Shows. No education or training will turn a bull-dog into a pointer, yet the human educator expects to work quite as great changes in human beings. From systematically ignoring the laws of cerebral physiology, both the educating and breeding of human beings are the merest chance and empiricism, and our liberty is thereby as much limited in some directions as that of the lame to run or the blind to see.

The first thing then to aim at is a healthy and well-developed body and brain; and next, to see that the force generated by the healthy activity of the bodily functions shall be applied to the purposes intended, and properly distributed, in due proportion, according to the offices to be performed. This balance between muscular, vital, and nervous power—between bodily labour and head work—has never yet been attained, if it has ever been attempted. This has been mainly owing to ignorance of the fact that vital forces are the correlate of physical forces, and mental of vital, and that "from given amounts of such forces neither more nor less of such physical and psychical changes can result."

We seldom, therefore, attain the *mens sana in corpore sano*; either the body or mind is stunted and imperfectly developed. Below a certain temperature the tadpole grows, but does not develop into the frog; so some human beings, from want of the due balance of force, remain great tadpoles all their lives, while the hot-bed of civilization precociously transforms others into the smallest possible frogs. Herbert Spencer, in his admirable chapter on Physical Education, says, "It is a physiological law, first pointed out by M. Isidore St. Hilaire, and to which attention has been drawn by Mr. Lewes in his essay on *Dwarfs and Giants*, that there is an antagonism between *growth* and *development*. By growth, as used in this antithetical sense, is to be understood *increase of size;* by development, *increase of structure.* And the law is, that great activity in either of these processes involves retardation or arrest of the other. A familiar example is furnished by the cases of the caterpillar and the chrysalis. In the caterpillar there is extremely rapid augmentation of bulk; but the structure is scarcely at all more complex when the caterpillar is full-grown than when it is small. In the chrysalis the bulk does not increase; on the contrary, weight is lost during this stage of the creature's life ; but the elaboration of a more complex structure goes on with great activity. The antagonism, here so clear, is less traceable in higher creatures, because the two processes are carried on together. But we see it pretty well illustrated among ourselves when we contrast the sexes. A girl develops in body and mind rapidly, and ceases to grow comparatively early. A boy's bodily and mental development is slower, and his growth greater. At the age when the one is mature, finished, and having all faculties in full play, the other, whose vital energies have been more directed towards increase of size, is relatively incomplete in structure ; and shows it in a comparative awkwardness, bodily and mental. Now this law is true of each separate part of the organism, as well as of the whole. The abnormally rapid advance of any organ in respect of structure, involves premature arrest of its growth; and this happens with the organ of the mind as certainly as with any other organ. The ' brain, which during early years is relatively large in mass but imperfect in structure, will, if required to perform its functions with undue activity, undergo a structural advance greater than is appropriate to its age; but the ultimate effect will be a falling short of the size and power that would else have been attained. And this is a part-cause—probably the chief cause—why precocious children, and youths who up to a certain time were carrying all before them, so often stop short and disappoint the high hopes of their parents." Properly speaking there is no *antagonism* between growth and development when the animal force is duly distributed; it is only when the balance is disturbed, and one is carried on at the expense of the other. If any passion—amativeness especially, that being the greatest consumer of force of all,—is precociously developed, and indulged, it is at the expense of the growth of the body. Early precocity is the use of mental force at the expense of the vital, and unless the balance is restored, the children cursed with it seldom live. On the other hand, agricultural labourers. and the nomad population generally, have vital power at the expense of the mental; consequently any injury to the bodily system is more easily repaired, but the mind is sluggish, and the feelings dull, and the sense of pleasure and pain is less keen, and approaches nearer to that of the brute creation.

In our Educational systems due regard must be had to the requirements of growth, development, and training, and great care must be taken to preserve the balance of power, so that one shall never be allowed to go on at the expense of the other. During rapid fits of growth, there is both bodily and mental prostration, and neither can be forced without injury to the whole system : there is but a limited supply of vital energy, and if the demands are great in one direction, a reduction must be made in some other. The intellectual forcing systems of our Schools, where mental effort alone is looked for and appreciated, are altogether at variance with these principles, and the consequences are lamentable in the extreme, although unobserved or misunderstood from ignorance of the law we are explaining, and of the principle that education is the drawing out—the developing, strengthening, and perfecting of *all* our natural powers, and not a mere strain upon the memory and intellectual faculties, at the expense of the others.

When growth and development are finished, the same fatal error attends the distribution of force in after life, and parts of the mind are exercised at the expense of the others, until many of our highest and most delicate faculties die for want of sustenance, and we have only a crippled and imperfect human being.*

Let us glance at the natural direction of some of our faculties, and see how they are misused and misdirected.

First. With respect to Woman and the still much-disputed point of her greater or less superiority to man. Probably each is superior to the other in the position nature has assigned them; the difficulty has been to find that position, and for each to be satisfied with it. A man's brain weighs on an average 3lbs. 8oz.; a woman's only 2lbs. 11oz.; and, as power is in proportion to the size of the organ, that settles the question as to the relative strength of mind ; but woman's brain, if it has less power, has generally more sensibility and delicacy of perception, and is calculated to do some things better than a man's. With respect to her

* " You dwarf the remaining faculties, when you develop one to abnormal size and strength. Thus have men been great preachers, but uncommonly neglectful parents. Thus have men been great Statesmen, but omitted to pay their tradesmen's bills. Thus men have been great moral and social reformers, whose own lives stood much in need of moral and social reformation. I should judge, from a portrait I have seen of Mr. Thomas Sayers, the champion of England, that this eminent individual has attended to his physical to the neglect of his intellectual development. His face appears deficient in intelligence, though his body seemed abundant in muscle. And possibly it is better to seek to develop the entire nature—intellectual, moral, and physical— than to push one part of it into a prominence that stunts and kills the rest. It is better to be a complete *man*, than to be essentially a poet, a statesmen, a prize fighter. Such an inordinate growth in a single direction, is truly morbid."

place and position in the world,* much has been
said of late days about the "independence of
woman," and so far as the law has aided to consign
her over to man as his property, too much cannot
be said about her emancipation; but in fact neither
man nor woman were intended to be independent.
Woman, like the ivy, is supported by the stronger
trunk of the man, and if when such support fails
her she sometimes shoots up into an independent
tree, she more frequently, like the ivy, crawls along
the ground. Man on the other hand requires
softening and refining by the woman. Bachelors
and spinsters are not complete in themselves;
man is not made by a given number of legs, arms,
and other parts, but by the mind; now one-third
of the mental faculties lie unused and undeveloped
in the single man, and this observation applies with
still greater force to single women. It requires,
then, one man and one woman to constitute one
human being; and together as much as possible
let them do the work of the world between them.
Let the business of the world be equally divided,
but each keep in their own department; each is
highest, best, strongest, and first there. Let both
take their own road, but let not these roads be
competing lines. Women should have work, but
not in competition with men. From her peculiar

---

* The following remarks on Woman's place and work, with
but little alteration, formed part of a paper read at the first
meeting of the Social Science Association, October, 1857.

organization, she has her sphere ; let her work be found in it. If she feed us, clothe us, bring us into the world, educate us, nurse us, and make a home what it ought to be, this is her work ; and if it be done properly, surely she will have enough to do—it is at least one half the business of life. If she will do this well, she may well be released from all harder work, whether of mind or body.

Let us consider each of these points. By feeding us is not meant earning our bread, but cooking it Whatever it may suit transcendental young ladies to say, gastronomy is of far more importance to us than astronomy ; and whatever truth may be found in astrology, the stars have less influence upon us than our daily pudding. Cooking is a science, and ought to be treated as such—as much so as chemistry. It has been said that if a man drinks beer he thinks beer ; and whether this be true or not, we *do* know that different meats and drinks affect the mind as well as the body differently, and we ought to be fed according to the requirements of our systems. We change not with " the breezy call of incense breathing morn," or ." still evening " and " twilight grey," so much as with our dietary and the state of our digestions, and moral conduct at present has more to do with eating and drinking than with principle.; for as Dr. Reid says, " He whose disposition to goodness can resist the influence of dyspepsia, and whose career of philanthropy is not liable to be checked by an obstruction in the hepatic organs, may boast of much deeper and firmer virtue than falls to the ordinary lot of human nature." Cookery, then, is a department of science open to women. I do not mean to say that they must all turn cooks, but all ought to understand the Chemistry of Food, and the Science of Gastronomy and good digestion.

The departments of nursing and early education belong alone to women, and these cannot go on properly with any employment away from home. Probably the "*Mens sana in corpore sano*" depends more upon the first year's nursing than upon all the other years put together. Whatever the lowly may think who go out to work, or the high who transfer the office to asses or other wet nurses, it is an office that cannot be performed by deputy. The mother only can properly nurse her own child, and her arms alone can furnish the cradle it requires. The same may be said of the earliest years of childhood. Women know how "to rear up children," but so far only as instinct and tradition teach them. All science were useless without such instinct; but do they know with true insight all the "wondrous powers that lie folded up" in the little being they have brought into the world—the enfolding and developing of which depend principally upon themselves? What do women ordinarily know of Physiology and Psychology, and the proper use, and therefore the abuse, of each bodily and mental faculty; of the education of the body and the education of the feelings which especially belong to their department ?

It is woman also that must furnish nurses for the sick. But this also òught to be a scientific profession, and it is time the race of Mrs. Gamps were only fossil specimens. Here a medical education to enable · the nurse the better to aid nature and the doctor would be very useful, and some kind of medical degree might attend it, without assuming the masculine M.D., and such qualified practitioners might perhape better "minister to the necessities of delicate young womanhood" than the other sex. Nursing is peculiarly a woman's element, and in the arrest of disease as much perhaps depends upon good nursing as upon the physician.

Women should clothe us, or at least their own sex and children. Women are no longer spinsters, not even the unmarried. The time was when the spinning and weaving of sheets, shirts, and broad cloth were done at home ; but now this is done by the steam-engine. A man by the aid of steam and machinery can do 200 times the work his wife formerly did ; and surely the amount of increased production ought to have enabled him to keep his wife and children without their being obliged to add to the weekly income ; and so it would undoubtedly have done if a National System had *obliged* the father to send his children to School till the time the boys should be apprenticed to skilled labour, and the girls consigned to the mother's care to be instructed in woman's work. The wife would thus have found quite enough to do without working at a trade.* But our industrial system has now absorbed a large portion of both wife and children, and to retrace our steps will be very difficult. But if machinery now does the spinning and sewing, it was thus intended to release women to some higher occupation. Let them, then, spin the clothing for the mind. To the man belongs strength—to the woman delicacy of perception and sensitiveness: her spring of mind is more highly tempered, and vibrates to the slightest touch and to the music of the spheres. Her instincts may be trusted rather than her reason. The most beautiful thing in creation herself, it is her place to beautify all around— to add the ideal to the real. To her, then, particularly belongs the Art of Living.

The Art of Living is the most important department in life, and it is the least understood. To the strength of man belongs Production — the transforming the rough and raw material into all that the world requires. To the woman belongs the ordering and administering of these things, so as to produce the greatest economy and the

---

* Women cannot be brought up to trades, where highly skilled labour is required, without a long apprenticeship, and surely this would be lost labour in at least three cases out of four.

largest amount of enjoyment at home. If the wife of a poor man understood this, it would save him much more than he now gets by her earnings either away from home or at home. Too often she does not know how to buy food economically, or to cook it, or to cut out clothes, or to nurse and attend to children's complaints, or to do anything else that shows she understands the art of living happily and economically. In the higher classes, if this were understood, it would banish at once the present expensive style of living that is the curse of English society, and all the snobbery that belongs to it; and instead of a heavy, dead, cumbrous, enervating, stifling luxury, we should have beauty and grace, and poetry and the fine arts, and whatever should bring vividly before the mind all that was best worth remembering in the past, or looking forward to in the future. When women understand the art of living, they will be able to make a heaven of home upon a third of what it now requires to support our present costly conventionalism. In thus advocating the domestic employment of women, we by no means advocate their dependence upon men; what we contend for is, mutual dependence. To the women we give the highest department of all,—the Art of Living, —of making life happy; and to them also will generally belong the next highest, the cultivation in man of the spiritual and the æsthetic. The

man is too much occupied with the real to have
time for the ideal, except through and by the aid
of his other half—the woman.

Surely, then, there is enough for woman to do
to make her properly independent in these departments, if the work is to be done well, without her
appearance on the Stock Exchange, or in the
farmers' market, or at the merchants' desk, or in
the factory, or in competition with our parsons,
lawyers, or physicians. Here is half the work of
the world, if it were well done ; but it has seldom
been well done. Women are not educated to work
well, and too many think it a degrading thing to
work at all, at least at any useful occupation. Mrs.
Bodichon in her excellent pamphlet on " Woman
and Work," very truly says, " People are grasping
after some grandiose task, something ' worthy ' of
their powers, when the only proof of capacity they
give is to do small things badly."

But women, we are told, want work, and 6d. and
1s. a day at shirt-making and slops is but poor pay;
but all unskilled labour is badly paid, and an
agricultural labourer gets little more. Let them
qualify themselves to do their own work in the
way it ought to be done, and the supply, as the
Economists tell us, will beget the demand.

But the law, it is said, " has tied the hands " of
one-half of mankind, and condemned the larger
number of women to " inactivity and frivolity."
We suspect there is considerable exaggeration here;

but if there are such unjust laws, they should be repealed, and women be placed before the law upon a perfect equality with men. Nature has legislated upon this subject, and so distinctly that man may save himself the trouble. A woman's proper work can be found only at home. Napoleon said long since, " The old systems of instruction are worth nothing," and when he asked what was wanting that the youths of France should be well educated, Madame Campon replied " Mothers." But mothers have not been supplied, for where are women qualified to bring up their own children properly, and able in the other departments we have mentioned, to make a home what it ought to be ? If a man's wife goes out to work, he has no home ; the house is dirty, the children uncared for, there is no cookery, no comfort, and the public-house parlour is the working man's home. The factory system, and the way in which women are employed in England, make a home impossible, and with it goes every social and moral tie, and society falls to pieces. The only thing that enables a working man to rise, and the foundation therefore of all his other virtues, is providence, and it is in a home that this must have its source ; it is there it first rises—that is the centre of all his thrift, around which everything accumulates. Many women, however, have no homes, and we are informed (I do not know on what authority) that 43 per cent. of women in England and Wales at

the age of 20 and upwards are unmarried. If
those who have no homes would qualify themselves
professionally to help those that have, there would
be no fear that their qualifications would remain
idle, be unappreciated, or badly paid. Let them
improve the quality of what they have to offer,
and its importance will be recognised, and it will
be more in demand. This is the way to make
them really "independent," to make them of more
importance, and thus ensure to them more respect
and better treatment. But by bringing their
labour into competition with men in the already
over-stocked labour market, they drag the married
women and children in also. Instead of trying to
introduce more women into trades and manufactures, our efforts ought, I think, to be directed
towards extricating those who have already got
themselves involved, not only without any real
increase of wages or other measurable advantage
to themselves, but to their positive injury : for, as
John Stuart Mill truly says :—" *Cæteris paribus*,
those trades are by far the worst paid in which
the wife and children of the artizan aid the work.
The income which the habits of the class demand,
and down to which they are almost sure to
multiply, is made up, in those trades, by the
earnings of the whole family, while in others the
same income must be obtained by the labour of
the man alone. It is even probable that the collective earnings will amount to a smaller sum than

those of the man alone in other trades ; because the prudential restraint on marriage is unusually weak when the only consequence immediately felt is an improvement of circumstances, the joint earnings of the two going further in their domestic economy after marriage than before."

With half the work, then, that peculiarly belongs to women, from constitution and circumstances, undone, and the other half badly done, employment in trades, and manufactures, and in professions, as is the present custom in France, would be a step backwards in civilization, not forwards.

Man has no more at present found his place and position in the world than woman ; and the civilization of the present day, after all, is but a civilized barbarism.

Our great aim should be, the predominance and habitual activity of those feelings that peculiarly distinguish us as human beings ; instead of which men ordinarily seek Wealth, and with it Power and Distinction, and we have occasional glimpses only of higher feelings and motives. A savage King visited a discovery ship in stark-naked majesty, with an old navy cocked hat on his head and a pair of tarnished epaulettes on his bare shoulders, the gift of some previous European visitors. All the world is now seeking distinction in the same way, only with *more* of the same things—fine clothes, a large house, many servants, luxurious carriages, rich carpets, easy chairs, soft beds, rich wines, costly banquets Suppose even that we reach perfection in this laudable "end and aim" of our existence, where shall we ultimately arrive? We might rival George the IV. perhaps, who was the most perfect gentleman in Europe, so far as such things could make him! *

"We thus spend our incomes," says Emerson, "for paint and paper, and not for the things of man. Our expense is almost all for conformity. It is for cake that we run in debt; 'tis not the intellect, not the heart, not beauty, not worship, that costs so much. Why needs any man be rich? Why must he have horses, and fine garments, and handsome apartments, and access to great houses and places of amusement? Only for want of thought. Once waken in him a divine thought, and he flees into a solitary garden or garret to enjoy it, and is richer with that dream than the fee of a country would make him. We dare not trust our wit for making our house pleasant to our friends, and so we buy ice-creams. Parched corn eaten to-day that I may have roast fowl for my

* "But *this* George what was he? I look through all his life, and recognise but a bow and a grin. I try and take him to pieces, and find silk stockings, padding, stays, a coat with frogs and fur collar, a star and blue ribbon, a pocket-handkerchief prodigiously scented, one of Truefitt's best nutty-brown wigs reeking with oil, a set of teeth, and a huge black stock, under-waistcoats, and then more under-waistcoats, and *then nothing.*"—*Thackeray.*

dinner on Sunday, is a baseness; but parched corn and a house with one apartment, that I may be free of all perturbations of mind, that I may be serene and docile to what God shall speak, and girt and ready for the lowest mission of knowledge or good will, is frugality for gods and heroes." True freedom requires that we should be unshackled in our bodily powers, in our affections, in our understanding, in our reason and will, that the highest powers and influences of our nature may have full play; and depend upon it we are in the wrong path for this, and we have become slaves to the very worst kind of "necessity,"—to the hardest of all task-masters—conventionalism. Like Gulliver, the Lilliputians have tied us down with innumerable small strings, and if we make any effort to free ourselves, they let fly a perfect shower of their tiny arrows upon us.

What we have to seek is not wealth, and the bondage it confers, but the True, the Good, and the Beautiful. The present slaving after wealth is but selling our souls to the devil for what is *falsely* considered worldly prosperity. "All these things will I give you, if you will fall down and worship me," and how many unconsciously do so, until every high and noble and true human feeling is gradually obliterated in the all-engrossing and all-absorbing pursuit! Truly "how hardly shall they that have riches enter into the kingdom of heaven." *Exclusive* attention to business or money-making, or to any passion or sensual pursuit, absorbs all the nervous "force;" and it is difficult, if not impossible, to revive the æsthetic and more refined susceptibilities when this has been long continued. Considering the sustained attention that the daily calling requires in the great majority, to maintain the due balance is almost impossible; still a complete character developed on all sides is what we have to aim at. The too great predominance of the æsthetic would unfit us for the commoner and coarser duties of life : and yet constant activity, steady, habitual, persevering occupation in the path of duty,* is the secret of happiness. We all desire success, and that is dependent upon strenuous effort, and effort upon mental training. No kind of excellence is easy of attainment. Then—

> " Into life's goblet freely press,
> The leaves that give it bitterness;

and let us not forget in this conduct of ourselves, that "There are no birds in last year's nests." We have our Spring, Summer, Autumn, and Winter, and when we have arrived at the Autumn

---

* "We are made up of activities nine parts and passivities one—being capable of only one part in pleasure to nine parts in duty ; and unless we prey upon something external, internal cravings will prey upon us. In other words, the satisfaction of active and benevolent exertions is almost inexhaustible ; whereas pleasures cloy, and by repetition souring, turn to pain. Labour is the doom of all. You may avoid the manual, but you increase the mental. You may avoid the burden of the shoulders, but you increase the burden of the heart and spirits."—Elkerton Rectory," by the Rev. James Pycroft, p. 415.

or Winter of life, we cannot go back to Spring or Summer, as too many fondly hope to do who spend all their early life in making a fortune; putting off the enjoyment of it till their old age. They find too late that the tastes and pursuits that belonged to their youth cannot be renewed.

The faculties have each a distinct and diverse action upon the body and health. The predominant action of the moral and æsthetic feelings produces an internal sunshine which adverse circumstances can scarcely cloud:—

> "What nothing earthly gives, or can destroy,
> The soul's calm sunshine and the heartfelt joy,"

is the immediate result. It:—

> "Lays the rough path of peevish nature even;
> And opens in each heart a little heaven."

As our feelings increase in strength with exercise' this state ought to become habitual as we grow in years, replacing the more active pleasures of youth. On the other hand, the objects of the propensities fail as we grow older, and if we have trusted to them, we have the full sense that "all is vanity and vexation of spirit." The abuse of the propensities, or these feelings in excess, constitute envy, hatred, malice, jealousy, anger, fear; and all act injuriously on the human system. Pale with fear, sick with love, bowels of compassion, &c., are no metaphors, but indicate the different ways in which the body is affected. It is better not to "bottle up" such feelings, but to let them off as harmlessly as possible; as the Apostle says, "Be ye angry and sin not." We should discharge our anger and grief in talk or muscular exercise, or else they cloud the mind and keep out mental sunshine for hours. As Jean Paul Richter says, "for a little indignation, 'The devil!' or 'All the devils!' is sufficient; but for the splenetic fever of anger, I would prescribe, 'Satan and his hellish grandmother!' and go on increasing the power of the remedy by the addition of a little 'thunder' and 'blasting.' since the healing power of the electric fluid is so well known."

Each feeling or set of feelings has its natural term of greatest activity,—the propensities in early life, the sentiments at its close. Thus it has been beautifully said, "Love is the shadow of the morning, which decreases as the day advances: friendship on the contrary, is the shadow of the evening, which strengthens with the setting sun of life." With respect to the sentiment of love which moralists so much exalt, to the exclusion almost of all others, we must not forget that we are as much called upon to hate the evil as to love the good, and that probably the former feeling played the more useful part in the earlier ages of the world; and also we must not forget that love, hate, faith, belief, are no more voluntary than the toothache is; they are not therefore the proper subjects of command. We cannot love that which appears hateful, or hate that which appears loveable, or believe that which appears incredible. We are commanded to love God and our neighbour, but we cannot love God if his character is drawn only to excite fear, nor our neighbour from a sense of duty. He must be loveable if we are to love him. "A mere revulsion from that which is wrong would never make a fine people; and the scarecrow method of frightening folks from sin is in every way below the natural method of making them love goodness and virtue."*

Happiness is about equally dependent upon our own selves and external circumstances, and attends the legitimate exercise of every mental function. Our true interest then is to maintain the due balance between them, and to keep all our faculties in exercise with as little labour and trouble as possible. If we duly cultivate the subjective elements of our nature, we may well do without the costly objective, for our surroundings are felt according to the qualities which *we*, not they, possess, and the most essential elements of happiness, like air and water and sunshine, are God's free gifts. We may be satisfied with less than "society" at present considers a *respectable* position; we could do even without "society" itself by the aid of daily intercourse in our libraries with the great and good of all past ages. We must learn to look up to worth rather than to wealth, and to choose our acquaintance and friends from their

* Slack's "Philosophy of Progress in Human Affairs," p. 197.

talent and refinement and sympathy with our higher qualities, and not for their mere social status. In fact, we must emancipate ourselves from the slavery of conventionalism, and we may then begin to live a really honest life, in harmony with the circumstances requisite for the development and exercise of our best feelings. In this alone is true freedom, this alone would give us power "to think or not to think, to move or not to move, according to the preference or direction of our own mind:" and as mind is manifested only under certain conditions of body, we must secure as much as may be the perfection of the instrument, and keep it tuned in harmony to itself and all things around us; we must keep it out of the sphere of little troubles, and engaged as much as possible on great, or at least, unselfish objects,—if only in the search for one single truth, and in making it a little more bright for the world's cognizance—so that not a string shall jar discordantly, and then—

> " The meanest floweret of the vale,
> The simplest note that swells the gale,
> The common sun, the air, the skies,
> To us are opening Paradise."

We must not conclude without considering what bearing the principles we have laid down and applied to our knowledge of man, have also on our knowledge of God—to Deism or Theism. It is impossible to accept contradictions, such as the doctrines of Necessity and Free-will, or the doctrine that God is all in all, and man and nature something besides. Neither is it necessary that such contradictions should be held, except to retain ancient superstitions in Ethics and Theology, which fall to the ground immediately we dare to be true to ourselves and to the supreme reason given us for our guidance. We have previously seen, then, that

" Nothing comes to pass without a cause. What is self-existent, must be from Eternity, and must be unchangeable ; but as to all things that *begin to be*, they are not self-existent, and therefore must have some foundation of their existence without themselves."

" Force can neither come into existence nor cease to exist. Each manifestation of force can be interpreted only as the effect of some antecedent force ; no matter whether it be an inorganic action, or animal movement, a thought, or a feeling. Either this must be conceded, or else it must be asserted that our successive states of consciousness are self-created."

" When we view the world as one universal effect, we are at once led to the contemplation of a Universal Divine Agency. Does not the infinite act on every atom ? * * God never delegates His power : He cannot transfer divinity to a substance : there is no power therefore separated from Himself."

The Great First Cause must, therefore, be equally the Great Last Cause of all things—the only real and efficient power in the universe. To be logically consistent, we must come to the conviction that God does everything or nothing. There is no such thing as Nature and God — all is God. Individuality, or anything separate from Him, is a mode of thought, and has no real existence ; and this conclusion that man is nothing, —God is all—is no new doctrince, only it has never been logically and consistently carried out.

"Those modes of the Unknowable which we call motion, heat, light, chemical affinity, &c., are alike transformable into each other, and into those modes of the Unknowable which we distinguish as sensation, emotion, thought ; these, in their turns, being directly or indirectly re-transformable into the original shapes." And " these as they change, are but the varied God."

"All these effects, which we commonly say are the effects of the natural powers of matter and laws of motion, of gravitation, attraction, and the like, are indeed (if we speak strictly and properly), the effects of God acting upon matter continually and every moment.' *

"He is the universal Being, of which all things are the manifestations. Every thing is a mode of God's attribute of extension ; every thought, wish, or feeling, is a mode of His attribute of Thought." The whole sensitive existence is but " the innumerable individual eyes with which the Infinite

* Dr. Samuel Clarke's Works, vol. 2, p. 698, folio.

World Spirit beholds Himself." In the constancy of what we call the laws of nature, we satisfy ourselves with second causes, and cease to recognize their all-sustaining source. What we call the qualities or properties of matter, are mere force or power, and the existence of matter itself is assumed on the supposition that there must be something to which those qualities pertain or belong; but we may do without this assumption altogether, if the above view be correct, for the qualities are qualities not of matter, but of God. What we call "ultimate atoms," and their extraordinary tendencies, may as well be mere laws of force as of matter. There cannot be God *and* matter, for that which is Infinite can have no limitation;—we cannot bound or limit the infinite by anything without or beyond itself; God *must* be all in all. No doubt we shall be accused in this work of materialistic tendencies, and yet we find no room for matter at all: its existence is a mere hypothesis which we can do as well without, as it is not at all a necessary link in the chain of sequences. We find only force or power, and that not separate from its source, or from God. The only *reality* we find underlying all things is the Great Unknown.

> " There lives and works
> A soul in all things, and that soul is God."—COWPER.

The world is created within our own minds. The starry heavens, the blue canopy, the boundless ocean, the beauties of sunshine and of the green earth, are the result of some unknown cause without us, which we call matter, but it is thus that God mirrors Himself within us—a much more perfect representation than any which man creates after his own image.

We thus regard the universe as the "manifestation of some transcendent life, to which our separate individual life is related;" and as with it we have been from Eternity, to Eternity we must remain. From God we came, and when the prism of our present individuality is broken, to God we must return. Our senses give us but a glimpse of that "vast chain of being which with God began." Philosophers tell us that in what appears solid, inert matter to us, the ultimate atoms are separate from each other, and revolve in constant motion round a centre, like our solar system, and it was Sir Isaac Newton's opinion that the solar universe might present, to some sense, an appearance like that which solids present to us, for that the distances of the stars from each other are probably not greater in proportion than the atoms of what we call solid matter. As far as we can trace it, the same law, the same force, pervades the whole: the universe is one: from an atom to a world.

> "To Him no high, no low, no great no small." ·

The differences that *we* make in that respect are purely subjective, the result entirely of our own form of intelligence. It is true we have nothing before us but individual phenomena; "but examine all these individual phenomena, and you will find that each one exists only as a part of some whole; you will find that the whole is as necessary to the parts, as the parts to the whole; and it is this unity that brings us to the great truth,—that a Divine Idea lies at the origin of all things." *

"The true doctrine of Omnipresence is," as Emerson says, "that God re-appears in all His parts in every moss and cobweb : thus the universe is alive. Everything in nature contains all the powers of nature." All the phenomena of the universe have also their counterpart in man's organization. As the ancients held, "he is microcosmos, an abstract or model of the world." We have the most varied mechanical, and the most delicate chemical action, incessant circulating fluids, life, sense, and feeling ; and thought governing the whole, like the Great Soul of Nature. Thus did God make man in His own image, for it is as impossible to disconnect God from the material living universe, as it is to disconnect the soul from the material living body. All we see is but the vesture of God, and what we call laws of mature are attributes of Deity.

And now it may be asked, are we to rest here ? What of Religion ? And it would appear that the

* Thorndale, p. 416.

principles laid down do not tend to separate us from Him, but rather to bring Him nearer to us; for "we are indeed the offspring of God,"—direct and immediate, and inseparable from Him. "In Him only do we live, and move, and have our being," and "we feel within ourselves His energy divine." We cannot speak too modestly where—the order of nature being all we can know, we must feel at every step beyond our depth, and where the most we can say is that this or that view appears to us the more probable. It is true we have little sympathy with that phase of Christianity which expresses itself in the cry of "Save your souls; each man his own dirty soul for himself," which Kingsley says is the cry of modern Christendom; or with the childish anthropomorphic view by which man creates God, instead of God man—making a sort of Jupiter Tonans in human lineaments, and invested with human passions; but we feel ourselves a part

> " Of that stupendous whole,
> Whose body nature is, and God the Soul."

But where so great a mystery remains still unveiled, we feel that the Poets are the best theologians, and best express our creed. Accordingly we say with them :—

> " I cannot go
> Where universal love not smiles around—
> Sustaining all yon orbs, and all their suns ;
> From seeming evil still educing good,
> And better thence again, and better still,
> In infinite progression."—THOMSON.

"What prodigies can power divine perform,
More grand than it produces every year,
And all in sight of inattentive man ?
Familiar with the effect, we slight the cause ;
And in the constancy of nature's course,
And regular return of genial months,
And renovation of a faded world ;
See nought to wonder at. * *
All we behold is miracle ; but seen
So duly, all is miracle in vain. * *
From dearth to plenty, and from death to life,
Is Nature's progress when she lectures man
In heavenly truth ; evincing, as she makes
The grand transition, that there lives and works
A soul in all things, and that soul is God.
The beauties of the wilderness are His
That make so gay the solitary place
Where no eye sees them. And the fairer forms,
That cultivation glories in, are His.
He sets the bright procession on its way,
And marshals all the order of the year ;
He marks the bounds which Winter may not pass,
And blunts his pointed fury ; in its case,
Russet and rude, folds up the tender germ,
Uninjured, with inimitable art ;
And ere one flowery season fades and dies,
Designs the blooming wonders of the next."

COWPER—Task : 6th Book.

"Cease, then, nor order, imperfection name :
Our proper bliss depends on what we blame.
SUBMIT.—In this or any other sphere,
Secure to be as blest as thou canst bear :
SAFE in the hand of one disposing Pow'r,
Or in the natal, or the mortal hour.
All nature is but art, unknown to thee ;
All chance, direction, which thou canst not see ;
All discord, harmony, not understood ;
All partial evil, universal good."—POPE.

APPENDIX.

APPENDIX.

THE following portion of the original work, which formed a third section on "Social Science," is here reproduced on account both of its historical interest and of its practical application of the foregoing principles to important social problems.

ON THE PRESENT CONDITION OF SOCIETY. We have examined the Constitution of Man, and the laws of his Physical, Moral, and Intellectual Being: and we have observed that the laws of Mind are equally fixed with those of Matter.

Morality we have defined to be the science which teaches men the means by which they may live together in the most happy manner possible, the fundamental moral law being the production of the largest sum of enjoyment to all; and we have shown that man must necessarily obey such laws, when he discovers the connexion between them and his own well-being, as it is the law of his existence to follow that which will produce the greatest happiness.

The province of Moral Science is thus to teach us what our duties are, and it is the province of Social Science to place us in circumstances that will best enable us to perform them.

We have first, therefore, to examine the present condition of Society, in order to ascertain how far it is in accordance with those principles which have been shown to be essential to the production of the greatest amount of happiness. As the working Classes are by far the most numerous part of the population in all countries, their condition must constitute the principal object of regard. Hitherto the Working Classes have seldom been viewed in so important a light; they have been looked upon (too much by Political Economists, and their Rulers), as means only to the production of the largest amount of wealth, not as means to the largest amount of happiness. Political Economy is without a moral sense; it has no conscience, and its calculations are based upon the supposition that each man as necessarily seeks his own individual interest as that a stone falls to the ground; but Trade Unions and Co-operative Societies show that the Working Classes are gradually coming to the conviction that there is a higher law, which will not allow us to pursue our interests separately, and which makes it imperative that we should do as we would be done by, and seek the good of our neighbour *as well* as our own. When this conviction becomes general Political Economy will require to be re-written. Athens, in the time of Pericles, contained 30,000 free citizens and 400,000 slaves : what these slaves were to the free state of antiquity, have the working classes been to us; for necessity has been, and is now, a harder taskmaster than any mere instrument of human tyranny. But the time for their emancipation must come, when the steam-engine shall take the place of the slaves, and do the drudgery of Society, and when all the higher and nobler parts of their nature, that peculiarly distinguish them as men, shall have full scope, and they shall no longer be regarded as the mere hewers of wood and drawers of water.

DENSITY OF THE POPULATION. With a single exception, England is the most densely peopled country in Europe. On good authority we have—

	Area.			
England	... 50,153	 16,921,880	= 337 persons to 1 sq. mile.	
Wales,	... 8,167	 1,005,721	= 123	,, ,,
Islands in British Seas	394	 143,126	= 363	,, ,,
Scotland	.. 31,324	 2,888,742	— 92	,, ,,
Ireland	32,512	 6,515,794	= 200	,, ,,

Without going minutely into detail with other countries, we learn that Belgium has 382 inhabitants to the square mile ; Saxony 328 ; Holland 242 ; Italy 208 ; Germany and Prussia 188 ; France 171 ; Austria 145 ; all Europe 82 ; Spain 81 ; Turkey 71 ; Russia 27 ; Norway and Sweden 16.

NUMBERS.—In absolute numbers, the population of Great Britain and the islands in the British seas, was on the 31st March, 1851, 21,121,967 ; and of the United Kingdoms 27,637,761. As to the rate of growth, it has been calculated that the population of the same countries was, in—

1651	... ...	6,378,000
1751	...	7,392,000 = 1,014,000 increase in the century.
1851	...	21,185,000 =13,793,000 ,, ,,

The course of events, during the last fifty years, is well worthy of attention. The numbers of the people were, in—

1801	 10,917,433	1831	16,564,138
1811	 12,424,122	1841	18,813,786
1821	 14,402,643	1851	21,121,867

Thus, within the half century there has been an addition of ten millions of people, which nearly equals the produce of the preceding eighteen centuries.

Between 1841 and 1851, 27 counties in England and Wales showed sensible diminution, which extended itself more or less over the greater part of Ireland, the north of Scotland, the north of Wales, and the west of England.*

"Above a third of the population of England and Wales resided in 1851, in towns, having a population of 20,000 and upwards. In 1851, the Population of towns in Great Britain, was 10,556,388. In the villages and detached dwellings in the country, 10,403,109. In England and Wales there were 5.5 individuals to a house; while in the great towns there were 6·5, and in the Metropolis there were nearly 8 individuals to every house."—M'Culloch.

WEALTH. Sir Archibald Alison, in his Principles of Population, vol. 2, p. 48, tells us that "the returns of the Income Tax, in 1812, showed in Great Britain

127,000	persons with an income from			£50	to	£200
20,000	,,	,,	,,		£200	to £1,000
3,000	,,	,,	,,		£1,000	to £5,000
600	,,	,,	above £5,000;			

152,600 persons in all, possessing an income of above £50 a year; or 60,000 souls dependent upon persons in that situation. To so small a number is the immense wealth of Britain confined." The number is now, he says, greatly increased, but probably does not exceed 300,000. On the other hand, there are 3,440,000 heads of families, and 16,800,000 persons, living on their daily labour. "These facts," says Sir Archibald, "are deserving the most serious consideration. They indicate a state of society which is, to say the least, extremely alarming, and which, in ancient times, would have been the sure forerunner of national decline."

* For the above facts, and for several others in this section, we are indebted to a paper by Jno. Gates, Esq., F.R.G.S., read before the British Association, "on our National Strength," and published in the Journal of the Statistical Society, December, 1855.

Mr. McCulloch estimates the whole income of the Kingdom at £370,000,000.

With reference to the mode in which the Annual Income is distributed, from the best sources of information at my command I come to the conclusion that one-seventh of the population take rather more than three-fifths, that one-third take two-thirds, and that thus for the use of land, machinery, capital, for superintendence and liberty to work, for distribution and protection, the working man gives eight hours' labour out of every twelve. He appears to give to the land-owner and capitalist half or six hours; to the retailer one hour, and to Government one; that is supposing he pays half the taxes—Government expenses being about one-sixth of the whole annual income. I presume the annual income of the Kingdom and the annual produce mean the same thing; and that for all we receive from abroad we give an equivalent in our produce in exchange. Commerce, then, merely means exchange, and exchange, although it facilitates production, really adds nothing to it; neither does trade, which is distribution. The actual producers bear a smaller proportion to the whole population of the Kingdom than is generally supposed, although the actual number as shown by the last census (1861) is not yet at my command.

" The wealth of England has been estimated, but it must only be taken as an approximation to the true amount. The value of the cultivated soil, that is, the labour and wealth that is in the soil, is estimated at £1,700,000,000; mines, at £120,000,000; roads, canals, and other means of communication, at £500,000,000; dwellings, factories, and kindred erections, at £550,000,000; annual agricultural produce in land, the surplus of former years, and agricultural implements,

at £230,000,000 ; horses, cattle, sheep, and other live
stock, at £242,000,000 ; manufactured goods, new and
in use, at £200,000,000 ; mercantile shipping, at
£40,000,000 ; foreign merchandize paid for, at
£50,000,000 ; fisheries, foreign and domestic, at
£5,000,000 ; being a total of nearly £3,700,000,000.
Now this is a sum of which few persons understand the
extent. But suppose it was before us in sovereigns, and
that we could count twenty in a minute for twelve
hours in the day, it would take about 800 years to get
through them. This immense sum, however, does not
include the coin which is in circulation in the British
Isles. The gold and silver is nearly £40,000,000,
besides copper, bank notes, bills, and other mediums of
circulation. The gold, also, which is in the coffers of
the Bank of England is not included. The amount of
this fluctuates, but it is seldom less than £15,000,000.
Now this £40,000,000 of gold and silver, which is in
actual circulation, and the £15,000,000 in the Bank of
England, and other sums similarly situated, will amount
to nearly £60,000,000 more. Here, then, we have a
realized capital of £3,760,000,000 of ˈproductive property in the British Isles. This amazing sum is all at
work in the three kingdoms, and forms our capital in
trade. But besides this, we have an enormous sum in
what may be called unproductive property. This may
be enumerated as follows :—Waste land, public build-
ings, churches, chapels, hospitals, prisons, arsenals, forts,
military stores, dockyards, ships of war, &c. All this is
estimated at being equal to the national debt, about 750
millions. It may, therefore, be said that, notwithstanding our enormous debt, which we must remember is not
owing to foreigners, but to Englishmen, we have the
entire of our productive capital of three billions seven

hundred and sixty millions clear, independently of what other nations owe to us. Now this large sum, which represents everything that is useful and agreeable, and which affords subsistence and comfort to twenty-eight millions of people, is the result of labour. In other words, it is the difference between a desolate country, such as this once was, and its present condition. What mine, therefore, was ever so rich in gold, as the mine of industry? England has maintained all her inhabitants, supported all her wars, repaired all her disasters, and, after all, has a clear property of £3,760,000,000 in hand, or £134 sterling per head for every man, woman, and child, in the three kingdoms, besides her foreign property. It is also supposed that Great Britain and Ireland are saving, upon an average, about £60,000,000 every year."

OCCUPATIONS. With regard to the occupations in Great Britain, and number of Persons engaged in them, from the Census in 1851, some curiosities occur. The milliners and dress-makers, for one sex only we may presume, nearly equal the boot and shoemakers for both sexes. In time of peace the carpenters and joiners outnumbered the forces both by land and sea. The tailors outnumbered the butchers, bakers, and brewers, taken collectively. The laundresses nearly equal the tailors, and, according to Dr. Lyon Playfair, the washerwoman's interest in a dozen shirts amounts to £7 16s., or more than double that of the producer, the cotton-spinner, and the shirt-maker. Messengers, porters, and errand-boys are 101,425. For every inn-keeper, licensed victualler, or beershop-keeper, there seems to be a poor seamstress or shirt-maker. The coopers are rather more than the clock and watch-makers (20,245 and 19,159.) Medical men and their assistants are 18,728. The brewers are

18,620. The clergy of the Established Church 18,587. The police 18,348, Lawyers 16,763. The druggists and the surgeons differ little in numbers, but there are rather more drug-vendors than milk-sellers.

HEALTH. The *mean* lifetime, or the average number of years that males live, in England, is rather more than 40 years   Hence the majority of us live only about two-fifths of the years others attain to, (100) or, may we not rightly say, three-fifths of our appointed time?   The average duration of life is 45 years in Surrey, but 25 only in Manchester and Liverpool. Thus, one individual in the former place is equal nearly to two in either of the latter.

Great as is our infant mortality and sickness, yet the proportion of children constantly ill is not by one-third so great as it was a century ago.

" Relative vigour will not increase in the same ratio as population, in consequence of sickly children reared.

"There are on an average 2·5 years of sickness to every death, or, 2·5 persons constantly ill, to one annual death : and in a population of 17,000,000 in 1846, there must have been about 744,600 persons down with sickness : one million and a quarter in the United Kingdom. The mortality in the Metropolitan Workhouses, was 29·1 per 1,000 ; in the country, 18 per 1,000.

Mr. Cowper, in his defence of the General Board of Health, in Parliament, said, " he had a list of 45 towns in which sanitary works had been completed, and it appeared from that list that there was a great decrease in the rate of mortality, since the completion of those sanitary works. In Coventry, the mortality had fallen from 27 to 24 per thousand ; in Darlington, from 28 in

1852, to 23 ; in Derby, from 28 to 23 ; in Swansea, from ?2 to 19 ; and so on. The Registrar General, in his Report, said that the effects of the sanitary measures which had been recently taken were beginning to be apparent, and that the mortality in 1,000 had fallen from the average of 23, in the ten years between 1846 and 1855, to 21 in 1856."

" The physiological changes in the human body intimate that it was framed to continue in healthy action for 70 or 80 years : yet owing to hereditary weakness, or a vicious tendency, and the imperfect adaptation of parts of the external world to its organization, a certain number of every generation fall sick, and of these a certain number die at all ages ; in such a ratio, however, that from birth to the age of puberty, the sickness and mortality decline ; while from puberty they increase slowly, in a geometrical progression, up to the 50th or 60th year, and then more rapidly to the end.

According to Mr. McCulloch, the 'average mortality of the Kingdom in six years, ending 1846, is 1 in 46.

Dr. Farr calculates that there are, every year, over 100,000 premature or avoidable deaths in England, and more than 1,000,000 persons who suffer from serious illness, also the direct result of neglecting the laws of health. In the extra-metropolitan portion of Surrey, less than 18 persons in 1,000 die annually, while in certain manufacturing districts, the death rate is twice as high, or about 36 in 1,000 ; and throughout the whole of England, it is now, on an average, 22 in 1,000. In comparing the districts in which the death-rate is low with those in which it is high, some particular form of disease has been found to characterize the latter. In certain districts in England six times more people die from disease of the lungs than in others, owing principally to want of proper ventilation, and to the action of certain work and manufactures upon the lungs. In many cases, now, this has been partially remedied, nevertheless, "Phthisis, or consumption, is the greatest, the most constant, and the most dreadful of the diseases that afflict mankind, and is the cause of nearly half the deaths between the ages of 15 and 35" The total number of deaths registered in the year 1857, under this head, was 50,106; if we add to these the deaths from all other diseases of the lungs, the number amounts to 124,082, or 30 per cent. of the whole number of deaths. This fearful mortality from one disease Mr. Porter ascribes to the following causes:—

1. The unhealthy nature of certain employments.

2. The bad arrangements, as respects ventilation, in manufactures and works of all kinds in which large bodies of the labouring classes are employed.

3. The quantity of drink taken by this class of people.

4. The apathy shown to the position in which they are placed as to sanitary matters, and the prejudices on the part of the operatives generally against all suggestions for the removal of the causes of the evils that injure them, in many conditions of life, particularly in the case of printers, millers, stonemasons, and persons employed in the manufacture of metals.

5. The defective sanitary arrangements as regards the Army.

6. The propagation of the disease by the marriage of those hereditarily affected with phthisis.

Compositors we are told frequently fall victims to phthisis at the early age of 30, and probably 40 would be too high a mean age to assign to them as a body.

Dr. Knight, of Sheffield, has shown that the grinding

and polishing of steel causes phthisis in an unusually short period ; and that out of 250 workmen engaged in the occupation of polishing steel, 154 suffered from affections of the chest; and that there was no case of a person engaged in polishing forks reaching his 36th year, —magnets, wire masks, currents of air, and moisture, having been successively tried for the purpose of arresting the passage of the metallic particles to the lungs, but without diminishing the mortality.

To give an idea of the excessive mortality among the operatives employed in the Sheffield grinding trade, I may mention that, in the fork-grinding branch—which is stated to be the most destructive—Dr. Holland found that, out of 1,000 deaths occurring among persons between the ages of 20 and 30, while the proportion in England and Wales was 160, among the Sheffield fork-grinders it was 475. In the next decade of ages, 30 to 40, a similar disparity was observed, the proportion in England and Wales being 136, among the fork-grinders 410. The mortality in this branch of the trade was, therefore, very nearly three times as great as that among the general population of the country ; the death-rate from pulmonary affections, per 100,000 males, being, for England and Wales, 569, while for Sheffield it was as high as 839, and nearly the same for Birmingham, viz., 838.

The Registrar seems to consider that the great mortality among butchers may be owing to the decaying matter by which they are surrounded in the slaughter-house and its vicinity. About this, however, there seems some difference of opinion. The Registrar observes that the red injected face of the butcher is an indication of disease—to the ordinary observer this

W

might be an indication of robust health. Similarly with respect to brewers' draymen; their appearance would indicate that they were blessed with strong constitutions; this is not, however, the case.

The workmen employed in flour mills are grievous sufferers from a spasmodic affection of the lungs, caused by the inhalation of minute particles of dust with which the atmosphere of most flour mills, as usually constructed, is impregnated.

Hugh Miller, himself originally, I believe, a stone-mason, states that few of the Edinburgh stone-cutters pass their 40th year unscathed, and not one out of every 50 ever reach their 45th year. It is considered, however, that there is scarcely any employment where proper precaution would not very much reduce the present evil consequences, and that ignorance greatly increases the excessive mortality. From the 20th Report, published in 1857, it appears that the number of persons signing the marriage register with marks was no less than 105,778—the proportions per cent. being of the men 72, and of the women 61 only, who were able to write their names. The percentage has doubtless greatly increased during the last five years still the ignorance was dense enough to make Mr. Close, the Dean of Carlisle, declare that, in his opinion, the education of the children of the working classes should be made compulsory. He says, "slowly and reluctantly, and after struggling against this necessity for nearly 40 years, I am an absolute convert to this necessity." This opinion has doubtless long been shared by many other sensible men.

Mr. Porter says, however, "Notwithstanding the evident unnecessary sacrifice of life in this country, there is no doubt that a gradual progressive increase in the mean duration of life has been maintained for some centuries past—with one exception, the 17th century—but it is probably only within our own time that any considerable increase in the longevity of the mass of the population will be apparent; and this will be owing as well to the improved habits of life of the people as to the reform in sanitary matters—to the improvements in the dwellings of the labouring classes —the greater atten-tion that is now being paid to drainage—the abolition of intramural interment—the establishment of baths and wash-houses—to the shorter hours of labour that are becoming daily more general, owing in a great measure to the exertions of the " Early Closing Association,"—to the establishment of national play-grounds, and the encouragement to indulge in manly exercises, of which the shorter hours of labour now more readily admit— and to the greater care that is now devoted generally to the promotion of the well-being of that large section of the community which the labouring classes form.

GENERAL CONDITION OF THE WORKING CLASSES. M'Culloch says that "the labouring classes have been the principal gainers by the improvements in the arts and sciences, as well by the large numbers of them who have succeeded in advancing themselves to a superior station, as by the extraordinary additional comforts that now fall to the share even of the poorest families." That they have been large gainers there can be no doubt, and that the poor can now obtain many things that were considered, fifty years since, as luxuries, even by the rich, and which even kings could not two centuries ago command, cannot be denied ; still the classes above them have undoubtedly had the largest share of the enormous wealth that has been created in England from the commencement of the century. The condition of the

working classes, however, has very much improved
during the last twenty years, since the publication of the
first edition of this work, and a higher standard of
living and comfort has been permanently established
among a great many of them. They are better clothed,
fed, lodged, and have increased habits of providence and
forethought.

By the working classes I mean those who are
dependent upon wages, and the difference in their condition among themselves is as various almost as in the
classes above them. This depends principally upon the
nature of the occupation. Unskilled labour, and the
occupations that admit of the employment of women
and children, are the worst paid. Mr. J. S. Mill truly
says, " those trades are by far the worst paid in which
the wife and children of the artisan aid the work. The
income which the habits of the class demand, and down
to which they are almost sure to multiply, is made up,
in those trades, by the earnings of the whole family,
while in others the same income must be obtained by the
labour of the man alone. It is even probable that the
collective earnings will amount to a smaller sum than
those of the man alone in other trades; because the
prudential restraint on marriage is unusually weak when
the only consequence immediately felt is an improvement of circumstances, the joint earnings of the two
going further in their domestic economy after marriage
than before. Such accordingly is the fact in the case of
hand-loom weavers. In most kinds of weaving, women
can and do earn as much as men, and children may be
and are employed at a very early age; but the aggregate
earnings of a family are lower than almost any other
kind of industry, and the marriages earlier."

These facts are strikingly exemplified in Coventry,

where the population is divided between the Watch and Ribbon Trades. In the former women are not employed, and are generally to be found at home in attendance upon their families and husbands; children also are not employed, except as apprentices; in the latter women and children are both employed, and at a very early age. Both work in factories, but in the watch trade men only are employed; in the ribbon trade men, women, and children are indiscriminately mixed together. Early marriages are the rule, and young children are left at home in charge of a child or old woman, and a fearful infant mortality is the consequence.* If a girl of 14 or 15 disapproves of the conduct of her parents, from their not being sufficiently tolerant of the morals of the young gentleman with whom she keeps company, or from other causes, she will leave home and take lodgings, sometimes even next door. The 8s. to 12s. a·week which she earns makes her thus early independent. If it is the latter

---

* Speaking of these children Dr. Greenhow says, children left by their mothers during so great a part of the day are fed in their absence on artificial food, which is for the most part unsuited to their digestive powers. The children are thus almost entirely spoon fed, the mother being able to nurse them only at night and early in the morning. To remedy the illness caused by mismanagement, various domestic medicines are administered, more particularly some kind of opiate, such as Godfrey's Cordial, or laudanum. From a return procured by the Mayor, at Dr. Greenhow's request, it was ascertained that twelve retail druggists, in Coventry, sold at least ten gallons of Godfrey's Cordial weekly; equal to 12,000 doses. Coventry is probably no exception to other manufacturing towns. In what country does infanticide prevail to a greater extent than here, for I understand that half the children die before the age of 5 years? Think also of the weakened constiutions of the children who do survive! No wonder that our manufacturing population grow up feeble, sickly, and small in stature; there is enough in this cause alone to counteract all our improved sanitary arrangements, so that if we have an average longer life, we have a deteriorated race in the factory districts. The spread of hereditary constitutional diseases through cow-pox matter may also tend to this result in the country generally.

sum she earns, she will probably spend 8s. a-week in
board and lodging, and 4s. in dress and nightly
dissipation; if the former sum, the additional income
may perhaps be derived from some other source—not
always moral. But there is a great improvement going
on even in this class; for as the provident operative
soon becomes a small master, so the most respectable
weavers save, purchase their own machinery, leave the
factories, and bring up their families most respectably.

The Agricultural Labourers are put down at
1,460,896, and it is calculated that 26 per cent. of the
men and 8 of the women, twenty years of age and
upwards, with 8 per cent. of the boys and 3 per cent.
nearly of the girls, under twenty years of age, are
employed in agricultural pursuits. To these may be
added the 375,551 who call themselves labourers only.
Since the large influx of the Irish has ceased, and
emigration has been more systematically carried on, the
condition of this class has much improved, still we do
not hear that an able-bodied man gets more than 12s· 6d.
per week (except at harvest times), and not that all the
year round, as the days during which he is unemployed
must considerably reduce the annual average. National
Schools, the influence of the Clergy, Clubs, Clothing
Societies, &c., are acting very beneficially on this class,
and the children, at least, are growing up a different
race.

The most numerous class of operatives is that
employed in the manufacture of clothing of all sorts,
cotton, silk, ribbons, trimming, cloth, hose, linen, lace,
&c., and when the factory system and factory operatives
are spoken of, it is to this class the terms are usually
applied.

The Domestic Servants, as long as they continue

servants, are comparatively well off, as they are at least well lodged, clothed, and fed, and it is from this source the funds in the Savings' Banks are principally derived. Servants who marry, having been accustomed to the comforts and luxuries of the higher class, and not having been brought up to any trade, are frequently worse off than their fellow operatives.

The Builders would appear to constitute the flower of our working classes. As this calling requires both strength and skill, and women are not employed, it is the best paid of all, and a man, if he is steady, usually earns enough to keep his wife and home comfortable, and to educate his children. A man knows exactly what he can earn, and what therefore he has to depend upon, and he is more provident and thrifty than those whose " comings in " are attended with greater uncertainty.

It is the Agricultural Labourers and Factory Operatives whose condition appears to be much the worst. The following statements, descriptive of the condition of these classes principally, and of the effects of the incessant toil to which they are reduced, in the deterioration of the race in both bodily and mental constitution, were made by Dr. John Conolly, of Hanwell, in a course of lectures on Education, delivered at the Philosophical Institution, Birmingham, in the spring of 1839,* and their interest and value principally depend upon their being founded on personal experience, derived from long practice amongst the poor in both

---

* These lectures were never published, and I am considerably indebted to their author for having allowed me to use them so extensively. I have retained the account here given in my 2nd edition because, although undoubtedly great improvements have taken place both in factories and among the country labourers, yet too much of it is still true, and it shows the condition of things from which we started less than a quarter of a century ago.

town and country. The enlightened and philanthropic lecturer defined the end of Education to be the improving and perfecting of every human being, in every bodily and mental faculty ; and his object in the following quotations was to show the counteracting circumstances which make education in this sense quite unattainable by the mass of the people.

" The large manufactories of Lancashire, and some parts of Scotland, present a combination of the evils incidental to the condition of the working man, and on a large scale.

" Too early employment—too long employment—too much fatigue—no time for relaxation—no time for mental improvement, —no time for the care of health—exhaustion—intemperance— indifferent food—sickness—premature decay—a large mortality."

" There is every reason to believe the frame of body and mind of persons employed in manufactories, where they are on their feet all the day, in a heated atmosphere, and living on poor diet, becomes so feeble and irritable as to lead, as a matter of course, to intemperance and disorderly passions, and to an actual degeneration of the species ; so that the mortality becomes very great, and the sickly and imperfect state of a great proportion of the children who *are* reared, is such that a greater and greater deterioration in each generation is inevitable. The visitor to the large manufactories sees little of the misery they entail. The sick and feeble are at home ; in miserable houses or in cellars. Those who are present are interested by the coming of strangers, and their general appearance, it is only fair to state, bespeaks animation and pretty good health. The visitor sees them for half-an-hour, but he cannot forget that *as* he sees them—on their feet, and in continual, although not perhaps laborious exertion, they remain during the whole of every day except Sunday. For the consequences he must go to their homes ; he must inspect their food ; their lodging, accommodations ; he must observe what are their relaxations, and, if they can so be called, their pleasures. Still more—he must examine their children, and particularly when all the causes acting upon them have brought them into the public Charitable Institutions ; and then he will see what neglect and over-work can do for an industrious, and even an intelligent class of people.

"He will find these children, for the most part, not deficient in intelligence ; but also for the most part, *sickly*. The remarkable thing, indeed, if the poorest children are looked at, in the workhouses and asylums (the children of parents reduced to indigence, or gone to an early grave, entirely worn out)—the remarkable fact is, that there is an *universal* appearance of sickliness among them ; a healthy face and figure is an exception :—the spectator is surrounded with pale blue, flabby faces, inflamed eyes, diseases of the scalp.   Many little creatures sit over the fire, with faces of old people ; shrivelled, wasted, wretched objects, with slender limbs, a dry, harsh, loose, coarse skin ; large joints, prominent eyes and jaws :—these little creatures are cold and feeble and fretful, and utter plaintive cries like a suffering animal.   Ask the medical officers concerning these circumstances, and you will learn that the children are well fed, well lodged, well clothed, and allowed proper exercise in the open air, and the older children are instructed in a school. Education, physical and moral, is not neglected ; but it is working on materials too imperfect to be much improved.   The organization is frail and incomplete · the stock of life is barely sufficient for a few years.   If the children are attacked with acute illness, they can neither bear the disease nor the remedies : the loss of a little blood is fatal to them.   Chronic affections cling to them.   Curative processes cannot be set up.   The medicating power of Nature is not active in their frames.   The tissues of their bodies are all unfinished pieces of Nature's workmanship, and prone to disease : their hearts are feeble, and blood is not vigorously circulated, nay, it is not healthily elaborated in their bodies ; and the regulating nervous system is as faulty as the rest of their economy.   Herded together, without parental care, and the thousand little offices comforting to early childhood, their affections have a small range, and their countenances are blank and melancholy.   They are even the victims of diseases never seen amongst the comfortable classes of society.   Every common disorder leaves consequences not to be got rid of— measles and smallpox leaving opthalmia and blindness.

" All this is distressing, but not wonderful.   In many a region, misery and exposure produce a marked physical degeneration, and even create diseases scarcely known in other circumstances.

" It might lead me away from my immediate subject, if I were to state how often epidemics of all kinds prevail among the poor alone. Yet you cannot be too often reminded that as such diseases find a reception in miserable courts and alleys, and from thence spread over the more happily circumstanced families, *so also* the moral infirmities allowed to grow among any part of a population, spread their infectious influence all around. There is, however, another, and a very large portion of our community, whose state, although often boasted of, is not, in my opinion, more favourable to the preservation of *perfect* life of body and mind than that of the manufacturing poor. I mean the labouring poor of agricultural districts. What I say concerning these poor people is the result of much observation of them, and I consider it a duty to lift the veil from a subject surrounded by many respectable prejudices. I know that they are kindly visited and assisted by the wealthier classes living in the country, and charity waits upon them in every shape, in sickness, or for the education and clothing of their children. Indeed but for this charity—and often, but for the boundless charity of the clergyman alone—the people would be utterly lost. But their extreme poverty, and their constant labour, so influence them, that the majority—I am sure I speak within bounds—have never the enjoyment of health after forty years of age. A thousand times in the course of dispensary practice, I have felt the mockery of prescribing medicines for the various stomach complaints to which they are so liable, and which are the product of bad food—insufficient clothing—wearing toil—and the absence of all hope of anything better in this world."

" The peasant's home is not the abode of joy or even of comfort. No 'children run to lisp their sire's return, or climb his knees the envied kiss to share.' The children are felt to be a burden, ill-fed, ill-clothed, and lying on beds worse than the lower animals; they are ragged or clothed by charity; untaught or taught by charity; if sick, cured by charity; if not starved, fed by proud charity; of which they bear the marks in the fantastic uniformity of their dress, or in the prison-look imparted by the general order under which they live, that their clustering hair shall be cut close to their heads, lest they should grow up fond of admiration. Observe their look of humility, of discontent,—their abject curtseys. In such a habitation—in the poor-house—is it possible to apply Physical and Mental Education? Its very elements are repelled from such a place. Dulness of the mental faculties, obtuseness of the moral feelings, and sickly bodies, can alone be formed."

"In agricultural districts, boys are very early employed in the fields; and their minds become utterly vacant. The scenes in which they live have no charms for *them* They toil early and late in certain services; *never* live well; are condemned to poverty if they marry. For them also physical and mental education is quite out of the question.

"The girls are no better off—many of them work labouriously; and marry the poor labourers we have spoken of. Others become servants. Servants in underground or back kitchens—no out-of-door exercise—no friends—no followers—no visits to others—no mental or other variety—yet every virtue expected from them, and a good humour which not even the inconsideration and injustice and caprice of others can ruffle."

"In the case of the manufacturing labourer, the necessary poverty is, I presume, by no means so pressing; their wages are better; they buy provisions in towns, at better advantage; but their exhaustion from over work, and their living surrounded by temptations to sensual gratifications, and particularly to intemperance, conspire to make them as destitute as the agricultural labourer. The latter, excluded from many temptations, *never* receives enough to support a family : his food is just sufficient to prevent divorce of soul and body for the best years of his sad life; if sickness assail him or his children he has no hope but the poor-house; and after toiling until he is old, the yawning poor-house still awaits him. On the brink of that gulf he has ever been, and he sinks into it at last."

"I lately accompanied a friend over a large and well-conducted Union Workhouse in an agricultural district. The persons whom I saw there were of two kinds; aged and helpless men who had toiled with the certain prospect of pauperism before them all their lives long; and younger men, who appeared to be deficient in intellect. Of the women, several also were old and helpless; a few were young, and of these, several, I am inclined to think more than half, were idiotic. There were nurseries and schools for the boys and girls. In the nurseries I was shocked with the spectacle of little laughing idiots, the children of idiotic mothers; but in the older children, with a few exceptions so striking that

one felt surprised to see them there, the children presented
coarse features ; their heads were singularly low and broad, as if
they had a broad shallow brain ; and in several instances the
upper dimensions of the head were so evidently defective, that
no one could help observing it. Every physiologist, nay, every
ordinary observer, would say, of such a shaped head, that it was
associated with very small intellectual power ; and the figure of
the head, taken with the faculties and expression of the face,
was too manifestly such as every observer would say prophesied
ill for the future character of the individual. Great care might
possibly do much ; but when you consider these evils of birth,
and the unavoidable privations and neglect to which these human
beings must be exposed as they grow up, the *awful* consideration
presents itself that they are pre-doomed, from childhood—from
birth—*before* birth—to ignorance and helplessness, or to crime ;
to the lowest toil—to want—to premature death, or to pauperism
in age."

" As in the agricultural workhouse, we find the human brain
brought to a very low state of development, and the faculties of
the mind very limited, so in the manufacturing workhouse we
find the results of causes of degeneracy acting on a population
whose faculties are kept in greater activity, but whose bodies are
deteriorated, and whose offspring are prone to every evil that
belongs to an imperfect structure of every tissue of the body,
and to the imperfect action of the organs which circulate the
blood, or which elaborate the chyle, or which should renew and
repair the perpetual waste ; so that, even in them the brain cannot long continue healthy and efficient. If the children in the
agricultural workhouse were tken out and brought up ever so
carefully, I believe that a very small proportion of them would
exhibit a capacity of much mental improvement. If the children
in the manufacturing workhouse were separated, and brought up
in families where every article of diet and regimen was very
carefully attended to, many of them would be found incapable of
continued life beyond a few years. They might escape some of
the worst forms of disease which now carry them off in infancy,
but a considerable proportion would eventually perish of some
form or other of tubercular disease—consumption—or disease of
the mesenteric glands. With these, then, you see how limited
must be the effects of the best physical and moral education that
could be devised, even if it could be at once and in every case

applied. And so long as these classes remain in this state, disease and premature death, and many moral evils which disfigure life, *must* be perpetuated. Of both these classes of the poor a proportion will still live to be thirty or forty, and become, unhappily, the parents of children who will inherit their infirmities of mind and body, and their tendencies fo disease ; until, by the gradual augmentation of the evil, successive families are extinguished. Less time is required for their total extinction than is commonly supposed. Sir A. Carlisle says, that where the father and mother are both town-bred, the family ends with the third generation.

" My reason for dwelling on these points is, that I would fain show the mockery of expecting, by anything which philanthropy can devise, the production of mental power, or even of virtue, any more than of healthy bodies, in the children of a very considerable portion of all the most civilized communities of Europe, in their present condition ; and that until this condition is so modified that the human economy can be healthily exercised, no physical education—no general instruction—no scheme of benevolence—can train these children into healthy adults. *You cannot engraft virtue on physical misery.* To hope to plant Temperance, Forethought, Chastity, Content, in a soil where the body and soul are corrupting, where the materials of the body are advanced towards death, and incapable of the full actions of vitality, is the dream of benevolence. You must secure good food, clothing, lodging, and cheerful mental stimulus to *all* classes, before you can raise them above that condition in which they will be glad so forget their misery in any sensual gratification that offers. Until then, they must continue feeble and sickly, discontented and fretful, and prone to fly for consolation to stimulants ; and, becoming parents, their children will inherit their imperfections, some dying early, others living in such a state that at length, perhaps, the intolerable magnitude of the physical and moral evil may suggest a remedy, and the means of effecting that first object of education, the formation of a healthy and virtuous people.

" It seems scarcely credible that in an age which, compared with feudal days, appears civilized, thousands of children are every year born only to be the prey and victims of disease, of early death or public punishment ; their parents not able to support the life they have created, and the wretched progeny being consigned, one may almost say, before birth, to fill the hospitals and jails ; to be swept away by diseases from which all the comfortable classes are comparatively protected, or to linger out a wretched age in the poor-house. There is no physiologist who contemplating these things, can complacently conclude, that it is *not possible* to do something better for the health and life of *every* child that is born into the world.

" I anxiously wish to avoid being betrayed into exaggeration on these points ; and I would say, generally, that there are not many occupations which would be in themselves unwholesome, if it were not for the number of hours in which it is requisite for those to be employed who live by the labour of their hands, or even by the exercise of their minds, in business. The merchant's desk, the professional man's study, the author's library, the artist's studio, the manufactory, the shop, possess nothing deadly to mankind, if human beings are not in them too long at one time ; or too laboriously exercised whilst there, or not exposed to fatigue at too early an age. It seems a sad result for an honest and industrious house-painter, that his hands and feet should become paralyzed, and that he should be liable to attacks of excruciating pain and delirium. It would seem cruel to consign a youth to such a business. but with care and cleanliness these results are, generally speaking, avoidable ; and if time be allowed in which good air may be breathed ; the working clothes laid aside ; they may be altogether escaped. Scarcely any of the evils arising from trades and occupations are unavoidable in themselves. The circumstance, therefore, that constitutes the hardness of life of the working classes, is not so much the nature of their work ; for in this, and the muscular or mental exertion required for it, there is actual benefit to the health, and pleasure to the sensations, and recreation to the mind ; but it is the absorption of *life itself into labour*, so that the body and the mind are no longer educated. no longer heeded, when life's toil has fairly begun, and the health of both must be sacrificed, and men *must die to live.*

" It would occupy too much time to take even the most passing view of the poor of large cities *not* employed in manufactures. Dr. Bateman, who wrote so much and so well on the diseases of London, tells us, what we may well believe, that in hot weather their houses are so heated and ill-ventilated, as to produce a state of faintness, depression of spirits, langour, pains in the back and limbs resembling those from fatigue, a fluttering in the region of the stomach, vertigo, tremors, cold perspirations, and various symptoms of indigestion ; with a feeble pulse. Impure air, fatigue and anxiety, contribute, he says, to produce these effects ; which they chiefly do in woman. How these must influence the temper, affections, and habits, and how interfere with the proper care of their children's bodies and minds, I am sure you will readily imagine.

"Visit the same poor people in winter ; you will find every cranny closed, and fever carrying off its victims in great numbers.

"Often, very often doubtless, moral evils flow from hence to the better quarters-of the town, and poison the peace of happy families : often, very often, the infection of fevers there cherished, floats over the luxurious parts of the capital, and awakens the great and wealthy to the sense of the common lot of humanity.

"Nor can we from these evils ever be free until *all* receive the benefits of physical, and moral, and mental education, which they *cannot do* so long as they are steeped to the lips in poverty.

"You must give them—the poor citizen—the manufacturer— the agriculturist—*leisure* for instruction, and comforts which will prevent their being reckless ; and then, fear not that they will *refuse* to be comfortable. Then they will become provident, careful of their health, prudent as to marriages, temperate, content—in short, reflecting creatures, exercising that now dormant brain, that capability and God-like reason, which their good Creator gave them, not to rust in them unused.

"From the observations I have made, you will gather that I do not believe the world to be so constituted that a large portion of mankind must, from the very necessity of nature, be con- signed to constant poverty, ignorance, suffering, disease, vice, and premature death.

"I even confess, that I am shocked when I hear the sacred writings quoted with comfortable satisfaction over 'good men's feasts,' as affording assurance that there must ever be 'hewers of wood and drawers of water ;' for without at all denying the necessity of these services, I have never found any reason to believe that hewers of wood and drawers of water must, as a matter of course, be starved, and sickly, and vicious, and limited in this life to half of the allotted years of men. I fear we dishonour the Great unseen Father of all his creatures by suppositions of this kind; and wrest the words of Scripture to some purposes which He is far from approving.

"Valueless, indeed, in my opinion, would all our own advantages be, if we could still cherish the selfish belief that for us and for our children alone such gracious advantages were conferred.

"There is nothing in the structure and capacities of any portion of mankind to sustain the notion that the same Deity who endowed them with feelings, affections, appetites, sensations, and intellect:—the same Being who accorded to rich and poor alike the gifts of light and air, has still ordained, that to any one class, and for ever, are to be denied the power to enjoy, not mere physical life alone, exempt from many miseries now incidental to their share of it, but also those pleasures of contemplation and reflection, those upliftings of the mind to Him, and all that intellectual and spiritual life, which alone give mere physical life any solid value to us. Feeling, that for us the delights of existence are increased a thousand-fold by the possession of health and by opportunities of instruction, whereby are developed countless sources of pure and elevated enjoyment, we must not—we cannot—ungratefully turn round and say that, except for a small number, the blessings of good air, good food and clothing, immunity from epidemic diseases, leisure and freedom of heart, healthy and peaceful old age, and a disposition to seek after immortal good, are for ever and absolutely denied."

The condition of the people in other countries varies considerably from our own as their industrial system differs. It approaches neither extreme of either comparative wealth or poverty. It is much more equitable and much less stirring. The changes of condition are less fluctuating: there is little change from father to son; consequently, although there is less material comfort than in England, there is more forethought and providence. In Norway and Sweden, the peasantry live a great deal in the families of their employers, and cannot and do not marry until a house falls to them in the course of nature through the death of the previous occupier.   In Germany, people are prevented from marrying early by the necessity of serving for three years as soldiers, and in many States by law, until the persons wishing to marry can show a reasonable expectation of the means of subsistence for their offspring.

Von. W. H. Reihl tells us that many vicissitudes have lately changed the dull current of German peasant life, and that "many disintegrating forces have been at work on the peasant character, and degeneration is unhappily going on at a greater pace than development. In the wine districts especially, the inability of the small proprietor to bear up under the vicissitudes of the market, or to insure a high quality of wine by running the risks of a late vintage, and the competition of beer and cider with the inferior wines, have tended to introduce that uncertainty of gain which, with the peasant, is the inevitable cause of demoralization." With the German peasant he says "Custom holds the place of sentiment, of theory, and in many cases of affection." But he adds, "The more deeply we penetrate into the knowledge of society in its details, the more thoroughly shall we be convinced that a universal social polity has no validity except on paper, and can never be carried into successful practice. The conditions of German society are altogether different from those of French, of English, or of Italian society, and we cannot apply the same social theory to these nations indiscriminately."

In France, Mill tells us the peasant proprietors, of which, including their families, there are some 21 millions, know exactly what inheritance they have to leave their children; "the peasant knows that the law will divide it equally among them ; he sees the limit beyond which this division would make them descend from the rank which he has himself filled, and a just family pride, common to the peasant and to the nobleman, makes him abstain from summoning into life children for whom he cannot properly provide. If more are born, at least they do not marry, as they agree among themselves which of several brothers shall perpetuate the family."

In Switzerland, a similar prudential check prevails.

The working classes in America are generally very well off, as unskilled labour is much in demand, and, therefore, highly paid; but there is a great mass of squalid poverty in New York and other large cities of the Union, and the best of our working men and cleverest operatives who go out there often return. It is not the rate of wages, but what can be purchased with them, that is the criterion of well-being.

Of the mere material condition of the poor of other countries, however, Sir A. Alison says—

"It has been observed that the paupers of England are better fed than the labouring poor of the Continental States; it may be safely affirmed that, in every gradation of rank above the workhouse, the difference is still more remarkable. Mr. Young observes that 'the labouring classes in France are 76 per cent. worse clothed, fed, and lodged, than their brethren in this country; and it is a remarkable fact, that, with the increase of agricultural wealth in the former country since the Revolution, a corresponding change in the diet of the peasantry has taken place. Notwithstanding this change, however, it is calculated by the latest political writer in the two countries, that the quantity of butcher-meat, butter, and cheese consumed in Britain is 50 per cent. greater than in France. A comparison of the food of the poorer classes in Poland, where the peasantry live entirely on inferior grain, while their splendid harvests of wheat are transported untouched to the London market, with that which is consumed by the same classes in Sweden and Switzerland, where ages of comparative freedom have diffused opulence through the rural population; or of that daily in use among the Irish poor, with that which for ages has subsisted among the opulent yeomanry of England, is sufficient to demonstrate the truth of these observations.' "

" ' Traversing the country South of Moscow,' says Clarke, 'it is as the garden of Eden, a fine soil, covered with corn, and apparently smiling in plenty. Enter the cottage of the labourer, and you find him, though surrounded by these riches, often in want of the necessaries of life. Extensive pastures often furnish no milk to him ; in autumn the harvest affords no bread to his children ; every road is covered with caravans bringing the pro- duce of the soil to the lords of Petersburgh and Moscow, while the cultivators who raised it are in want of the necessaries of life.' "

In the rich and fertile plain of Lombardy, where three crops annually repay the labour of the husbandman, and the means of perpetual irrigation are afforded by the streams that descend from the adjoining mountains, want and indigence generally prevail among the peasantry. Inhabiting a country which abounds in wine, it is seldom they drink anything but water ; their clothing is scanty and wretched ; their dwellings destitute of all the comforts of life. On the public roads, in the villages, in the cities, the traveller is assailed by multitudes of beggars, whose squalid looks and urgent importunity attest but too strongly the abject distress to which they are reduced. On the mountains, as on the plains, he perceives the traces of a numerous population, and the benignity of the climate clothes the wooded slopes with innumerable villages, whose white walls and elegant spires give a peculiar charm to Italian landscape ; but within their walls he finds the well-known features of public misery, and the voice of distress supplicating for relief, in scenes which, at a distance, appear only to teem with human happiness."

" Provisions are incomparably cheaper in Poland and in Russia than in this country ; but are the Polish or Russian peasants half as comfortably fed, lodged, or clothed, as the corresponding classes in this country ? Every one knows that, so far from this being so, or obtaining any benefit whatever from the cheap price of provisions in their own country, they are in truth the most miserable labourers in Europe, and feed upon scanty meals of rye bread, in the midst of the splendid wheat crops, which they raise for the more opulent consumers in this country. In the Southern provinces of Russia, wheat is often only ten shillings a quarter, form the total want of any market. But what is the consequence ? Why, that wages are so low that the Cossack horseman gets only eight shillings and sixpence a year of pay from Government. Wheat and provisions of all sorts are much cheaper in Ireland than in Great Britain; but nevertheless, the Irish labourers do not enjoy one-half the comforts or necessaries of life which fall to the lot of their brethren on this side of the Channel."

"The mere necessaries of life are sold almost for nothing in Hindostan and China; but, so far from 'obtaining any benefit from that low rate of prices, the labouring classes are so poor as to taste hardly anything but rice and water; and wages are so low, seldom exceeding twopence a day, that every sepoy, foot-soldier, and horseman has two, and every native, three, attendants to wait upon his person."*

WAGES, AND THE LAWS WHICH REGULATE THEM.— Thus we see that the majority of the people in all countries, with differences dependent upon local situation, government, laws, and institutions, are everywhere the same—they are everywhere poor, ignorant, and over-worked; although a great improvement has taken place in their condition during the last quarter of a century.

We have seen that in this country the working man gives for the use of land, machinery, capital, for super-intendence and liberty to work, for distribution and protection, eight hours' labour out of every twelve.

Society, at least in this country, is divided into Capitalist and Labourer — into those who possess everything, and those who possess, comparatively, nothing. When the poor man comes into the world, he finds it already occupied; every part of it, except uncultivated regions inaccessible to him, is already appropriated. All the means by which labour is made available to production are private property, and all that is left to him is the strength of his body, the use of his limbs. His labour, therefore, is all that he has to

---

* Alison, vol. 1, pp. 202, 200, 435, 454; vol. 2, 419, 420.

exchánge for the means of subsistence, for lodging, food, and clothing; what he shall receive for it, will depend upon the bargain he shall be able to make with those who possess the means of setting him to work. This bárgain will be more or less in his favour as his labour may be more or less wanted. But should the capitalist have no need of labour, should he already have as many things as he wants, or as many for the time as he can profitably dispose of, he who has only labour to give in exchange for food, must stárve, or depend upon charity for support, although, if set to work, he could produce many times as much as he can consume.

No one would cultivate a field if another might reap what he had sown, and the fruits of the earth would scarcely be allowed to come to maturity, if no one were interested in preserving them to their full time.

Man has to earn his bread by the sweat of his brow, and labour is in all cases necessary to production. Without the labour of cultivation, the earth would support very few inhabitants. However abundant the raw materials for clothing and lodging, labour must fit them for the purposes required. There must also be capital, land, houses, implements, and machinery, to make this labour available to further production. There must also be an accumulation of capital, that is, more than enough to meet the wants of existing individuals; for the rising generation, the young unable to produce for their own support, must be provided for.

The object of the institution of the present law of property was, therefore, to provide for this accumulation, and it is a very clumsy instrument for this purpose, and, as we have seen, a very unequal division of the produce of labour takes place under it.

Now what is the law by which this division takes

place? The Political Economists tell us. Mr. James Mill says—

"In the greater number of cases, especially in the more improved stages of society, the labourer is one person, the owner of the capital another. The labourer has neither raw material nor tools. These requisites are provided for him by the capitalist. For making this provision the capitalist of course expects a reward. As the commodity, which was produced by the shoemaker, when the capital was his own, belonged wholly to himself, and constituted the whole of his reward, both as labourer and capitalist, so, in this case, the commodity belongs to the labourer and capitalist together. When prepared, the commodity, or the value of it, is to be shared between them. The reward to both must be derived from the commodity, and the reward of both makes up the whole of the commodity. Instead, however, of waiting till the commodity is produced, and abiding all the delay and uncertainties of the market in which the value of it is realized, it has been found to suit much better the convenience of the labourers to receive their share in advance. The shape under which it has been most convenient for all parties that they should receive it, is that of wages. When that share of the commodity which belongs to the labourer has all been received in the shape of wages, the commodity itself belongs to the capitalist, he having in reality bought the share of the labourer and paid for it in advance."

This at once shows very plainly the source of the power of the capitalist; for why does it suit the convenience of the labourer to receive his share in advance? Simply because having nothing but the fruits of his labour to live upon, he cannot wait till the "joint property" is realised, and he is obliged, therefore, to take whatever the capitalist, who can wait, chooses to give; and if he did not—so plentiful, ordinarily, is the supply of labour—another would. I am quite aware of, and fully appreciate, all the advantages of Capital, as explained by the Economists; its tendency to fly away if not well treated, and how much more easily it takes wing than Labour can do. I also fully appreciate a wise and energetic superintendence and direction of Capital, and I know that accumulations will not be made, and Capital will not increase rapidly unless there be sufficient inducement. Still I am of opinion that, if one-seventh of the population take two-thirds of the "joint produce," it is a little more than can be said justly to belong to them; and that whenever it may "suit the convenience" of the workmen to take a little more of that which they are at least *equally* instrumental in producing, there is a wide margin left for the improvement of their condition.

But what determines the share of the labourer, that is, the wages he shall receive? The demand for labour, and the supply—that is, the work to be done, and the number of hands to do it.

" Let us begin by supposing," says Mill, "that there is a certain number of capitalists, with a certain quantity of food, raw material, and instruments, or machinery; that there is also a certain number of labourers : and that the proportion in which the commodities produced are divided between them, has fixed itself at some particular point.

" Let us next suppose, that the labourers have increased in number one-half, without any increase in the quanity of capital. There is the same quantity of the requisites for the employment of labour ; that is of food, tools, and materials, as there was before ; but of every 100 labourers, there are now 150. There will be 50 men, therefore, in danger of being left out of employment. To prevent their being left out of employment they have but one resource ; they must endeavour to supplant those who have forestalled the employment ; that is, they must offer to work for a smaller reward—wages, therefore, decline.

" If we suppose, on the other hand, that the quantity of capital has increased while the number of labourers remains the same, the effect will be reversed. The capitalists have a greater quantity than before of the means of employment ; of capital, in short ; from which they wish to derive advantage. To derive this advantage they must have more labourers. To obtain them, they have but one resource—to offer higher wages. But the masters by whom the labourers are now employed are in the same predicament, and will of course offer higher to induce them to remain. This competition is unavoidable, and the necessary effect of it is a rise of wages.　.　.　.　.

"From this law, clearly understood, it is easy to trace the circumstances which, in any country, determine the condition of the great body of the people. If that condition is easy and comfortable, all that is necessary to keep it so is to make capital increase as fast as population; or on the other hand, to prevent population from increasing faster than capital. If that condition is not easy and comfortable, it can only be made so by one of two methods; either by quickening the rate at which capital increases, or retarding the rate at which population increases; augmenting, in short, the ratio which the means of employing the people bear to the number of people.

"If it were the natural tendency of capital to increase faster than population, there would be no difficulty in preserving a prosperous condition of the people. If, on the other hand, it were the natural tendency of population to increase faster than capital, the difficulty would be very great ; there would be a perpetual tendency in wages to fall ; the progressive fall of wages would produce a greater and a greater degree of poverty among the people, attended with its inevitable consequences, misery and vice. As ʳpoverty and its consequent misery increase, mortality would also increase. Of a numerous family born, a certain number only, from want of the means of well-being, would be reared. By whatever the proportion the population tended to increase faster than capital, such a proportion of those that were born would die : the ratio of increase in capital and population would then remain the same, and the fall of wages would proceed no farther.

"That population has a tendency to increase faster than, in most cases, capital has actually increased, is proved, incontestably, by the condition of the people in most parts of the globe. In almost all countries, the condition of the great body of the people is poor and miserable. This would have been impossible if capital had increased faster than population. In that case wages must have risen ; and high wages would have placed the labourer above the miseries of want.

"This general misery of mankind is a fact, which can be ac⁻ counted for, upon one only of two suppositions: either that there is a natural tendency in population to increase faster than capital, or that capital has, by some means, been prevented from increasing so fast as it has a tendency to increase. This, therefore, is an inquiry of the highest importance."—Mill, p. 43.

The *natural* rate of increase in a population is about 3 per cent., at which rate it is doubled in 24 years. The actual increase in our population has been 1.329 per cent. annually for the fifty years 1801-1851, and it has doubled in 52 years. The question is, has capital increased as fast? The value of real property assessed to the property and income tax for Great Britain was, in 1851, £105,524,491 ; in 1814-15 it was £60,138,323 ; so that it has at least doubled in 50 years, the same time that population has,—for personal property has increased in about the same proportion or perhaps a little faster than real. At 3 per cent. per annum, compound interest, the value of capital is doubled in 24 years, so that while 100 people have become 200 in 53 years, £100 invested and *allowed to accumulate* at 3 per cent. would become £479. "If we take this indication," says the report of the Census Commissioners, "the means of subsistence have increased faster than the numbers of the population." We cannot say that we see what indication this furnishes, as it gives no data as to how much of the capital of the country was *allowed to accumulate* or how much was consumed ; it only tells how much it would be if allowed to accumulate. The increase of capital depends upon what is saved, and it is scarcely likely that 3 per cent. of the whole income of the country would be saved ; about half that seems to accord with actual fact. But population has not increased at half the rate it has a *natural* tendency to do, and it has probably therefore been kept down by its pressure on the means of subsistence. That capital has increased as fast as population has *actually* increased, is no proof to the contrary. Political economists are probably right, then, when they say that the cause of the poverty of the working classes and the general misery consequent upon such poverty is owing to " the *natural* tendency in population to increase faster than capital," and which natural tendency therefore requires to be checked and to be brought, like all our other natural propensities, within the bounds of reason ; but "that capital has, by some means, been prevented from increasing so fast as it has a tendency to increase " is also true, and the impediments to this increase require to be removed.

Division of the Produce of Labour. The consequence of the present mode of division of the produce of labour is that the working classes are always kept so near the borders of poverty that causes are constantly arising to push them over, and we have seen the evils to which this poverty gives rise ; and on the other side we have all the luxury, the folly and extravagance and waste which enormous wealth produces in the classes above them.

There are two ways by which it is thought a more just division of the produce of labour may be brought about. The one recommended by the Political Economists is, so to raise the condition of the operatives that they may feel the advantages of their improved condition and resolve to maintain it by provident marriages and providence in all other departments. By thus checking the increase of their own numbers, labour will become scarce, and they can make better terms if not their own terms, with the capitalist. This plan is not at present popular with the workmen. The other plan is that the working classes should possess them. selves of land, capital, and machinery, either by clubbing their joint means or borrowing at interest, and then dividing the joint produce of their labour either equally or in proportion to capability and earnings. This last plan is the much dreaded Communism and Socialism, and it has attained a firm footing in the imagination of the operatives both here and abroad. It might be .thought that there was a third course—an appeal to the justice of the employers of labour themselves. But the employer *could* not if he would, and *would* not if he could, raise wages. He could not, because competition will not allow one capitalist to pay much higher wages than another ;* and although there are exceptions, it is not easy to make friends of workpeople—the master is obliged to keep a tight hand, or he would soon be put at a fatal disadvantage with his competitors ; and he would not if he could, because he considers the present arrangement between capitalist and labourer as the natural and proper order of Providence, and because he knows that, with the present standard of Education among working men generally, more time and additional wages would. by the majority, be probably spent in dissipation, to the injury of the workman himself. So far as this is true it shows that, besides the root of the evil, the soil in which the root is placed is of equal consequence, and that the working classes must work

* As an illustration of the effects of a rise of wages, we may mention that a halfpenny a yard upon a ribbon is 1s. 6d. per piece, and as a weaver makes 10 pieces a-week of broad ribbon, if this halfpenny a-yard were added to his wages, it would be 15s. per week—about double his present income. This would soon be again given to the public by the large looms which are now being introduced, and which will enable a workman to make 15 pieces where before he made 10.

out their own salvation, and in the process they will be fitted for maintaining any more elevated position to which they may attain Wherever, from peculiar circumstances, the masters have been in the hands of their workpeople, the trade has always been damaged ; the workpeople objecting to the introduction of machinery, or to a greater sub-division of labour, or in other ways preventing its extension.

Co-operation and Organisation of Industry. With reference to the two plans already mentioned, for a more equal division of profits, they may be said to represent the objective and subjective, that is, what a man can do for himself, and what can be done for him by external circumstances. The feeling of society is now divided between these two theories ; the few being of opinion that a man can only help himself, and that very little can be done for him—in fact, that everything must come from within, whilst the many are of opinion that a great deal depends upon circumstances and upon the organisation of industry. In my opinion, these are but different *points of view* of the same question—the different sides of the same shield—and both parties are right and both wrong. That " action and reaction are equal and contrary," applies as much to the moral world as to matter ; and the two states, the internal and external, act and re-act equally upon each other. The last twenty years have witnessed a great change for the better in the condition of the working classes. A nearer approach to free trade, and an extensive emigration, have kept them well employed, and, in some instances, made labour scarce. Many have raised themselves to the condition of masters and capitalists, and great savings have been made and invested in Freehold, Building Land, and other Societies. As much as 200 thousand pounds have been saved in such Societies by the working classes, in Coventry, during the last 15 years, and there is a general air of increased comfort in lodging, clothing, and food, and this improved condition in very many cases, in my opinion, is likely to be maintained. On the other hand, all attempts at Co-operation, and for the working classes to become their own masfers, have hitherto failed. Mr. Robert Owen's "New Moral Worlds," both in America and England, the Leeds Redemption Society, and other experiments in Communism, have all failed. Whenever there has been a sufficient tie, either of Religion or Fanaticism, to keep men together, such Societies have always been an economical success; but among the working classes at present there is no tie,— there is no principle strong enough to overcome the individualism, the selfishness, and ignorance, that pretty universally prevail. When the moral nature, which is at present all but rudimentary, shall be fully developed, —when a man's desire to do right is as strong as his propensities now are,—when he is as much pinched by his conscience if he neglects to do right, as he now is by his stomach if he neglects to work for his living, some form of such Societies may become possible : but not before. The working classes have attempted various other minor forms of Co-operation. Tailors and other trades have combined to work for themselves, and divide the profits between them. Others have associated to supply themselves with the necessaries of life at first-hand, and have become their own millers, grocers, and provision and coal dealers, but at present with very little success, and, perhaps I ought rather to say, with a marked want of success, as success has been the exception and failure the rule. The Co-operative stores at

Rochdale,—where I understand there is a large-headed and large-hearted manager, who gives, almost gratuitously, the whole of his time to the Society,—have been a great success; also there has been success at at Leeds. At Coventry, a Society, numbering 1,000 men, under my own presidency and inspection, has failed. Mr. Vansittart Neale also, I understand, has lost many thousand pounds in his benevolent efforts to establish and aid such Societies over the country at large. The principle at present, in my opinion, most likely to succeed in giving the workman a more just share of the joint produce, is to give him a share of the profits in the establishment in which he works This is successfully practised, I am told, in many trades in Paris. Under this system he is paid his wages as usual ; is not allowed to interfere in the management; and the additional profits he receives are a premium upon his good behaviour and additional skill. I am glad to find the attention of the first of our Political Economists, Mr. John Stuart Mill, called to this question. Writing on the "Probable Future of the Labouring Classes," he says, "confining ourselves to economical considerations, and notwithstanding the effect which improved intelligence in the working classes, together with just laws, may have in altering the distribution of produce to their advantage, I cannot think it probable that they will be permanently contented . with the condition of labouring for wages as their ultimate state. To work at the bidding and for the profit of another, without any interest in the work,—the price of their labour being adjusted by hostile competition, one side demanding as much and the other paying as little as possible,—is not, even when wages are high, a satisfactory state to human beings of educated intelligence, who have ceased to think themselves naturally inferior to those whom they serve.

"The problem is, to obtain the efficency and economy of production on a large scale, without dividing the producers into two parties with hostile interests, employers and employed, the many who do the work being mere servants under the command of one who supplies the funds, and having no interest of their own in the enterprize except to fulfil their contract and earn their wages."

" It is this feeling, almost as much as despair of the improvement of the condition of the labouring masses by other means, which has caused so great a multiplication of projects for the 'organization of industry,' by the extension and development of the Co-operative Joint-Stock principle : some of the more conspicuous of which have been described and characterised in an early chapter of this work. It is most desirable that all these schemes should have opportunity and encouragement to test their capabilities by actual experiment. There are, in almost all of them, many features in themselves well worthy of submitting to that test ; while, on the other hand, the exaggerated expectations entertained by large and growing multitudes in all the principal nations of the world, concerning what it is possible, in the present state of human improvement, to effect by such means, have no chance of being corrected except by a fair trial in practice. The French Revolution of February, 1848, at first seemed to have opened a fair field for the trial of such experiments, on a perfectly safe scale, and with every advantage that could be derived from the countenance of a Government which sincerely desired their success. It is much to be regretted that these prospects have been frustrated, and that the reaction of the middle-class against anti-property doctrines has engendered for the present an unreasoning and undiscriminating antipathy to all ideas, however harmless or however just, which have the smallest savour of Socialism. This is a disposition of mind of which the influential classes, both in France and elsewhere, will find it necessary to divest themselves. Socialism has now become irrevocably one of the leading elements in European politics. The questions raised by it will not be set at rest by the mere refusal to listen to it ; but only by a more and more complete realization of the ends which Socialism aims at, not neglecting its means so far as they can be employed with advantage. On the particular point specially considered in the present chapter, these means have been, to a certain extent, put in practice in several departments of existing industry ; by arrangements giving to every one who contributes to the work, whether by labour or by pecuniary resources, a partner's interest in it, proportionally to the value of his contribution. It is already a common practice to remunerate those in whom peculiar trust is resposed by means of a per centage on the profits ; and cases exist in which the principle is, with the most excellent success, carried down to the class of mere manual labourers."

"The value of this 'organization of industry' for healing the widening and embittering feud between the class of labourers and the class of capitalists, must, I think, impress itself by degrees on all who habitually reflect on the condition and tendencies of modern society. I cannot conceive how any such person can persuade himself that the majority of the community will for ever, or even for much longer, consent to hew wood and draw water all their lives in the service and for the benefit of others ; or can doubt, that they will be less and less willing to co-operate as subordinate agents in any work, when they have an interest in the result, and that it will be more and more difficult to obtain the best workpeople, or the best services of any workpeople, except on conditions similar in principle to those of Leclaire (who gives in Paris a share in the profits.) Although, therefore, arrangements of this sort are now in their infancy, their multiplication and growth, when once they enter into the general domain of popular discussion, are among the things which may most confidently be expected."

Of course Mill is here alluding only to what is possible in the future for the labouring classes ; all who know the present low moral and intellectual condition of the great majority must know that any change of that sort is impossible at present, except in exceptional cases. " To that complexion may they come at last," but it must be through years of discipline. Measures for improving the condition of the people at present, have only had the effect of increasing their numbers, without much improving their moral state. They have not maintained the advanced position ; but have only peopled up to it. Mill most truly says "no remedies for low wages have the smallest chance of being efficacious, which do not operate on and through the minds and habits of the people. While these are unaffected, any contrivance, even if successful, for temporarily improving the condition of the poor, would only let slip the reins by which population was previously curbed."

I have worked with the working classes at all measures for improving their condition for a quarter of a century, but have never yet found them capable of conducting their own affairs. If their affairs were of a trading kind, they were jealous and niggardly of the pay of those who were principally instrumental in making them succeed, and what was ordered by a Committee one week or month was too frequently undone the next. There was no permanency or persistency. If their affairs were of other kinds they fell out among themselves, and could not long be kept together. The worst feature of ignorance is intolerance, and the worst of the working classes is that they cannot agree to differ. They are for the utmost freedom of thought and liberty of opinion, but denounce as knave or fool every one who does not think as they think. They are too generally suspicious of each others' motives, and find it very difficult to rise to the comprehension of a disinterested feeling. I have heard a philanthropist defined as a person who acts from no motives at all. I have heard the most damning denunciations of government pay and patronage,—of aristocrats helping themselves and their relations out of the public purse; but I have known the same persons order a larger quantity of tea and sugar for a tea-drinking than could possibly be used, that they might divide it among themselves at *half* price afterwards. Of course there are many and glorious exceptions. During the last 20 years I have witnessed great improvement in the condition of the working classes; year by year the state of a large number is permanently improved, and if the present peaceful and prosperous state of the country should continue this must rapidly increase. From the small number of producers and the unequal mode of distribution there is ample room to improve the physical condition of the operatives, and although I have lost all faith in any single remedy for all their ills, I have an increasing conviction that no effort is thrown away, but that all measures for their improvement are working together for their good; gradually and slowly bringing about a time in which all may enjoy what hitherto has been the exclusive privilege of the favoured few. I say *slowly*, because conduct depends more upon individual organisation than upon opinion, however enlightened, and the organisations have yet to be grown.

MEASURES PROPOSED FOR THE AMELIORATION OF THE CONDITION OF THE PEOPLE. We cannot now complain that the interests and condition of the people are neglected; but an immense amount of philanthropy is thrown away from being misdirected. The evils we have pointed out are now forcing themselves into general recognition, and all parties have their pet schemes for their amelioration, in Political or Social Reforms, in Emigration, and Education.

POLITICAL REFORM. The people have lost their faith in Reformed Parliaments, and there is a very general feeling that Government can do little more than it has done, and that the people must take their affairs into their own hands. They see that in all countries the condition of the great body of people—of the working classes—is, with slight differences, the same. In all, the wages of labour are—relatively to what each produces, and to what such wages will purchase—equally low: and yet some of the countries to which we have before alluded possess all for which politicians of the Liberal school are contending. If wages are higher in America than in the old world, it is owing, not to their liberal institutions, or to anything in which their Government may differ from ours, but to the scarcity of labour in proportion to the vast tracts of half-cultivated and uncultivated land. But the lower wages in England will purchase there more of all that is best worth living for than the higher wages of America will in that country. Our political agitators and first-class workmen are quite aware of this, and refuse to go.

CHARTISM. Consequently, we hear very little now of the Charter. The late Union, however, of the working men for the purpose of obtaining what is called the Charter, the chief object of which is an extended suffrage, demonstrated how utterly incapable this class was of undertaking the management of its own affairs. Whatever may be the opinion with respect to the desirableness of placing political power in the hands of the majority, it cannot be doubted, that in the hands of a majority such as our working classes in their present condition constitute, it would tend more to their injury than benefit. Whatever exception may be made in favour of some few amongst them who have far outstripped their brethren in reason and intelligence, it may be asserted that, as a class, they have no knowledge of the foundations upon which society is built; of the steps by which we have arrived at our present stage in civilization; of the original necessity to the advancement of the race of that which now strikes them as a glaring abuse; of the mutual sacrifice of our natural liberty which is hourly called for, to ensure to us the advantages of living in society at all. They have no knowledge of the causes of the evils that oppress them, and where, therefore, the remedy should be sought. Scarcely any two among them agree as to what should be done, had they the necessary power. It is quite impossible, as society is now constituted, that they, with their limited means of acquiring information, and the incessant toil to which they are subjected, can acquire sufficient knowlege for their own governance, or perhaps even to choose those who are qualified. Legislation requires more knowledge than any other profession. A legislator ought to be intimately acquainted with the constitution of human nature ; the constitution of society ; the history of civilization ; with the particular character of the people, and of the institutions of the country for which he would legislate. This is a know. ledge to be acquired only by long and arduous study, the time for which is denied to the multitude. Universal suffrage, including all that can make that suffrage available, will be excellent and necessary, when the people know how to use it ; but a great improvement in their physical condition must take place before this can be the case. Changes brought about by the representa tives of the people in ignorance of the causes of oppression, would only make things worse, by affecting the order, tranquillity, and security necessary to the spread of knowledge, and to the improvement which can be based only upon such knowledge.

EXTENSION OF THE SUFFRAGE. A judicious exten- sion of the suffrage is certainly called for, and would make the legislating class more dependent upon the people and therefore more solicitous to educate them and to attend to their interests ; but this extension ought by no means to be overwhelming in its influence, swamping all other classes in mere numbers, or ignorance and prejudice would rule instead of knowledge.

Is not this, therefore, evidence of some fallacy in the views of this party, if indeed the object of their measures be to raise the condition of the people ? In questioning, however, whether the measures of what is called a liberal and enlightened policy do often or always con- duce to this end, and in endeavouring to show their exact bearing upon the condition of the people, we would not wish to appear to condemn such measures, or to represent them as containing no good. It is impossible not to be aware of, and to appreciate, the benefits that have been and will be conferred by them upon all possessing property; it is obvious also that increased production must reflectively, and in a minor degree, benefit those who have no property, but who live by the wages of labour; and that it will raise many of the latter class into the former; but that such policy will not materially ameliorate the condition of the majority, may, we think, be demonstrated.

TAXATION. First among the remedies of this class to which the people are taught to look for relief, is the lessening of Taxation, Cheap Government, and the taking off the duties on everything that the working man finds necessary for the support of his family. The national debt and our heavy taxation, it is said, press down our people into the dust. But in those countries where there is no national debt, and where taxation is light, is the condition of the people better? It appears a hard thing that the working man should have to pay 3s. 6d. of every pound that he earns, in direct or indirect taxation, and out of an income of £50, to pay £8 towards the government of his country, and the interest of its national debt; and yet, supposing the same rate of taxation to affect the capitalist, and that his income is £1,000 a-year, he pays only £166, leaving in the one instance £42 a-year, and in the other £834; thus reducing one party to the point of starvation, and leaving the other with every means of luxury. But were the working classes relieved from all taxation, and were those who are much better able to bear the burden made so to do, how would it affect the former? At first, and for some time, the operative would find that his pound per week would go much farther in supplying his wants ; it would not only yield necessaries, but comforts. But soon the inevitable fluctuations in trade, a lessened demand for labour, or the increase of his own numbers, would throw him out of employment, and in order to obtain his share of the work that remained, he would offer his labour for less and less remuneration, until within a short period his wages would again be reduced to the lower rate, as we find to be the case in other countries where the necessaries of life are cheap. " The money rate of wages, wholly independent of the price of provisions from year to year, is entirely regulated by it, other things being equal, from ten vears to ten years."*

One advantage he would derive—but that would also be fleeting, although, perhaps, not equally so—the demand for his labour would be more steady in consequence of additional markets abroad being opened to his employer. This, however, in many cases, would throw people out of employment elsewhere, or if their wages admitted of any reduction, would grind them down to meet this additional competition.

Under the present system the working classes are merely the instruments of production, and to relieve them of taxation would have exactly the same effect upon production as improvements in machinery ; as they would be able to live for less, they would be enabled to produce for less. This would lead to increased demand, depending, of course, upon the cheapness of the produce. No increase, therefore, of wages would take place, but a great increase of population, similar to that which has taken place in Manchester, Glasgow, Leeds, and other large towns, where improvements in machinery, and our consequent power of producing cheaply, have enabled us to command extensive markets. But in a short time population would be upon a par with this increased demand, and foreign competition, over-speculation, fluctuating currencies, and all the various causes that disturb our commercial atmosphere, would again throw the people out of employment, and produce the results for which we now seek a remedy.

The great political questions of the day are questions concerning more or less representation—more' or less taxation—whether this or that section of the aristocracy shall have power and patronage ; but they are not questions that tend ultimately to raise the condition of the people ; the utmost that we can expect from the satisfactory solution of them is, that by enabling us to produce more cheaply, increased demand may give employment to the working classes for a time, when otherwise there would be none, and thus afford leisure to introduce gradually and securely other measures which can alone be effectual to the desired end.

THE FUNCTIONS OF GOVERNMENT. There is much discussion in the present day regarding the proper sphere of Government, and there are those who seek to confine its functions simply to the protection of life, limb, and property. They would have the people govern themselves in their municipalities, as they did in olden times, and they live in great dread of the foreign system of centralization and government by Bureaucracy and Functionaryism. But surely we are as much self-governed in this country by the Central Government as we should be by our local Municipal Council ; and the same people who elect the Municipal Representative, elect the Parliamentary one : and no abuse now escapes the eyes of party or the press. The foreign system no doubt is wrong, and it would be better that men should govern themselves badly, than have everything done for them, as it is on the Continent. In America we have the opposite extreme, and the lower minds rule and give the tone to society. But it would be impossible to introduce the Continental system into this country ; our circumstances are so widely different. There is no attempt here to take the government of the people out of their own hands, only to systematize and direct it, and to lay down principles based upon science and a large experience, which they are invited, not forced, to carry out. Perhaps the last place in which reforms are likely to emanate, are the localities in which they are most needed ; the people are born in and are used to their condition, and like grubs see little beyond the leaf on which they feed, and rarely dream of the " butterfly " life to come. Government, aided by the first talent, should inspect, inquire, and lay down principles ; it should be the head, the localities the hands—the head should think and originate, the hands should administer, and, in this sense, where the Government is elected by and under the control of the people's Representatives, Centralization seems to be a thing much needed in this country ; for we want knowledge, order, system, science, as opposed to prejudice, ignorance, and short-sighted selfishness and jobbery. We have no fear for the liberties of the Anglo-Saxon race ; we fear more lest the liberty of every man, as in America, should run to excess. Those who advocate falling back upon our ancient Municipal liberties seem to forget that the Railway, Steam, and the Electric Telegraph have made the nation what the Municipality used to be, and the civilised world what the nation used to be. Whatever tendency there may be towards Co-operative industry, the tendency of the age is towards the Individuality of the Individual, and the disintegration of the old forms of society; and where this has been completely attained, and each atom (or person) in society has been relieved from its former attractions and repulsions, it will again form new combinations—it will crystalize into new and more healthful shapes. Voluntaryism is no doubt the right principle. A MAN should be allowed to do as he pleases consistently with the same liberty to others, but it is the duty of Government to see that there are no impediments in the way of his becoming a *man*. The protection of children and youug persons, therefore, properly belongs to Government, and it ought to be held responsible for the public health and education, and whatever else is required to develope it subjects into healthy bodily and mental manhood. To Government also belongs the protection of animals and lunatics. In the recognised departments of Government, in the protection of life and property, much requires to be done. Our Laws want simplifying, codifying, and amending, and if that were properly done, half the lawyers' offices in the kingdom might be shut up. The lawyers have proverbially been the conservators of " old and barbarous usages,', but this " vested interest " must be relinquished.

FREE TRADE. The one thing with which the Government has certainly no right to interfere, and with which it can only interfere injuriously, is the freedom of trade. To make at home what we can buy cheaper abroad is a waste of labour, and to be obliged by law to buy the dearer article is an injustice. All monopolies, bounties, and prohibitions, therefore, should be abolished, and trade allowed to flow into its natural channels; each country furnishing that for which nature has best qualified it, and which costs, therefore, the least labour to produce. We should not be obliged to grow wheat upon land unfitted for it, any more than we should attempt to grow grapes and oranges in our Northern latitudes.

We must bear in mind, however, that the principal economic advantages to be derived from free trade are increased cheapness and increased demand from extended markets. Now Manchester possessed all the advantages in this respect that free trade could possibly give to any town or country. Improvements in machinery by Watt and Arkwright, and peculiar advantages of situation, opened to it the markets of almost the whole world. It was enabled to import its raw material from India, to manufacture it, to send it back again, and yet undersell the Indian who works for twopence per day, in his own market. In this department of cotton-spinning, the improvements in machinery enabled one man to do the work that it required 200 men to do before; and here one would think that if the extra produce were divided fairly between the capitalist, or owner of the machine, and the operative, there was plenty of room for the improvement of his condition. But did it increase his leisure? No. Were his wages increased for doing 200 times more than he did before? But very little; for the competition for employment of those who were at first thrown out of work by the extra productiveness of the machine, obliged him to work the same number of hours, and to be satisfied with nearly the same rate of wages as before. Where then was the advantage? The extra number of pieces produced went to the warehouse of the capitalist, and by reducing them in price, he forced them over all the markets of the world. The reduced price occasioned a greatly increased demand; capital flowed in that direction; manufacturers and merchants multiplied and grew rich; and the number of hands employed, instead of being ultimately decreased, was increased until it reached the number of about 1,200,000, with whose condition Parliamentary enquiries have made us but too well acquainted.

The greatest advocates for freedom of trade can scarcely expect that it can do more for the country at large, than improvements in machinery and other peculiar local advantages have already done for Manchester, Leeds, Glasgow, and some other of our large manufacturing towns, and hitherto it has only had the effect of increasing the numbers of the people, without much improving their moral state; they have not maintained their advanced position—they have only peopled up to it. But the economical advantages of free trade are daily becoming greater, and year by year a large number of the operative class either become masters or are otherwise permanently raised in the scale of society. Free commerce, and increased facilities of transport on the iron way, now put the whole world under requisition for the house, clothing, and food of all classes—even the poorest. It is true that with it comes "unlimited competition," but with that also comes increased cheapness, so that the same money rate of wages goes much farther. The great drawback is, that one country may become dependent upon another for the raw material, upon the making up of which its very bread depends. As long as the highways of the world or its productive power are liable to be stopped by passion or prejudice or misrule, this will always be a difficulty. The cotton famine, consequent on the American war has left whole districts in this country and on the Continent without the means of subsistence. But relations based on slavery could not be expected to be permanent. Whole districts also, by present arrangements, are made dependent upon the caprices of fashion, the effects of which no prudence or forethought can obviate. But notwithstanding those drawbacks, the world gains greatly by freedom of trade, and the moral advantages derived from it cannot be over-estimated.

UNION OF AGRICULTURE AND MANUFACTURING INDUSTRIES. The joint effect of the want of country air and exercise and of solid food, is the predominance of the nervous system at the expense of the muscular energies, which begets mental disorder and the necessity for constant excitement, found generally at the gin and beer shops, and leading, with the precarious nature of their employment, to the improvidence which characterises so many of the class. This degeneration of the great body of our manufacturing operatives has now proceeded very far, and for that, among other things, we must seek a remedy. The foreign operative, although inferior in position to our English workman in many respects, has this advantage over him, that he is not solely dependent upon the sale of his labour for a livelihood, but has the means of using his labour to furnish himself with everything necessary to his physical well-being. His labour will always supply him with the necessaries of life, often with its comforts, and even a surplus to exchange for foreign luxuries. There is no doubt that he is in want of many things that our operatives possess, but he is not subject to the same fluctuations of income, and can

therefore calculate better his own resources, and there is
little question but that upon the whole he is a more
contented and happy being. The result of the circumstances in which he is placed upon his constitution, is
just the reverse of the case with our operative, viz.,
physical predominance over the mental constitution.
Now if we could unite the two states or conditions, one
would so correct the other, that we should have all the
advantages of both without the evils which each engen-
ders separately. Our labourers and artizans have been
divorced from the soil and made solely dependent upon
the sale of their labour, the demand for which is
dependent upon fluctuating causes, and will therefore
frequently not furnish them with the necessaries of life.
So far let us return to the old system as to put them
back upon the land. Let us endeavour to unite the
advantages which the rapid progress of civilization and
improved machinery have already brought to the
operative, with the advantages of country residence
and the health of mind and body derivable from
agricultural labour. Machinery is daily displacing the
adult operative, and his labour will soon be too expensive
a material to work into manufactures : let him therefore be employed in the garden cultivation of the land
to supply his family with the necessaries of life, and let
only his own surplus time and that of his family be
employed in watching power-looms to furnish comforts
and luxuries. Agriculture and manufactures never
ought to have been divorced. Employment *solely* in the
one department, injures the mind ; in the other the
body. There is not now, if there ever has been, the
necessity for it. Machinery has been invented, and can
be invented, to do all for which skilled labour is required.
When a nation becomes a nation of manufacturers and

dependent upon other nations for its agricultural produce, it gives up more than it can ever receive in return, viz., the health and strength of body acquired from out-door labour. If the people of the Continental States, during the six months they are compelled to work in-doors, were to abandon their primitive mode of manufacturing, and by the aid of a factory in each district, were to make use of steam and our improved machinery, might not their condition be prosperous in the extreme? For, the same amount of labour they now employ might produce a large surplus to exchange for every foreign article required; whereas, almost all that they can now purchase after supplying themselves with the needful allowance of their own manufactures, is tobacco, tea, coffee, and sugar. If our own population, now dependent upon wages alone, could be supplied with allotments of land, either by purchase or upon lease, so that by spade cultivation their labour should always furnish the first necessaries of life, they would then have something to fall back upon during the fluctuations to which trade is, and always must be, liable. Secure of the means of supporting life, and of making it not only endurable but pleasant, they would have less to fear from the freaks of fashion, from the closing of this or that market, from this monetary crisis, or that war. In order to make the great extension of our foreign trade, implied in the Free Trade principles, *safe*, and to the ultimate interest of the majority, all—whether by this means or any other that can be suggested—should be made *independent of foreign markets*, so far as the first *necessaries* of life are concerned.*

* The *Times*, July 31, 1862, writing on the debate in the Commons on the Lancashire distress, says:—"Let us not deceive ourselves by talking of the Cotton Famine and the Civil War in America. What we now behold we have several times seen

To the thorough Free Trader this may appear to be a retrograde movement and perfectly chimerical. To carry it out immediately, to the extent contemplated, may be impossible and undesirable, and we would wish rather to point to it as an object towards which our policy should be directed for the future. To the master manufacturer, who wishes always to keep the supply of labour above the demand, and by that means to keep the operatives wholly dependent on him—greater slaves to the necessity of living than any we have lately emancipated in the West Indies—the plan may appear objectionable altogether, as interfering with the supply of labour, and consequently with our manufacturing supremacy. We do not anticipate, however, that the effect would be to raise the price of labour; because, having other means of subsistence, the operative could afford to sell his manufacturing skill for less. But even should the objection be admissible, we think with Mr. Laing, that

before, and shall see again. The more numerous the people engaged in the cotton manufacture, the better the machinery, the greater the enterprise, the more overflowing the prosperity under favourable circumstances, the greater will be the reaction certain to follow soon or late. Nor is there any surety that the next season of agricultural distress, whatever the time, the cause, or the name, will be one whit less serious, shorter, or less extensive than what we now witness. It is time, therefore, to consider what remedies are to be applied to a recurrent calamity beyond the resources and the arrangements of our Poor Laws. It is the case of an employment fluctuating between very great prosperity and equal collapse, between enormous profits and enormous losses, between wages at least twice the agricultural scale and no employment at all. The object is to make the good years help the bad years, and it is far better the good years should do this by anticipation than by making up arrears, inasmuch as savings are better than debts. From all accounts, the Lancashire operatives have been provident, but not provident enough for a calamity beyond their expectation. But it is the aggregate industry that must be made to insure itself against such reverses. How is that to be done? The problem has hardly been touched in the debate which has run on the Cotton Famine; but it is one which we shall undoubtedly have to meet."

"there may be a greater national good than the cheap-ness, excellence, and extension of a manufacture. The wealth of a nation, that is, of its State or Government, may depend much upon productive labour well applied, and upon great accumulations of manufacturing capital to apply it; the happy condition and well-being of a people seem to depend more on the wide distribution of employment over the face of a country by small but numerous masses of capital." *

Let our steam factories be uniformly built in the open country, as is now very generally done in Lancashire, and let cottages for the artizans be also built in an airy situation, around the factory, with land attached to each. Most of the evils attendant upon the extension of the factory system might thus be avoided, and a high state of external prosperity and internal order, intelligence, and morality be introduced. Employment would thus be found for the male adults, forty or fifty thousand of whom, trained from early childhood to factory labour, are yearly turned adrift, and whom machinery every day tends more and more to supplant. Let this employment be principally upon the land, and the father of his family may still be its head, and enabled to supply its members with the necessaries and comforts of life, with-out its being essential to their subsistence or England's supremacy that his daughters under 18 and young children should work ten and a-half hours per day at the mill. We may then perhaps discover that our national existence does not depend upon our selling manufactured cotton at a farthing per ell cheaper than any other people. As Carlyle says, "a most narrow stand for a free nation to base itself on—a stand which, with all the corn-law abrogations conceivable, I do not think will be

* Residence in Norway, p. 299.

capable of enduring." The factories at Lowell, in the State of Massachusetts, United States, are worked principally by the daughters of farmers in the surrounding States, of the age of from 17 to 24, and they exhibit a high state of prosperity, morality, and intelligence. Our own Gregs, Strutts, and Ashworths, have also set a noble example of what may be done towards improving the condition of the factory operatives under their charge. In the ameliorated condition of their workpeople the manufacturers will find their own interest, and they will never have reason to regret any degree of pains and attention directed towards the increase of their physical comforts and the improvement of their minds. The strength and welfare of a State is best based upon a contented and happy peasantry ; the condition of our own labouring classes would indicate that, notwithstanding our apparent prosperity, we have still much to fear. We have made mention chiefly of the manufacturing poor, not because we are unaware that the condition of the agricultural poor is even less prosperous, but because we consider that our proposed remedy is equally applicable to the amelioration of the condition of all who are dependent upon wages. Instead of the children of the agricultural labourer going into the town to be exposed to all its moral and physical deteriorations, the factory, or the steam power to each dwelling, might be brought to them. It is quite true that more perfect freedom of trade, and increased facilities of intercourse between nations, render the fluctuations in trade less and less frequent ; still employment upon the land—the Union of Agriculture and Manufactures, is not the less desirable. Most of the physical and moral diseases, induced by a perverted civilization among our factory population in the large towns, are consequent upon their divorce from the land, and the best remedy, if not the only one, will be found in the return to it, either at home or by emigration to our colonies.

The Free Trade principle, "that we should never produce in one country what can be produced at less cost of labour in another," should be received as admitting of many exceptions, because where labour would probably be to spare, such occupations would be˜chosen as were most conducive to health and happiness rather than always those that the circumstances of the country rendered most productive. At present production is considered only, without reference to health, and the produce of one hour's labour in our manufactories is exchanged for the produce of one hour's labour upon land abroad ; such land being twice as productive as our own, one hour's labour on manufactures here produces by the exchange double the quantity of corn that could be produced by the same labour upon our own soil. But may not the question fairly be asked, whether two hours' labour upon land be not more to the interest of the labourer, if he had his due share of the produce, and all other influences being taken into consideration, than one in a factory? That system must be had which takes no account of the health of body or mind in the *saving of labour*.

> " A time there was, ere England's griefs began,
> When every rood of ground maintain'd its man ;

and to this state we should return, with the differences indicated.

COLONIZATION AND EMIGRATION. That population hitherto has pressed upon the means of subsistence,— that mankind, governed more by brute instinct than by reason, have not limited their numbers within the means provided for their support, is well for the world at large, as it has driven numbers from their native hearths and the comforts of home and civilization, to fight with and subdue nature to their use in new and untrodden regions of the earth. It has been found that disease and crime increase in proportion to the number of the people on a square mile, and more than proportionately to the increase of numbers, and as the only way to raise wages is to make labour scarce, it is most desirable that the road to our colonies should be made as short and as easy of access as possible. That wages are high in America is not owing to its democratic institutions, but that its surplus population is drafted off to the prairies of the far West. We ought to have our far West to thin the population of our densely crowded cities, and to transport our underpaid mechanics and agricultural labourers to new countries where their labour is the thing most wanted ; to rescue the former from all the temptations to which a large city subjects them, and to transport both to new regions where |their labour shall produce for them at least every necessary of life. The evils generated in the hotbed of civilization are best cured by labour on land and in a new country, and Government should see that Australia and New Zealand and Canada and our other colonies, by a well-organised system of emigration, are put within the reach of our working classes. Since the potato failed in Ireland, emigration has been very rapid, not only from that country, but from England and Scotland, and it has done much to raise the condition of the operatives who remained at home. Our Colonies should be systematically fed from our Reformatories, both for children and adults : the old country is no abiding place for the criminal class ; society has little faith in their amendment, and will not receive them, and they are cast out too often with no means of support but by returning to their old vicious courses.

EDUCATION. The most important of all measures for the improvement of the condition of the people is the improvement of the people themselves through the means of education, and this we are glad to find is now very generally recognized; but while our religious guides have been trying to agree as to *what* religion shall be taught in the common schools and *how* it shall be taught, anything deserving the name of education has become almost an impossibility for the mass of the people. If on the great expansion of our national industry by steam all children had been obliged by law under a national system of education to go to school till the age of 12 or 14, then education of some kind would have been possible to all, and the rate of wages would have adapted itself to the consequent lessened supply of labour ; but now the children have been absorbed into the industrial employments of the country, and wages have fallen so low that parents cannot do without their earnings, and children are therefore kept from the schools. But this is not the worst ; the mothers as well as the children have been set to work, and the effect of the ignorance and neglect, consequent upon the mother's divorcement from domestic duties, is that more than 50 per cent. of the mortality in all great towns is of children under five years of age. For every such death there are at least 28 cases of sickness, and education in after life can do little towards counteracting the effects of influences so weakening and deteriorating to the whole constitution. We have thus in a large proportion of the rising generation a stunted growth, a nervously predominant bodily

system, an ill-balanced mind, and a perpetual craving for
unnatural and unwholesome stimulants.

But our semi-voluntary and wretchedly defective no-
system of education does not reach low enough down in
the scale of society to affect in the least the classes who
most require it. It passes over almost all who are
without the pale and influence of some religious organization. To remedy this defect Ragged Schools and
Reformatories for juvenile delinquents have been lately
established, and an Act has been passed by which young
vagabonds with no ostensible means of occupation can
be seized and forcibly committed to some school. But
this Act, I fear, is likely to remain a mere dead letter
for some time to come. The Annual Report of the
Committee of the Privy Council on Education has been
issued, June, 1862. It details their proceedings during
the past year, and shows that the number of schools, or
departments of schools, under separate teachers, which
were inspected, had been increased by 497, the number
of children by 65,758, of pupil teachers by 742, of
certificated teachers by 987 ; of students in training for
teachers, 43 ; and that new school accommodation was
created for 47,103 children. The sixty Inspectors
visited 10,900 daily schools, or departments of schools,
and found present in them 1,028,690 children (five boys
to four girls), 8,069 certificated teachers, and 15,498
apprentices. The Inspectors also visited 39
Training Colleges for teachers, occupied by 2,869
students, and examined these and 2,782 candidates ;
besides visiting 422 schools for pauper children,
containing about 30,000 inmates, and 58 ragged or
industrial schools, containing 4,411 inmates. The Privy
Council Committee notice that while making a certificated
teacher a condition of annual grants, they have provided

for the granting of certificates to younger and humbler classes of candidates for service in small schools, and that they are now engaged in revising the subjects wherein teachers are required to be examined. A hope is expressed that by the encouragement given to the instruction of infants as a foundation, and to the instruction of evening scholars as a continuance of the elementary day school, a road has been marked out for the solid and suitable education of the classes who support themselves in independence by manual labour. As for the education of the pauper and criminal classes, they are now dealt with by the Legislature as separate parts of the question, and with, by way of supplement, the missionary action of Sunday Schools and Ragged Schools, the Council entertain a confident hope that no part of the great field of education for the poor remains unknown or uncared for ; and that in the midst of many difficulties, and more differences, progress is being everywhere made.

Notwithstanding, our educational establishments are deficient in the quantity, and still more so in the quality of instruction supplied. With most who use the term, education means intellectual instruction, but rightly understood it is the improving and perfecting of every bodily and mental faculty. "It is," says Mackintosh, "a wise disposal of all the circumstances which influence character, and of the means of producing those habitual dispositions which ensure well doing."

SOCIALISM. We have hitherto spoken of Society as it now exists, and have considered how its shortcomings may be best remedied, but there are those who consider that its evils cannot be remedied—can at the best be only palliated, as they are inherent in the system itself.

The assailants of the present form and constitution of Society, based upon the law of individual property, have been called Socialists or Communists.

We have all been brought up under the present system, and are accustomed to all its abuses and to all the restraints it imposes upon us, as the bird to the cage in which it was born, and our aspirations after greater freedom are as little understood by us as by the poor prisoned bird.

Mr. M'Culloch may be said fairly to represent the school who support the present system ; in favour of it he says—

"We incline to think that the great inequality of fortune that has always prevailed in this country has powerfully contributed to excite a spirit of invention and industry among the less opulent classes. It is not always because a man is absolutely poor that he is perseveringly industrious and economical : he may have already amassed considerable wealth, but he continues with unabated energy to avail himself of every means by which he may hope to add to his fortune, that he may place himself on a level with the great landed proprietors and those who give the tone to society in all that regards expense. No successful manufacturer or merchant ever considers that he has enough till he be able to live in something like the same style as the most opulent persons. Those immediately below the highest become, as it were, a standard to which the class next to them endeavour to elevate themselves ; the impulse extending in this way to the very lowest classes, individuals belonging to which are always raising themselves by industry, address, and good fortune, to the highest places in society. Had there been less inequality of fortune amongst us, there would have been less emulation, and industry would not have been so successfully prosecuted. It is true that the desire to emulate the great and affluent, by embarking in a lavish course of expenditure, is often prematurely indulged in, and carried to a culpable excess ; but the evils thence arising make but a trifling deduction from the beneficial influence of that powerful stimulus which it gives to the inventive faculties, and to that desire to improve our condition and to mount in the scale of society, which is the source of all that is great and elevated. Hence we should disapprove of any system which, like that of the law of equal inheritance established in France, had any tendency artificially to equalize fortunes. To the absence of any such law, and the prevalence of customs of a totally different character, we are inclined to attribute a considerable portion of our superior wealth and industry."

On the other hand, Mr. Combe is not quite so satisfied, he says :—

" In Britain, that individual is fitted to be most successful in the career of wealth and its attendant advantages, who possesses vigorous health, industrious habits, great selfishness, a powerful intellect, and just so much of the moral feelings as to serve for the profitable direction of his animal powers. This combination of endowments would render self-aggrandizement and worldly-minded prudence the leading motives of his actions ; would furnish intellect sufficient to give them effect, and morality adequate to restrain them from abuses, or from defeating their own gratification. A person so constituted would feel his faculties to be in harmony with his external condition ; he has no lofty aspirations after either goodness or enjoyment which he cannot realize ; he is pleased to dedicate his undivided energies to the active business of life, and he is generally successful. He acquires wealth and distinction, stands high in the estimation of society, transmits comfort and abundance to his family, and dies in a good old age."

"The tendency of the system is to throw an accumulating burden of mere labour on the industrious classes. I am told that in some of the great machine manufactories in the West of Scotland, men labour for sixteen hours a-day, stimulated by additions to their wages in proportion to the quanity of work which they produce. Masters who push trade on a great scale, exact the most energetic and long-continued exertion from all the artizans whom they employ. In such circumstances man becomes at once a mere labouring animal. Excessive muscular exertion drains off the nervous energy from the brain ; and when labour ceases sleep ensues, unless the artificial stimulus of· intoxicating liquors be applied to rouse the dormant mental organs and confer a temporary enjoyment, which, in such instances, is very generally the case. To call a man, who passes his life in such a routine of occupation,—eating, sleeping, labouring, and drinking,—a Christian, an immortal being, preparing by his exertions here for an eternity hereafter to be passed in the society of pure, intelligent, and blessed spirits,—is a complete mockery. He is preparing for himself a premature grave, in which he shall be laid exhausted with toil, and benumbed in all the higher attributes of his nature, more like a jaded and maltreated horse, than a human being. Yet this system pervades every department of pratical life in these islands. If a farm be advertised to be let, tenants compete with each other in bidding high rents, which, when carried to excess, can be paid only by their converting themselves and their servants into labouring animals, bestowing on the land the last effort of their strength and skill, and resting satisfied with the least possible ,enjoyment from it in return.

" By the competition of individual interests, directed to the acquisition of property and the attainment of distinction, the practical members of society are not only powerfully stimulated to exertion, but actually forced to submit to a most jading, laborious, and endless course of toil ; in which neither time, opportunity, nor inclination, is left for the cultivation and enjoyment of the higher powers of the mind. The whole order and institutions of society are framed in harmony with this principle. The law prohibits men from using force and fraud in order to acquire properity, but sets no limit to their employment of all other means. Our education and mode of transacting mercantile business, support the same system of selfishness. It is an approved maxim, that secresy is the soul of trade, and each manufacturer and merchant pursues his separate speculation secretly, so that his rivals may know as little as possible of the kind and quantity of goods which he is manufacturing, of the sources whence he draws his materials, or the channels by which he disposes of his produce. The direct advantage of this system is, that it confers a superiority on the man of acute and extensive observation and profound sagacity. He contrives to penetrate many of the secrets which are attempted, though not very successfully, to be kept; and he directs his own trade and manufacture, not always according to the current in which his neighbours are floating, but rather according to the results which he foresees will take place from the course which they are following ; and then the days of their adversity become those of his prosperity. The general effect of the system, however, is that each trader stretches his capital, his credit, his skill, and his industry, to produce the utmost possible quantity of goods, under the idea that the more he manufactures and sells, the more profit he will reap. But as all his neighbours are animated by the same spirit, *they* manufacture as much as possible also ; and none of them know certainly how much the other traders in their own line are producing, or how much of the commodity in which they deal the public will really want, pay for, and consume, within any specific time. The consequence is, that a superfluity of goods is produced, the market is glutted, prices fall ruinously low, and all the manufacturers who have proceeded on credit, or who have limited capitals, become bankrupt, and the effects of their rash speculations fall on their creditors. They are, however, excluded from trade for a season,—the other manufacturers restrict their operations,—the operatives are thrown idle, or their wages are greatly reduced ; the surplus commodities are at length consumed, demand revives, prices rise, and the same rush towards production again takes place ; and thus in all trades the pendulum oscillates, generation after generation, first towards prosperity, then to the equal balance, then towards adversity,—back again to equality, and once more rises to prosperity.

"The ordinary observer perceives in this system what he considers to be the natural, the healthy, and the inevitable play of the constituent elements of human nature. He discovers many advantages attending it, and some evils ; but these he regards as inseparable from all that belongs to mortal man. The competition of individual interests, for example, he assures us, keeps the human energies alive, and stimulates all to the highest exercise of the bodily and mental powers ; and the result is, that abundance of every article that man needs is poured into the general treasury of civilised life, even to superfluity. We are all interested, he continues, in cheap productions, and although we apparently suffer by an excessive reduction in the prices of our own commodities, the evil is transitory, and the ultimate effect is unmixed good, for all our neighbours are running the same career of over production with ourselves. While we are reducing our shoes to a ruinously low price, the stocking maker is doing the same with his stockings, and the hat maker with his hats ; and after we all shall have exchanged article for article, we shall still obtain as many pairs of stockings, and as many hats, for any given quantity of shoes, as ever ; so that the real effect of competition is to render the nation richer, to enable it to maintain more inhabitants, or to provide for those it possesses more abundantly, without rendering any individuals poorer. The evils attending the rise and fall of fortune, or the heart-breaking scenes of bankruptcy, and the occasional degradation of one family and elevation of another they regard as storms in the moral, corresponding to those in the physical world, which, although inconvenient to the individuals whom they overtake, are on the whole, beneficial, by stirring and purifying the atmosphere ; and, regarding this life as a mere pilgrimage to a better, they view these incidental misfortunes as means of preparation for a higher sphere.

" This representation has so much of actual truth in it, and such an infinite plausibility, that it is almost adventurous in me to question its soundness ; yet I am forced to do so, or to give up my best and brightest hopes of human nature and its destinies. In making these remarks, I blame no individuals It is the system which I condemn. Individuals are as much controlled by the social system in which they live, as a raft is by the current in which it floats."*

It is true that society, as at present constituted, is a mere chaos of conflicting interests, born of chance and of selfish instinct, over the surface of which the spirit of reason, directing and arranging each part for the production of the greatest happiness, has never moved. That society should be founded upon laws by which *all* might live together in the most happy manner possible, has yet to be acknowledged. On the contrary, it has been left to form itself ; part has been added to part, as time and circumstances, the increase of mankind, and the formation of section after section, have called for it,—each portion fashioned after the individual interests of class, without any reference to the good of the whole. Thus it is we find " all mankind heaped and huddled

---

* Combe's Moral Philosophy, pp. 205, 216.

together with nothing but a litle carpentry or masonry between them ; crammed in like salt fish in their barrel ;—or weltering (shall I say ?) like an Egyptian pitcher of tamed vipers, each striving to get its head above the rest."* The immutable and resistless laws of nature have, however, been doing their work, and through the all-powerful influences of pleasure and pain, have been pushing man forward in the march of improvement, and like the forces which, in the course of many ages, laid stratum upon stratum and prepared the way for sensitive existence upon the earth, have gradually been preparing for the existence of man, not merely as a selfish animal, but in all the capacities of his physical, moral, and intellectual being.

If we trace back the progress of the development of man's resources, we find the foundation of the present social institutions laid at a time when, to prevent him preying upon his fellow like wild beasts upon each other, rights of property were established and maintained by the strong arm of force alone. The greatest want, and therefore the greatest blessing, was security of life and limb ; and the institution that could best afford it was the most desirable. Here, then, was the foundation of an aristocracy. The leaders chosen to head the different associations of men for their common protection maintained a kind of security, and "the strong man ' was in proportion respected. Kings were at first only the chosen leaders of armies ; valour and military skill were the virtues most in request ; protection became a *profession,* and a soldier as the representative of that profession, the most honoured.†

* Sartor Resartus.
† "All high titles come hitherto from fighting. Your Herzog (Duke, Dux,) is leader of armies ; your Earl (Jarl) is strong man ; Marshal, cavalry horseshoer. A Millenium, or reign of

But the power thus necessarily entrusted to an individual, was soon abused, assumed as a right derived from God only, and not from the people, and ultimately became irresponsible. A profession of arms having been established with leaders whose interests were at variance with those of the people, constant wars were necessary to find occupation for such a profession, to promote the individual aggrandizement of the leaders, and maintain the influence they had usurped ; and their real motives were concealed under the high-sounding names of Glory, Patriotism, and National Honour.

The power thus yielded by the people to ensure personal security when no better means could be devised, has never yet been recovered. Magna Chartas, Cromwellian Revolutions, Parliamentary Reforms, mark the progress which has been made towards it, and the barriers to liberty that have been removed. The problem to be solved is, how to make perfect liberty compatible with security to life and limb, and the fruits of industry.

In the first stage of society physical prowess was alone regarded ; but no sooner were the wild barbarous hordes that founded the present nations of Europe settled down into some quiet, than the influence of mind began to be felt, and then arose the power of the priesthood—a power sufficient, in some measure, to control the license of the feudal lords, and to weaken the arm of violence and blood, which was constantly uplifted in their mutual aggressions, or attacks upon the liberty of neighbouring States.

Oral teaching was then all-important, for when there were few books, and fewer still who could read, it

Peace and Wisdom, having been prophesied, and becoming daily more and more indubitable, may it not be apprehended that such Fighting titles will cease to be palatable, and new and higher need to be devised ?"—Sartor, p. 256.

was almost the only means of imparting instruction. The sole possessors and interpreters of the book which was supposed to contain the Revelation of God's Word, claimed and received universal dominion over the multitudes who knew no other source of light and truth ; but now that we are furnished with a more ample revelation of His laws unfolded by the experience of ages, and the written means of communicating it to the hearts of all, oral instruction is no longer the only method of making known the law of the Lord, and the more extended knowledge of His will, as revealed in His works.

As other wants of society took shape and form, the class through whom such wants found the means of gratification arose in importance. With personal security and comparative security to property, trade and commerce began to flourish ; and however much the pursuits connected with them were at first despised, as the dependence of society upon them for foreign productions, and even the comforts of life became recognised, they were first tolerated, and then protected, until an aristocracy of wealth has gradually arisen, which treads closely upon the heels of the aristocracy of birth.

When trade and commerce flourished, and the right of the strongest was no longer admitted, the laws of property became necessarily more complicated ; hence a class was called forth for the expounding of those laws, and their administrators rose in proportional importance. On the complexity of the laws depended the necessity for Lawyers,—make the laws plain, their occupation is gone. Consequently the simplest question, in their hands, assumes an intricacy which the strongest uninitiated intellect cannot unravel, and the plainest, most intelligible language of common sense and justice soon becomes that of an unknown tongue to the people.

Thus it appears that the right of each class of society to the distinction it claims was based upon utility ; but the world is changed, and society pays homage to the shadows of things that were. As each of these leading divisions became necessary to the good of society, its pre-eminence has been acknowledged ; and although the wants that gave rise to it may be now reduced in importance, it still maintains its rank in the social scale. With security and peace, the power of man over the earth and its produce has increased, until money, the representative of this produce, has become almost omnipotent, " and whoso has sixpence is sovereign, (to the length of sixpence,) over all men ; commands cooks to feed him, philosophers to teach him, kings to mount guard over him,—to the length of sixpence." Money; therefore, is the universal want, and respect in proportion is paid to those who have it—with it man is everything, and without it he is nothing.

The Military and fighting age has passed, and protection to property being secured, a Commercial age has commenced. Kings, no longer wanted as military leaders, their power is fast passing over to our commercial leaders. A Constitutional Sovereign has become a mere abstraction—the embodiment and representative of all the power and dignity of the state ; and the Rothschilds and great moneyed men possess the real power in the civilised world.

One class only has not hitherto been duly acknowledged—the working class ; but the signs of the times indicate the approach of a period when it *must* and *will* be recognised. "There is, however, something greater in the age than its greatest men ; it is the appearance of a new power in the world, the appearance of a multitude of men on that stage, where as yet the few have acted their parts alone."* Money, the representative of all the produce which flows from the labour of the multitude, has been the means of defrauding them of the rights resulting from their real weight and importance ; by the help of money the truth has been concealed that everything which gives support, accommodation, and luxury to life, comes through the medium of labour, and the tribute due to the labourers in return has been paid to the god of these latter days—Mammon. They will discover this, Mammon will be undeified and dethroned, the working classes in working for others will also work for themselves, and their claims will be then acknowledged. Yes, "he who first shortened the labour of copyists by device of moveable types, was disbanding hired armies, and cashiering most kings and senates, and erecting a whole new democratic world : he had invented the art of printing." * By its means the people will ultimately become wise enough to take their own concerns into their own keeping, to govern and protect themselves ; and *present* not *past* utility will be the only acknowledged title to distinction.

The Socialists say that to base society on competition, _—on individual conflicting interests and opposing objects, was a great mistake ; that it ought to be based on Community of interest and Unity of purpose, and that property, therefore, should not belong to individuals, but should be held *in trust by society* for the benefit of all.

They say it has been well ascertained that each healthy adult individual can produce considerably more than he can consume, if his labour be profitably directed.

* Dr. Channing's "Present Age." † Carlyle.

AA

" Taking the best data that can be had, it appears that
the labour of 19 families is required to produce annually
1,160 quarters of all kinds of grain, being at the rate of
61 quarters by each family."* According to this
estimate the labour of one family would support about
15, and these 15 families, therefore, might be spared for
manufactures. The productive powers of machinery in
manufactures are scarcely calculable; in the cotton
manufactory, already, one man by this power performs
the work of two or three hundred, and the whole
mechanical power of the country is estimated at that of
400, according to some, of 600 millions of men. This
power, it is said, properly economised, and the produce
of it properly distributed, is sufficient to supply all the
wants of society. This idea of community of property
and interests is not altogether new. To what extent it
has been carried out in practice at different periods of
the world's history I considered in the Appendix to the
1st Edition of this work. To such a system have the
hopes of mankind, during all ages, with more or less
distinctness, been directed. Sometimes the happy community was to dwell in a millennium of this earth, sometimes in a fellowship of the saints in heaven—the poet
dreamed of it in the Golden Age—the philosopher in his
Republic,—his Atlantis, his Utopia. Amidst all the
draperies of fancy and fable which have clothed the
vision, it still stands forth, a living form—a type of the
future brotherhood of man.

The change contemplated it is said would render it
unnecessary for the workman to sell his share of what
his labour produces for less than it is worth ; it would
give capital the most profitable direction towards further

production, and cause machinery to work *for* the labourer, never *against* him.

These objects could only be effected by the re-union of capital and labour—by the labourer himself becoming a capitalist, and the owner of the machinery with which he produces. It is proposed, therefore, that the working men should be encouraged and assisted to unite together in associations or communities, upon the principle of Joint-Stock Companies, in such numbers as convenience may dictate, for the production and equal distribution of all the necessaries and comforts of life.

It is easy to find practical illustrations of what is meant by organization of industry. The Post-Office is a familiar instance. By means of such an organization we can send a steam carriage with a letter to any part of the kingdom, and a penny really pays the costs and leaves a profit. Here the clear gain effected by organization is the difference between the penny and its profit and what it would cost an individual to send a letter himself by his own conveyance. Railways afford another powerful illustration of the advantages of industrial organization. By the present uniform system of arrangement, a person can go from London to Edinburgh in about ten hours,—a vast saving of time compared to a system of steam-travelling in which every person had to lay down the rails over his own land, according to his own ideas, causing an infinity of gauges and stoppages ; and yet the savings effected by order, arrangement, and organization in the Post-Office and in Railways, is probably not greater than would be effected by introducing order and organization into our present individual and disjointed efforts for the increase and distribution of wealth in all departments of industry upon our present system of *laissez faire*. The Post-Office and Railways keep comfortably all parties employed in and on them, and leave a large profit. The Clubs at the West-end of London are a result of organization of industry, by means of which gentlemen of refined tastes get palace accomodation, a splendid library, excellent attendance, the best wines, the simplest and most *recherche* fare at a third of the charges of the ordinary hotels. The model lodging-house is another instance of the advantages to be derived from the organization of labour. Large and airy rooms, baths, easy and economical methods of cleaning, washing, and cooking, are provided for the use of the poor, at a less cost than the miserable and ill-ventilated rooms in the back alleys of London. The large factories, warehouses, and trading emporiums of England are all evidences of what can be effected by a combination of industrial operations. In fact, the chaos of work is of itself gradually crystallizing throughout the empire, and the process only requires to be carried a few steps further to reach the working man.

Thomas Carlyle, our great philosopher, says, "This that they call 'Organization of Labour,' is, if well understood, the problem of the whole future, for all who would in future pretend to govern men ;" and the 19th century may see a considerable advance in this direction.* It is much easier to form theories than to

* While this was passing through the press, the following interesting letter appeared in the *Times* :—" Assington Hall, Suffolk, December 19, 1862. Sir,—The interesting article from your 'Own Reporter,' dated Rochdale, respecting Co-operative Societies, induces me to trouble you with a few lines on the same subject. About 30 years ago, upon a small farm in Suffolk becoming vacant, I called together 20 labourers and offered to lend them capital without interest if they would undertake to farm it, subject to my rules and regulations. They gladly availed themselves of my offer. In the course of ten years they paid me back my capital, so that I was induced to let another farm of 150 acres to 30 men upon the same terms. These have also nearly paid back the capital lent to them, and, instead of

work them out in practice. Making the best of the present system of separate individual interests, we may see in healthy country districts squares of 300 or 400 houses, with as much land attached to each house as each man could cultivate, with a steam engine in the centre of each square, with power conveyed to each house to do all hard and dirty work, or to work the loom or other machinery upon which the women and children might wait : or looking into the far future we may see the system of society changed to one of community of property and interest, of which our present country gentleman's seat should furnish the model. We may imagine a large house, on a sufficiently large estate, where each family had their separate rooms and common rooms for sitting and meals, and where, instead of the exercise and labour required for health being taken, as it now is, in hunting and shooting, it might be employed in the labour of the farm, and where the women, instead of riding, gossiping, and dressing, might have their mornings usefully employed also ; and where the labour of all properly directed, should furnish everything that the highest happiness requires, and where the community of interest should develop all the best feelings, and make a really united family.

eating dry bread, as I regret to [say many of the agricultural labourers are now doing, each man has his bacon, and numberless comforts that he never possessed before ; thus the rates are reduced, as these 50 families are no longer burdensome. The farmers are sure to meet with honest men, as conviction of crime would debar them of their share, and the men themselves have become much more intelligent, and present happy, cheerful countenances. If every country gentleman would follow my example distress among the agricultural poor would not be known. I merely add that I have no land so well farmed   I shall be happy to send you my plan, rules, and regulations, if required.
　　　　　"I am, Sir, your obedient servant,
　　　　　　　　　JOHN   GURDON."

What form society may ultimately take it is impossible
to say : one thing only is evident, that the morals and
intelligence of the working classes are at present unequal
to any but the lowest form of Co-operation.   When
their character shall be raised,—when they have felt the
advantages of comfort and civilization, and have
determined to maintain that state by keeping their numbers within what will make it possible, much more may
be got from the present form of society than has yet
been attained.   Probably that form will be ultimately,
preferred which gives the greatest amount of individual
liberty.   At present, the great majority of mankind are
slaves to work and to the necessity of living ; their
liberty is bounded by their wants and narrow means, and
at no time perhaps can they properly be said to be their
own masters ; and if, under a Co-operative system, they
gave up their liberty for half the day, so that they might
call the other half their own, they would be great gainers
in that respect.   On the *present system.*   "Each individual
of the civilised millions dwelling on the earth, (by the
appliances of Trade and Commerce, Art and Science,)
may have nearly the same enjoyments as if he were the
single lord of all."   All this is possible in this "old
immoral world" for individuals, and the mental qualifications that would make Socialism practicable, would give
to all what is now the privilege only of the few.   Still
Socialism appeals more directly to all our higher feelings,
and may perhaps be the last form that society will take
when the perfectibility of man shall have reached a
higher range on this earth ; and as regards the guarantees
for liberty, that is the fullest liberty which is exercised
according to known and recognised laws.   The nearer we
attain to perfect goodness and intelligence, the less choice
have we, as there is ordinarily but one *right* path.

But that we should be able absolutely to determine the best form of society is of less consequence, inasmuch as the growth of the world seems to have been little influenced by theories. If some wise Ichthyosaurus had clearly foreseen our present state, we must still probably have approached it by the intervening hundreds of centuries. It is not any grand and logical theory that has made mankind what they are, but the hundred million little causes or antecedents of which probably they have been altogether unconscious. Many old forms which have trammelled the progress of the race are now breaking up; we have attained to security of life and limb and to the perfection of mere animal life, and society seems now working towards the complete "Individuality of the Individual;" and when each atom of mankind has liberty to move equally in every direction, Society will crystalize into new forms more in accordance with man's higher and superior and essentially human nature. What we have now to do then, is not to neglect *any means* which are offered to us for developing and perfecting the individual; among which means Temperance and Education must stand first.

Lightning Source UK Ltd.
Milton Keynes UK
UKOW05f0040161116

287689UK00013B/431/P

9 781330 442777